REALITY
Isn't What It Used to Be

Theatrical Politics, Ready-to-Wear Religion, Global Myths, Primitive Chic, and Other Wonders of the Postmodern World

Walter Truett Anderson

HarperSanFrancisco
A Division of HarperCollins*Publishers*

To Mauriça and Dan, with love and hope.

Library of Congress Cataloging-in-Publication Data

Anderson, Walt, 1933–
Reality isn't what it used to be : theatrical politics, ready-to-wear religion, global myths, primitive chic and other wonders of the postmodern world / Walter Truett Anderson.
p. cm.
Originally published: San Francisco : Harper & Row, 1990.
Includes index.
ISBN 0–06–250017–1
1. Civilization, Modern—1950– 2. Postmodernism. I. Title.
[CB428.A64 1992]
909.82—dc20 91–55284
CIP

93 94 95 RRD(H) 10 9 8 7 6 5

REALITY
Isn't What It Used to Be

Pardon him, Theodotus: he is a barbarian, and thinks that the customs of his tribe and island are the laws of nature. (G. B. Shaw, *Caesar and Cleopatra*)

Contents

Preface

I stood one day on a cliff above the Pacific, looking down at a sea otter that bobbed in the surf far below. The otter floated happily and busily on its back in the water, holding an abalone in its forepaws and cracking the abalone's shell open with a rock.

The waves were coming in, and the otter was rocking about gently on the surface. The little animal was constantly being moved this way and that by the water, but seemed to pay no attention to this movement as it concentrated on its task.

And I thought, how different from mine its experience of life must be, living in a medium in such flux and so unlike the hard ground on which I stood.

But as I thought about it further, I realized that the medium in which I live is far more turbulent than anything the sea otter could ever conceive of—because, as a human being, I bob about in a sea of symbols, an ocean of words.

We humans find our loves and hates, our successes and failures, our status and identity and orientation to the world through use of symbols. Even our most primal drives (see sex) are channeled through ideas and images, shaped in the mold of culture.

In the long time scale of evolution, we are still new to this symbolic medium. We don't yet know how to get around in it very well. We hardly even know we are in it. We repeatedly create symbolic systems of meaning—religions, political ideologies, scientific theories—and then forget that they are our creations; we have a devilish habit of confusing them with the mysterious nonhuman reality they were meant to explain. We have constructed about ourselves (and within ourselves) an environment of symbols and cannot tell where symbol leaves off and nonhuman reality begins, cannot (as the general semanticists put it) tell the map from the territory.

For centuries, some of our greatest minds have sought to comprehend the nature of this symbolic universe—to make us see, first of all, that we live in such a medium, and then to show us its limits and its possibilities. This has been going on for a long time: it is some 2,500 years since the Buddha had his moment of profound insight into the illusory nature of human experience, and began trying (with indifferent success) to tell his followers, in words, the truth about words. The Buddha was the first deconstructionist. It was only a few decades after Buddha's time that Plato wrote *The Republic*, with its unforgettable metaphor of the people in the cave who see nothing but the shadows thrown upon its wall by the fire.

My subject in the following chapters is the social construction of reality: how societies created and maintained realities in the past, how postmodern ideas reveal the workings of the reality-creating machinery, how contemporary operators on the political and cultural scene create new realities before our very eyes.

We will mainly follow this story as it has unfolded within Western civilization, but occasionally I will direct our attention into the mirror of the East, to see what we can learn from traditions like Buddhism, Hinduism, and Sufism that grapple in their own ways with the ancient problem of social construction of reality. Those traditions have much to tell us, but no easy answers; followers of such paths are as easily ensnared in their symbols as we are in ours.

For Westerners, the issues are more accessible in such fields as the sociology of knowledge, cognitive science, and the body of thinking-about-thinking that has come to be known simply as "critical theory."

The cognitive scientists, a relatively scrutable band of explorers of the brain and mind, are struggling in new ways with the old question that occupied some of the best philosophical minds of past centuries: what is the match between *human* reality—all our history and science and systems of belief—and the objective reality of the cosmos?

The various answers to this question divide the cognitive scientists into two main camps. On one side are the objectivists, who see the human mind as capable of more or less accurately, more or less impersonally, mirroring external nonhuman reality; on the other side, the constructivists hold that what we call the "real world" is an ever-changing social creation.

The constructivists—whose thinking runs close to my own, and to the main themes of this book—say we do not have a "God's eye" view of nonhuman reality, never have had, never will have. They say we live in a symbolic world, a social reality that many people construct together and yet experience as the objective "real world." And they also tell us the earth is not a *single* symbolic world, but rather a vast universe of "multiple realities," because different groups of people construct different stories, and because different languages embody different ways of experiencing life. So, according to the constructivist view, people may have not only different political opinions and religious beliefs, but different ideas of such basic matters as personal identity, time, and space.

Such ideas and such divisions are surfacing in many fields. Richard Bernstein, a philosopher, writes of "an uneasiness that has spread throughout intellectual and cultural life." This pervasive disturbance, he says, "affects almost every discipline and every aspect of our lives. [It] is expressed by the opposition between objectivism and relativism, but there are a variety of other contrasts that indicate the same underlying anxiety: rationality versus irrationality, objectivity versus subjectivity, realism versus antirealism." Farther along in the same work he mentions another set of contrasts—absolutism and relativism—and describes this variously defined controversy (it seems appropriate to me, somehow, that everybody has a different way of describing it) as "the central cultural opposition of our time."[1]

In these contrasts and dialogues—amid this uneasiness—the difference between the worldview of the recent past and the worldview of the present and future begins to become clear.

A mere couple of centuries ago, most societies recognized a single official reality and dedicated themselves to destroying its opposition. You could get burned at the stake for suggesting that there might be more than one version of reality. Today, in some intellectual circles, you can get into trouble for suggesting there might be only one. There are, to be sure, plenty of people around who would not mind setting the torch to the constructivists and their many allies. Fundamentalists of all kinds would suppress such notions as socially dangerous, because they believe that there is no basis for social order without a fundamental agreement that some things are not just socially true but by God *cosmically* true, true for everybody and for all time.

Unfortunately for the cause of those who seek such an anchor for our wavering systems of value and belief, there is not, in most parts of the contemporary world, much of a consensus about what those truths are—if there are any—and it is rarely possible to enforce conformity in the good old-fashioned inquisitorial way. So the constructivists and their ilk—and, as we will see, it is a pretty big ilk—are permitted to go more or less freely about their heretical business.

These postmodern thinkers are in one sense revolutionaries, and in another sense conservatives. You can hardly call them stormers of the Bastille, because the Bastille has already been pretty thoroughly stormed. The old epistemology that equated human beliefs with cosmic reality is now a minority report. Ancient and not-so-ancient systems of eternal truth lie in ruins everywhere around us. The mainstream of social reality has shifted. Yet, although this news is out and many people are acting on it, the full import of the change has not quite found its way into public consciousness.

Most of us in the Western world slip and slide around in the territory between the objectivist and constructivist camps, without much of a clear idea of what we think about such matters. Our everyday experience tends to be objectivist, guided by what the philosophers call "naive realism": we generally assume that the universe is the way we experience it. But if asked to think about it, we turn into constructivists. Sure, we say, it's all relative; time and space and identity are subjective ideas—everybody knows that.

Well, yes, probably everybody does know that. But we don't all know we know it. We haven't yet quite figured out how to live with what we know, and we don't know what a curious piece of knowledge it is—part jewel, part bombshell.

Few of us realize that even to hold a *concept* of relative truth makes us entirely different from people who lived only a few decades ago, and we complacently overlook the evidence that many people living today profoundly hate the view of reality that seems so eminently tolerant and sensible to the Western liberal mind.

We do not comprehend what a stunning—and yet still incomplete—upheaval of thought has occurred in the recent historical past. Nor have we pursued our liberal tolerance to its logical conclusions, and accepted the enormous uncertainties and vast possibilities of the life it opens up before us.

We do not see the full dimensions of the upheaval, and yet the upheaval, fully comprehended or not, rumbles about the world and changes everything it touches.

This book is about that upheaval, and about getting to know what we know. My approach to the subject will be to get us acquainted with some of the main themes of contemporary constructivist thought, and then to use those as our intellectual guides and interpreters for a tour through the strange and wonderful new social world that is coming into being around us. And along the way I will attempt to share with you my conviction that there is much to hope for in this world. Amidst the chaos, there is progress toward a future in which people will live free of belief as we have known it, at home in the symbolic universe. We can see, if we look closely at the ideas and events of the post-modern world, a new sensibility emerging—a way of being that puts the continual creation of reality at the heart of every person's life, at the heart of politics, and at the heart of human evolution.

Walter Truett Anderson

Acknowledgments

Among the many people who read the manuscript at various stages and/or gave helpful suggestions are James MacGregor Burns, Elizabeth Campbell, Napier Collyns, Jim Dator, Jackie Doyle, Jack and Jeff Fobes, Tom Greening, Mary Gardiner Jones, Doug Lea, Abe Levitsky, Tom Mandel, Rollo May, Jo-Ann McDowell, Will McWhinney, Don Michael, Stuart Miller, Brian Murphy, Maureen O'Hara, Pat Ophuls, Mauriça Osborne, Hinkley and Elsa Porter, Theodore Roszak, Steve Rosell, Nancy and Paul Silverman, Huston and Kendra Smith, Keith Thompson, Art Warmoth, and Tom and Page Wilson. My special thanks to Sandy Close and Franz Schurmann and Pacific News Service, to Bill Kenkelen and Richard Rodriguez for material quoted in chapter 8, to the Ucross Foundation in Wyoming for an opportunity to spend a couple of quiet weeks getting this project started, to Lewis Yablonsky for getting me acquainted with psychodrama and sociodrama and the theater of life, to my agents Norman Kurz and Barbara Lowenstein and to the people at Harper & Row—Wendy Chiu, Georgia Hughes, and especially John Loudon—who did so much to make this book a reality.

Acknowledgments

PART ONE

THE COLLAPSE OF BELIEF

CHAPTER 1

Welcome to the Postmodern World

In recent decades we have passed, like Alice slipping through the looking glass, into a new world. This postmodern world looks and feels in many ways like the modern world that preceded it: we still have the belief systems that gave form to the modern world, and indeed we also have remnants of many of the belief systems of premodern societies. If there is anything we have plenty of, it is belief systems. But we also have something else: a growing suspicion that all belief systems—all ideas about human reality—are social constructions. This is a story about stories, a belief about beliefs, and in time—probably a very short time—it will become a central part of the worldview of most people. It will be the core of the first global civilization.

But it is not yet a core. It is more a seed of discontent. It fills our daily lives with uncertainty and anxiety, renders us vulnerable to tyrants and cults, shakes religious faith, and divides societies into groups contending with one another in a strange and unfamiliar kind of ideological conflict: not merely conflict *between* beliefs, but conflict *about* belief itself.

Politics has always rested on the construction and maintenance of social reality, but until recently we didn't talk much about that. The deep issues concerning the nature of human truth were left to the philosophers. Most of the conflicts that tore the now-ending modern era were between different belief systems, each of which professed to have the truth: this faith against that one, capitalism against communism, science against religion. On all sides the assumption was that *somebody* possessed the real item, a truth fixed and beyond mere human conjecture. The modern era brought us into a world with multiple and conflicting belief systems. Now the postmodern era is revealing a world in which different groups have different beliefs about belief itself. A postmodern culture based on a different sense of social reality is coming into being—and it is a painful birth.

In small towns all across America, modern and postmodern culture do battle: neighbor turns against neighbor in bitter disputes about whether children should be taught skills of "moral reasoning"—a very postmodern concept—or should instead be taught to accept unquestioningly some rock-solid American values and beliefs. In the circles of higher education, the case is stated by books such as Bloom's *The Closing of the American Mind*, which hammer at the postmodern relativism that (Professor Bloom says) abandons fundamental political principles in favor of a wishy-washy flexibility and recognizes "no enemy other than the man who is not open to everything." Bloom recognizes—and is alarmed by—the extent to which the old view of reality has eroded: "Almost every student entering the university believes, or says he believes, that truth is relative."[1]

Bloom's indictment is quite correct, in a way: most people in Western society today do hold a much more relativistic view of reality. And he is also justified in charging that few of them understand the full implications of this profoundly radical epistemology and instead wander around in a muddled good-guy liberalism that has no clear concept of truth and think all the world's problems would melt away if we just had a tad more tolerance. A postmodern worldview is present among us, yet unformed: it knows neither its own strengths, nor its own weaknesses. We do not know how to live in a world of socially constructed realities, yet we find it increasingly difficult to live in anything else.

The conservative indictment is correct, and yet the strategy that logically follows from it—to rebuild consensus, to get a core of standard values and beliefs in place in every American mind—is doomed to fail. To see that, you only need to look at the variety of things being offered by people who are in favor of some such consensus building: Professor Bloom offers a restoration of classical Western civilization, and his idea of culture leans strongly to the right. Frances Moore Lappé in her book *Rediscovering America's Values* pleads for a similar return to cultural roots, but her version leans equally to the left.[2] Robert Bellah and his coauthors of *Habits of the Heart* want Americans to become less individualistic, more settled and community based, to stop wandering around.[3] James

Fallows in *More Like Us* argues for restoring the old American "sense of possibility and openness," our tradition of mobility, our willingness to head for a new job or a new town and start all over.[4] E. D. Hirsch, Jr., in *Cultural Literacy* proposed a list of things we all ought to know about, from Hank Aaron to Zurich, in order to be "culturally literate."[5] Other writers criticize Hirsch's list for being too white- and European-oriented and propose other lists of items from non-European traditions. Still others counsel us to create and unite around new values based on feminism or ecology.[6] All of these proposals make sense, in a way. Each of them looks good to certain groups of people, particularly those whose values and beliefs are the ones being proposed for the national culture. And I am sure the great majority of Americans have never heard of any of these people, or their books.

Humpty-Dumpty is not going to be put back together again. Efforts to do so are ultimately self-defeating, because campaigns to make people choose any particular system of value and belief tend to have the subversive effect of informing people that they are free to choose systems of value and belief. All too often, indoctrinations—even indoctrinations into traditional principles—turn out to be de facto courses in postmodernism.

The metaconflict about beliefs has become a central theme in American politics, and it also echoes around the globe: we can see it in the travails of the Catholic church as it struggles to hold the line against radically new ways of looking at revealed truth, in the reluctant and explosive deflation of doctrine of Marxist nations, in the worldwide proliferation of spiritual and psychological cults that offer new certainties to people who have abandoned—or been abandoned by—the old ones.

We can also see an increasing theatricality of politics, in which events are scripted and stage-managed for mass consumption, and in which individuals and groups struggle for starring roles (or at least bit parts) in the dramas of life. This theatricality is a natural—and inevitable—feature of our time. It is what happens when a lot of people begin to understand that reality is a social construction. The more enterprising among us see that there is much to be gained by constructing—and selling to the public—a certain reality, and so reality making becomes a new art and business. And a very big business, if you consider how much money is spent (and made) in fields such as advertising and public relations and political campaigning.

These are signs of the postmodern world coming into being—a world that, as philosopher of science Stephen Toulmin says, does not know how to define itself by what it is, only by what it has just now ceased to be.[7]

Three major processes are shaping this transition.

The first, which has been going on throughout this century, is the breakdown of old ways of belief. It has been amply documented elsewhere; indeed, it is one of the major themes of literature and scholarship in this century. Yeats in *The Second Coming* summed it up well:

> Turning and turning in the widening gyre
> The falcon cannot hear the falconer;
> Things fall apart; the centre cannot hold;
> Mere anarchy is loosed upon the world,
> The blood-dimmed tide is loosed, and everywhere
> The ceremony of innocence is drowned;
> The best lack all conviction, while the worst
> Are full of passionate intensity.[8]

The result of this breakdown, now becoming increasingly apparent, is a kind of unregulated marketplace of realities in which all manner of belief systems are offered for public consumption.

The second process is the emergence of a new polarization, a conflict about the nature of social truth itself; epistemology joins the old family favorites—class, race, and nationality—as a source of political controversy. This polarization is evident in battles over education—especially moral instruction—and in several different intellectual disciplines.

The third process is the birth of a global culture, with a worldview that is truly a *world*view. Globalization provides a new arena (or theater) in which all belief systems look around and become aware of all other belief systems, and in which people everywhere struggle in unprecedented ways to find out who and what they are.

The decades just ahead will provide the stage on which these processes will unfold, and on which the human species will strive to build a new civilization based on a new sense of social reality.

Let's take a closer look at each of these three historical processes. First, the breakdown of old ways of belief.

FORCED TO BE FREE

In premodern societies, social constructions of reality took form slowly and invisibly, and the symbolic universes that people wove about themselves seemed to be permanent fixtures of life. The duty of persons in authority was to maintain the official worldview; that of everybody else, to conform to it. Most people do not appear to have known they had a worldview, nor to have felt in need of one. Premodern societies did not generally entertain the idea of any possible gulf between objective reality and social belief systems, much less the idea that it might be possible for other societies to have much different but equally good worldviews or that multiple worldviews (and views *about* worldviews) might coexist in the same social space.

In modern societies—born out of social and physical mobility, with people beginning to suspect that there were different possible realities—individuals and groups gained, or tried to gain, more options. And so were played out the dramas of recent centuries—inquisitions and revolutions, the explosive appearance of new ideas such as human rights and the separation of church and state. At a high cost of blood, with monumental investments of courage, many people gained the freedom to make their own choices about what to accept as real. They became consumers of reality who could select different values and beliefs and ways of behaving.

The modern era was a long period of transition, now nearing completion. As it ends, we are all thrust rudely—Adam and Eve thrown out of the garden again—into a new climate of freedom and stress. In the postmodern world we are all *required* to make choices about our realities. You may select a life of experimentation, eternal shopping in the bazaar of culture and subculture. Or you may forego the giddy diversity of contemporary life-style swapping and fall into step with some ancient heritage: be an Orthodox Jew or a fundamentalist Muslim or a Bible-toting Christian or a traditional native American. The range of such choices is enormous, but the choice is still a choice and requires an entirely different social consciousness from that of the Jews, Muslims, Christians, and native Americans who knew of no alternatives. The contemporary traditionalist may resemble in some outward ways the premodern individual, but the actual lived experiences of the two are utterly dissimilar. Today we are all "forced to be free" in a way that Rousseau could not have imagined when he coined that famous phrase. We have to make choices from a range of different stories—stories about what the universe is like, about who the good guys and the bad guys are, about who *we* are—and also have to make choices about how to make choices. The only thing we lack is the option of not having to make choices—although many of us try hard, and with some success, to conceal that from ourselves.

A new social consciousness is coming into being, and taking up residence within every one of us—including those of us who want no part of it. We all now live in our belief systems in an entirely new way. When we choose to adopt one, we know—even if we are terrified by the knowledge and do all we can to repress it in ourselves and others—that we could choose an entirely different one. The fundamentalist lives in eternal fear that he or she may lose the faith; the freethinking liberal lives in eternal fear that he or she may tire of freedom and fall into the arms of some ancient, modern, or postmodern belief system—anything from Islam to Scientology—that has a solid structure and ready answers.

The postmodern individual is continually reminded that different peoples have entirely different concepts of what the world is like. The person who understands this and accepts it recognizes social institutions as human creations and knows that even the sense of personal identity is different in different societies. Such a person views religious truth as a special kind of truth and not an eternal and perfect representation of cosmic reality. And—going beyond modern secular humanism—he or she sees the work of science as yet another form of social reality-construction and not a secret technique for taking objective photographs of the universe.

Many people are well into that postmodern understanding. Old ways of belief are collapsing within millions of minds. But we all have remarkable abilities for managing this internal transition, psychological tricks that help us remain sane and more or less socially conventional and that also conceal the enormity of what is going on in the world. It turns out that a collapse of old *ways* of belief does not necessarily—at least not immediately—result in a collapse of old *systems* of belief.

Like hermit crabs who skitter about in the tide pools wearing the shells of dead snails, we don old belief systems that do not always fit too well, and go about our business. Most of us now are not so much believers as possessors of beliefs. Conversion comes easy and often. The seeker after religious faith tries on not one religion, but any number of them. Conservative intellectuals point proudly to their renounced Marxism. And a dazzling tool kit of contemporary methods—everything from the brainwashing of individuals to the propagandizing of entire nations—is employed to get people to drop this belief, pick up that one, adjust the fit of another.

We all become consumers of reality (although, as in other forms of consumption, not with equal buying power), and greater numbers of us also become creators and merchandisers of reality. As the faith in old absolutes wanes, the season opens on the construction of new realities for those who do not care to be seen in the standard models. In earlier times, the invention of cultural forms was shrouded in mystery; now it becomes, for better or for worse, democratized. Individuals feel free to create new identities for themselves, and entrepreneurs of reality dabble gaily in the creation of new history, new science, new religion, new politics.

The mass media make it easy to create and disseminate new structures of reality. A new reality does not have to convert the entire society; it merely has to find its buyers, get a share of the market, and locate enough customers to fill up the theater. For example, recent books have been written seeking to demonstrate that in prehistoric times societies were goddess-worshipping and consequently peaceful, productive, and progressive. In *The Chalice and the Blade*, Riane Eisler tells us that early civilizations, under the influence of female-spirit religion, were wondrously benign and creative until—in the eleventh century B.C., apparently—macho barbarians from Europe and Asia came down from the hills bringing a new culture of violence and domination.[9] Her general conclusion is that societies based on a feminine ethos are superior, and that if we can establish that ethos worldwide everything will be fine.

This story is offered as a new reality for everybody—indeed a prescription for the future of all human civilizations—but it has not been accepted as such, even by feminists for whom it is obviously meant to be a manifesto. Rachel Sternberg criticized the book's "excesses of free association and sleight of hand."[10] Elizabeth Fox-Genovese dismissed it as full of "absurdities."[11] A reviewer of an earlier book with a similar thesis pointed out that prehistory is still prehistory, and thus a "playground" in which one can create just about anything one pleases.[12] Nevertheless, the thesis is widely, uncritically, even gratefully accepted by many people because—well, because it's a good story. It makes a case for a higher position for women in the world, and dramatically challenges the equally spurious construction of reality upon which male-dominated society is built. However, although offered as a universal, it does not sweep away that reality; it merely finds its following among people who think it's a nice thing and soon becomes the belief system of yet another subculture. In the collapse of belief, a thousand subcultures bloom, and new belief systems arrive as regularly as the daily mail.

Can a case on behalf of a decent position for women in the world be made on any less grandiose basis? Can we work toward equality of the sexes without believing that it is going to fix up all our problems? Or do we need to swallow whole another shakily assembled story about the past and another glib promise about the future? In the postmodern era, many people choose the latter—conclude that the best way to advance a personal opinion is to create a whole new reality around it, complete with new absolute truths.

The logic of reality-creation is the following: if people believe this, then they will do that. It is a somewhat dubious method of getting things done, since it requires that a lot of people believe, it assumes they will do what you want/expect them to do when they do believe, and it all too often carries a certain contempt for the intelligence of those to whom you plan to sell your story. It is flimflam—high-minded flimflam at best—and although it is being practiced as never before, it is also as old as Western civilization. It is the logic of what Plato called the "noble lie."

In *The Republic*, Socrates and his friends considered how it would be possible to obtain the loyalty of the guardians of the republic. It is one of the earliest recorded discussions of a deliberate social construction of reality. Socrates says that he will

> attempt to persuade first the rulers and the soldiers, then the rest of the city, that the rearing and education we gave them were like dreams; they only thought they were undergoing all that was happening to them, while, in truth, at that time they were under the earth within, being fashioned and reared themselves, and their arms and other tools being crafted. When the job had been completely finished, then the earth, which is their mother, sent them up. And now, as though the land they are in were a mother and nurse, they must plan for and defend it, if anyone attacks, and they must think of the other citizens as brothers and born out of the earth.[13]

And so, with a bit of what would later become known as brainwashing, Socrates offers his solution to the classic political problem of how to get young men to sublimate their natural urges toward self-preservation and instead go forth willingly to risk their lives in conflict with other young men who don't appear to be all that different from themselves. The noble lie is not a complete fabrication; it takes a core of what most of us believe to be true, our organic connection to the earth, and puts a different spin on it. But it is obvious that Socrates does not believe it himself; he just thinks it would be a good thing if others did.

We have many such noble lies, created out of the best of political intentions. We have always had them, and postmodern society is a fountainhead of new ones. The most recent is the story of Gaia, an ancient Greek myth hoked up anew in the guise of science to make us suitably reverent toward the biosphere. It, too, has a plausible, even in some respects obvious, core—the hypothesis that the biological processes on the earth affect geochemical and climatic conditions and, in effect, maintain the conditions for life. The hypothesis (or theory, as it is now being called) is quite worthy of our attention, and is easily the *least* important part of what could more accurately be described as the "Gaia phenomenon," the popular new belief that the earth is a living organism. The Gaia phenomenon rests heavily on myth and metaphor. The Greek myth carries an image of earth as goddess. The organism metaphor suggests that the earth must, if it is like other higher organisms, have its own mind. These ideas—which have very little to do with science—are the turn-ons, and they are what is being transformed into a new *faith,* a kitsch ecotheology complete with its doctrines and its priests and priestesses.

The job skills of the creator of social reality include not only storytelling, but playwriting and playacting and many varieties of stage management. As more people suspect that reality can be created, the world becomes a kind of theater in which competing groups offer competing plots, and people with political aspirations try to get themselves cast in good roles. Shakespeare saw this coming when he had a character say, "All the world's a stage"; today it is true in a way he could not have imagined.

In the collapse of belief, a thousand playwrights offer their versions of what is happening: here comes the revolution, here comes the Kingdom of God, here comes the New Age. One stage, different plays.

Tom Stoppard's *Rosenkranz and Guildenstern Are Dead* is one of the great myths of our time. It is not merely a play, or even a play within a play, but a counterplay about people who don't want to follow the prevailing story. Some murky tragedy involving a Danish prince is taking place over there on one corner of the stage, but our heroes are not terribly interested in that plot. They do their own thing, spin out a different script. And so it goes in the postmodern world: if you don't like the plot, you can always try your hand at creating another one and seeing if anybody wants to take a part in it.

It is not surprising, though, that controversies arise as to what is the *real* plot—or whether there is one at all. This kind of controversy has become a familiar feature of contemporary politics; it produces new and confusing situations, but amidst the confusion we can identify a pattern, a new political polarization. This is the second process.

THE NEW POLARIZATION

In the modern era, everyone learned to see politics along a left-to-right spectrum: the popular image had wild-eyed bomb-throwing revolutionists at one outer edge of the band and uptight my-country-right-or-wrong conservatives at the other. That spectrum had many shadings, but a basic polarization tended to emerge in all countries—particularly those with two-party systems. Gilbert and Sullivan summed it up admirably in their song about

> How nature always does contrive
> That every boy and every gal,
> That's born into the world alive
> Is either a little Liberal,
> Or else a little Conservative![14]

This polarization expresses deep psychological differences between human beings. Perhaps such differences exist in any society, modern or ancient; in any case the specific form it took, the form we know best, was a product of the Industrial Revolution. In that form it shaped the politics of most governments at most levels, from national to local. It also generated the capitalist-communist deadlock, which dominated decades of international politics.

Another political spectrum is now becoming visible—so visible, in fact, that you would have a hard time *not* noticing its presence. We commonly identify it also as a conservative-to-liberal spectrum, but it is not quite the same. The new spectrum has at one extreme those who hold firmly to a set of truths that they declare to be *the* cosmic reality. These enviably sure-minded citizens may be religious fundamentalists or hard-nosed scientists, Marxist ideologues or true believers in Gaia—epistemology makes its own strange bedfellows. All kinds of positions occupy the middle ground; some of them are moderate and most of them merely confused. Near the other extreme are the relativists and constructivists who hold all truth to be human invention. Whatever is out there, they say, remains for all time out there, and all our systems of thought are stories we tell ourselves about something that remains essentially unknowable.

And there is yet another position. The rush of postmodern reaction from the old certainties has swept some people headlong into a worldview even more radical than that of the constructivists. Many voices can now be heard declaring that what is out there is only what we *put* out there. More precisely, what *I* put there—just little me, euphorically creating my own universe. We used to call this solipsism; now we call it New Age spirituality. It is the world according to Shirley MacLaine, who apparently created us all.

Many variations. But, as in the modern era, a basic polarization emerges. A postmodern Gilbert and Sullivan might say that all the people who now exist are either a little objectivist or else a little constructivist. And the two find themselves totally unable to agree on such matters as educational policy: what beliefs and values we should teach in the public schools.

Conflicts about this concrete part of the social-reality question have broken out like angry wildfires in very ordinary American communities, little towns where a lecture on epistemology would not draw enough listeners to fill the back room of the bar. One such place was Lolo, Montana, a small rural community near the Idaho border, where people divided into opposed camps and engaged in a bitter and long-lasting battle about what was being taught in the local schools. Some parents feared that their children were getting "global perspectives" instead of patriotism, "moral reasoning" and "values clarification" instead of traditional Christian and American principles. They considered such ideas to be subversive, and the people advancing them to be enemies of society. A teacher who was fired in the Lolo dispute said that she finally understood what people must have felt like during the McCarthy era or the Hitler years.

What some parents found subversive was the proposition that values are *not* based on any utter certainty about what is true and right, and have to be worked out by fallible human beings in the midst of daily life. This is a fairly common theme in public-school texts. A home economics book that drew heavy fire in one such dispute had the following statement: "Values are subjective. They vary from person to person. You will be able to understand and get along with other people better if you keep an open mind about the value judgments they make."[15]

Another text said that "one cannot go to an encyclopedia or a textbook for values," that they "come out of the flux of life itself."[16] A handbook for values clarification activities told teachers that such learning could not even be graded: "The teacher may, and is encouraged to, evaluate how well a particular activity is going, but this can never be translated into an evaluation of students.... There are no wrong answers, and grading would only serve to stifle trust, honesty and a willingness to self-disclose."[17]

This sort of stuff, which to most of us might seem to suffer from no vice other than blandness, enrages fundamentalist critics, who say it comes perilously close to teaching that there is no right and wrong. In the fundamentalist worldview, there can be no values without an absolute source and authority; any instruction based on purely *human* moral reasoning, its critics say, has an "amoral, socialist bias."[18]

Fundamentalists have produced their own textbooks, based on absolutism instead of relativism. An ad for one announces:

> Many good books have been written about the danger of Secular Humanism. Now there is a book that does something to protect the mind of your child from its evil. *Escape from Sugarloaf Mine* is a power-packed, adventure story for children from pre-school through junior high school.
>
> This children's book actually counteracts—and neutralizes—the humanistic philosophy taught in Values Clarification. . . . Where Values Clarification teaches moral relativism, *Escape from Sugarloaf Mine* teaches decision-making skills based on God's moral absolutes.[19]

Controversies over this issue have torn apart many communities, and have surfaced also at the highest levels of government. In the Reagan administration, some officials pushed for an all-out White House crusade against any sort of relativistic values teaching.[20] It is a major concern of national organizations such as Citizens for Excellence in Education, which supports teaching of absolute values, and People for the American Way, which works for moral reasoning.

Running closely parallel to the educational wars are conflicts about religious faith. The Southern Baptist church—a denomination that was once a model of old-style American individualism—has been having a tumultuous battle born of the crusade of some of its members to impose upon all Baptists a single tightly defined set of religious doctrines.

Old-time Baptists are amazed to see such a battle going on within their church. For centuries the Baptist denomination championed freedom of religion, and practiced it. Its congregations were independent democratic organizations, its members guided by the old freethinking tenet of the "priesthood of the believer." Put two Baptists in the same room, a saying went, and you would get three opinions.

But then a faction within the church began strenuously advancing a doctrine of the literal truth of the Bible—one truth, one infallible and unerring truth. This position is known as inerrantism or literalism. Bill Moyers (himself reared as a Southern Baptist) interviewed its chief spokesman, the Reverend W. A. Criswell of the First Baptist Church in Dallas, for a Public Affairs Television series entitled *God and Politics*:

MOYERS: You call yourself a literalist. How do you define that?

DR. CRISWELL: Yes. I just think the Bible literally is true. Just from the beginning to the end of it.

MOYERS: Doctrinally?

DR. CRISWELL: Yes.

MOYERS: Scientifically?

DR. CRISWELL: Yes.

MOYERS: Historically?

DR. CRISWELL: Historically, yes.

MOYERS: In every way?

DR. CRISWELL: In every way.

MOYERS: And by liberal, you mean those people who say that Adam and Eve were not necessarily historical figures, that they were representative of the human race?

DR. CRISWELL: That's correct.

MOYERS: And people who say that miracles didn't necessarily happen, that they are parables of truth.

DR. CRISWELL: That's correct.

MOYERS: That's a liberal.

DR. CRISWELL: That's correct, that's correct, that's correct.

MOYERS: You mean liberal theologically.

DR. CRISWELL: That's right. For when the man starts going that way, it's not long until he puts his Bible down and he picks up psychology and sociology and political science, and the Lord only knows what all. You've got to stay by that Bible and what it says, and if you ever turn aside from it, you're going to turn into all those other things.[21]

Dr. Criswell and his followers mounted a well-organized campaign to take over the denomination and impose that truth on all its services, publications, and teaching institutions. Inerrantists gained majorities on several major committees, and succeeded in forcing the resignation of the president and the dean of faculty at Southern Baptist Theological Seminary. The new chairman of the seminary's board of trustees announced that from then on all new faculty members would be "people who believe that the Bible is without error."[22] This battle is still going on, and many of the older church leaders, people whom most of us would take for straight-backed conservatives, are hurt and bewildered to find themselves regarded by the inerrantists as a bunch of mushy liberals. They wonder why this is happening to them, and why it is happening now. Their agony, whether they know it or not, is part of the pain of the birth of a postmodern world.

Inerrantism is a counterrevolution. The inerrantists are in rebellion against contemporary life with its complexity and pluralism, its constant squabbles among different groups with different views of reality, its endless demand on the individual to make choices. They are in hot pursuit of a civilization with no uncertainties.

They have a political ideology, which they call Reconstruction. Reconstruction is popular among religious fundamentalists in many different denominations. Its agenda is fairly simple, and just what its name suggests: to reconstruct American civilization and make the literal truth of the Bible the public creed. All laws and public policies would be based on the appropriate scriptural passages. The Reconstructionists (who seem not to have heard of hermeneutics) operate on the touchingly naive assumption that there will be no political conflicts about how to interpret the passages or about who decides which chapter and verse to apply to which issue. So presumably there can be no possibility of anybody exercising political tyranny by being the official interpreter. The government will simply base its politics on all subjects—space exploration, biotechnology, Federal Reserve rates, energy policy, whatever—on plain readouts from the Good (instruction) Book.

What the Reconstructionists want is an error-free, choice-free society, and they believe it is possible. They see the truth as God-given, beyond all human construction—yet at the same time readily available, right there in the Bible. And they are united in their unmoving opposition to any suggestion that values and beliefs (and Holy Scriptures) are human creations.

Switch the scene to Iran, and the same polarization comes into focus. The news from Iran in the late 1980s told a story of religious persecution—in this case, violent and cruel persecution of members of the Baha'i faith. It was an ugly story that, reduced to its essentials, showed another conflict between absolutist and relativist worldviews—and vividly illustrates some of the general propositions of constructivist social theory.

In a society dominated by a single absolutist worldview, write Peter Berger and Thomas Luckmann in *The Social Construction of Reality*,

> the monopolistic tradition and its expert administrators are sustained by a unified power structure. Those who occupy the decisive power positions are ready to use their power to impose the traditional definitions of reality on the population under their authority. Potentially competitive conceptualizations of the universe are liquidated as soon as they appear—either physically destroyed ("whoever does not worship the gods must die") or integrated within the tradition itself.... The competition may also be segregated within the society and thus made innocuous as far as the traditional monopoly is concerned.[23]

The Iranian government tried a bit of all three of the standard methods of liquidation. Some of the Baha'is were tortured and executed. Others, those who held public office, were "integrated" by means of an edict that required them to renounce their religion if they wanted to keep their jobs. Others were rendered innocuous: the state deprived them of protection of the laws, stripped them of their property, and in various ways managed to push them toward the bottom of the social and economic scale. Many fled the country as refugees; the Iranian government had stopped giving them exit visas.

The conflict between the Islamic government and the Baha'i minority was not a conflict between similar opposing systems of thought. The government represented a fundamentalist wing of Islam. The Baha'i faith is an open-minded and humanistic religion that believes in the unity of all nations and races; its teachings advocate the abolition of extremes of wealth and poverty, universal education, equality between the sexes, and an "unfettered search for truth" embracing philosophical inquiry and modern science. It is especially postmodern in regard to religion and the state: it holds as equally sacred the scriptures of most world faiths—including Islam—and instructs its members to obey the laws of whatever society they belong to.

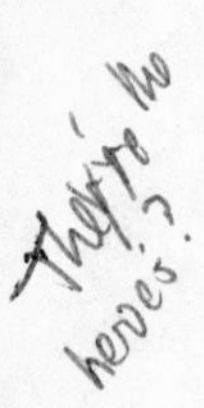

Obviously a bunch of troublemakers.

The Iranian government would not even recognize Baha'i as a religion. "It would be illegal to recognize as a religion any sect which is not recognized in the Koran," an Iranian official told an American writer, in a statement whose logic would please the author of *Catch-22*.[24] Thus the government absolved itself of guilt for religious persecution.

But note that the government felt the need to do so publicly, and note why: Iran's leaders were concerned about how the country would be perceived by other nations. Religious tolerance has some validity as a global norm, one that gets a bit of lip service even from a spokesman for a rigid theocracy that is in the process of violating it.

The Iranian government's treatment of the Baha'is was in part good old-fashioned religious persecution, but this aspect of it reveals that something new and different is going on: the conflict was not limited to the boundaries of Iran but was happening within the context of a global society that has some norms, however weakly institutionalized, of pluralism and religious tolerance. This is another feature of the postmodern world: because every society now operates within the global society, one slowly but inexorably developing its own culture, the task of enforcing a single official reality structure is extremely difficult. It is likely to fail in the long run, and the government that tries to do the enforcing will be oppressive and bellicose while it lasts—driven to the use of terror against its own citizens, justified in the use of terrorism against its external enemies because they are seen as enemies of truth and goodness itself.

The new polarization is a split between different *kinds* of belief, not between different beliefs. It divides those who believe from those who have beliefs. It pits fundamentalists—who may be fundamentalists of religion, science, ideology, or cultural tradition—against an opposition called relativists here, secular humanists there, religious liberals somewhere else.

This polarization has now become at least as widespread and explosive as the "East-West" rivalry between the capitalist nations and the communist nations, and the "North-South" tension between the developed nations and the Third World. It does not replace them, and it does not render them obsolete. It transforms them, and gives them new meaning and depth and emotional urgency.

GLOBAL MEMES

This polarization has an unmistakably global dimension to it. Even in the small towns where folks bicker with one another about how to run the schools, the local issues and rivalries are overshadowed by a general feeling that all social orders—definitely including small-town America—are being drawn into something much larger.

We all know that some kind of a global civilization is coming into being; this is one of the truisms of our time. And we dimly sense also that this must be an event of great significance, a turning point in human evolution. For hundreds of thousands of years, human beings dispersed around the world, developing different languages and religions and customs and political systems. Then, within an instant of evolutionary time, the process began to reverse itself, and that which had been flowing apart for millennia suddenly began to flow together. Today, all those cultures stand shoulder to shoulder on a single planet that now seems quite small, and another level of cultural evolution begins: it demands language about languages, religion about religions, custom about customs, and a civilization to encompass civilizations.

Everybody knows there is a global culture—an ever-growing web of ideas held together by the majority of human beings. Yet nobody has much of an idea of what it is. No team of social scientists has yet gone forth to do the global opinion survey that would tell us (at least those of us who believe in opinion surveys) what knowledge and values the world's 5.2 billion people share in common.

Such a project would be a grantsman's dream and a worthy addition to the public dialogue. Without it, is there any way we can begin to know the shape and form of this global culture, and sensibly evaluate its likely impact on our older systems of value and belief?

I will raise this question several times in the following chapters, and suggest a number of ways of answering it. At this point let us begin with the obvious, with things we see in the world news. Consider, for example, the image of a young Palestinian soldier that a reporter I know saw standing guard in the hills of Lebanon. He was fighting to preserve his ancient culture and its identity. He wore sneakers, blue jeans, and a Grateful Dead T-shirt. He carried an Uzi.

Or consider the photograph taken of a Chinese student in Tienanmin Square during the 1989 demonstrations. He was also wearing a T-shirt, inscribed, in English, "We Shall Overcome." Consider Zhao Ziyang, the later-deposed general secretary of the Chinese Communist Party, who was frequently seen wearing a Western business suit instead of the traditional Mao uniform that had been worn by his predecessors in that office. Consider, for that matter, the Mao uniform and what it says to wear one.

The semioticists, the scholars of signs, say that all the things human beings create are containers of meaning. A building is thus not only a shelter, but a statement. And a city is a veritable library. Every object that the eye falls upon tells something about its creator, and about the society, and is used to create meaning within the mind of the beholder. The British zoologist Richard Dawkins, working in the same general direction as the semioticists, coined the term *memes* to describe replicating mental patterns—the cultural equivalent of genes. As examples of memes he notes "tunes, ideas, catch-phrases, clothes fashions, ways of making pots or of building arches."

And so all the T-shirts and jeans and sneakers and suits are not only things but ideas. They carry (if nothing else) the far-from-trivial message that human beings everywhere have more or less similar bodies that can be encased in more or less similar pieces of clothing. And, since few of us make our own suits or sneakers (or Uzis), they announce that we are all consumers of things made by other people—probably other people we have never seen nor expect to see, quite likely people in other countries halfway around the world.

Most inhabitants of the planet, I am told, have seen at one time or another in their lives an image of the earth itself, know it is a photograph taken from a space vehicle en route to the moon. The idea that the earth is a planet is in itself a relatively new meme, another one whose impact we should not underestimate.

Here is a brief, almost-random list of a few other ordinary ideas that most people hold:

- That there is a human species, all of its members biologically capable of interbreeding with all the others, but not with members of different species.
- That the world is divided up into nation-states.
- That there are such things as atomic weapons, and that a global atomic war is possible.

- That there are many different religions, and that some people do not take any of them very seriously.
- That societies change, and keep changing.

All of these are stupefyingly conventional pieces of information to the Western mind, and most of us regard them as so obvious that they are scarcely worth heeding. Yet such homely propositions have everywhere arrived like earthquakes, bringing profound conflicts and stresses—and they continue to arrive that way in remote and relatively untouched regions of the globe.

Look for a moment at another obvious part of contemporary life: money.

Networks of money exchange are spreading over the planet with amazing speed, creating unprecedented patterns of human communication. Most of us devote a good part of our lives to having and getting money, or to worrying about it and dreaming about it. And many political analysts will tell you that economic activity is more or less synonymous with politics itself; this is known as hard-headed political realism.

And so it is, in a way. But money is a *socially constructed* reality, an abstract idea. The international money economy is a network of symbols, becoming more symbolic all the time. William Greider, in one of his "Annals of Finance" articles, noted: "Over the centuries, the evolution of money has been a long and halting progression in which human societies have hesitantly transferred their money faith from one object to another, at each step moving farther away from real value and closer to pure abstraction."[25]

Some African tribes used cattle as currency, but cattle were also valuable in themselves. So were the clam shells used by North American Indians, the tobacco used by some American colonists, the gold and silver out of which coins were made. But then we took a leap to currencies that only *represented* something of inherent value, and now, in the electronic bazaars of international finance, the postmodern money changers regularly invent new and more abstract ways to wheel and deal: options and futures and debt-for-equity swaps. Even in our personal everyday commerce, we become more and more accustomed to credit cards—which enable us to deal in representations of the representation—and are told by the futurists that money will someday become obsolete.

It is commonplace to observe that cultures change when the use of money is introduced. The observation is correct, yet it misses the point. Money *is* culture; it is a symbolic system of value and belief, a pocketful of memes. Even to learn that it exists is to transform your consciousness, to take a step toward modernism that you can never reverse. And the more we all abstract our use and understanding of money from any absolute value, the farther we travel into a postmodern worldview which recognizes that its reality is a social creation.

In thousands of such ways, many of them so prosaic that we scarcely notice them, we form a new worldview. A new superculture comes into being, wraps itself about the globe. Goods of all kinds move about in international trade. The rapidly growing networks of communication—print, radio, television, and all the rest—scatter images and ideas. Money in all its postmodern guises flows everywhere. And international organizations proliferate: since the end of World War II, the number of international organizations has risen from about eighty to more than four hundred. Multinational corporations and financial networks have grown and rapidly become more complex. Nongovernmental organizations spring up everywhere: in 1910 there were only a couple hundred NGOs in the whole world; now there are over five thousand—or, if you prefer a more generous definition that includes religious bodies, over twelve thousand.

Global subcultures such as those of science, business, and diplomacy also flourish and create new patterns of international society. Many people are more at home in these placeless subcultures than in any traditional culture or nation or tribe. And as the marketplace of reality becomes an international one, subcultures of all kinds forge links around the world—free-floating communities of shared interest and ideology and information.

This looks to some people like nothing more than the Westernization of the world. They're not entirely wrong, and the spread of Western influence is something you can view with dismay, or perhaps with a bit of hope. It includes not only junk food and junk bonds, but also concepts of democracy and human rights. And whether it's good or bad, it is still only a fragment of the whole picture anyway, because a more subtle Easternization is going on also. Every Westerner knows about tea and Zen and the thoughts of

Chairman Mao, and every Western businessman has heard about Japanese management. In California we have already had our first Buddhist governor, and I have no doubt that more are on the way.

Some parts of global culture brutally destroy and quickly replace the values and beliefs of traditional cultures. Modernism supplants premodernism; postmodernism supplants modernism. But other things, far more complex and fascinating things, also take place. Cultural change has always been an astoundingly multidimensional business, full of innovations and improvisations, ghosts and disguises.

We are indeed seeing in our time the birth of a global superculture that pours together bits and pieces of many different cultures. But it is not just a combination of pieces, and neither will it be merely an homogenization; human beings are far too inventive for that, and the human mind is far too complex. We are learning the infinitely subversive lesson that we don't always have to simply believe this and not believe that. Amid the collapse of old ways of belief comes the discovery that we are capable of creating many layers of belief and unbelief, of living partly in and partly out of socially created realities. The collapse of belief has already generated entirely new ways of being in cultures, and pluralism with a vengeance. Old belief systems live on, and new ones are created to suit every yen and every agenda. The postmodern world will be anything but dull, everything but monolithic.

The question—and it is one of the most important political questions of all time—is this: what will be the basic shape of the global culture? What values and beliefs will form the overall structure of global civilization? Many people are of course right on hand to offer quick answers to this, based on whatever their ideological preferences happen to be. There are even more prescriptions for the globe than there are for America. You can find books describing a global Marxist civilization, and books describing a Western-model "modernization" as a universal pattern of social order. Some Christian fundamentalists prophesy a whole world running smoothly and virtuously according to biblical instructions, and I recently heard a leader of the Hezbollah proclaim the coming of an Islamic world civilization. So it goes among the big thinkers.

But those are idle dreams. The world is not about to develop some grim doctrinaire culture to unite the entire human species under one of the old ideologies. And although some dreamers prescribe *new* ideologies of global scope, those prospects look equally dim: we are in no more imminent danger of all becoming Greens than of all becoming Marxists. For the foreseeable future, the global culture is going to be one with a thin, fragile, and ever-shifting web of common ideas and values, and, within that, incredible diversity—more diversity than there has ever been.

Yet so many people are convinced that global culture must be the great monolith that destroys old systems of value and belief. And conflicts between relativists and fundamentalists, even local conflicts, frequently turn into battles about globalism. In the American school textbook controversies, "international studies" and "global awareness" courses meet with the same heated opposition—and from the same sources—as do courses on moral reasoning. Those courses, as Citizens for Excellence in Education declares, are de facto indoctrination into "a one-world, anti-American point of view." And in Iran it is precisely the Baha'is, seekers after the unity of all nations and all religions, who are singled out for extermination.

In a way, the fearful fundamentalists are right: globalism does undermine systems of absolute value and belief. But in a way they are wrong: the systems of value and belief do not immediately disappear—people simply inhabit them in a different fashion, and sometimes the old ways turn out to have a surprising amount of life left in them. The human mind has a great repertoire of ways to accept and honor social constructions of reality without swallowing them whole.

Globalizing processes require us to renegotiate our relationships with familiar cultural forms, and remind us that they are things made by people: human, fallible things, subject to revision. Globalism and a postmodern worldview come in the same package; we will not have one without the other.

People who talk about the birth of global society often point to the picture of the earth as one of the great memes of the century, powerfully communicating its stark visual message that we are all in the same round boat. Others speak of human rights—the spreading idea that all people are entitled to some minimal conditions of freedom and dignity—as a central core of world civilization. The idea of the social construction of reality is at least as important as either of these.

It is an elusive idea, with a now-you-see-it, now-you-don't way of behaving. Some of the intellectual movements that deal with the subject have it pretty well pinned down, but for most of us it seems obvious one minute and invisible the next. Yet it is present among us for all that, a living part of global culture. And it will inevitably turn out to be the main meme, the idea that takes us beyond belief as we have known it into a new way of understanding ourselves and of thinking about that which is beyond our understanding.

THE THREAT AND THE PROMISE

The ideas we have been discussing here—rather abstract ideas, rather slippery ones—are, despite their intangibility, the keys to all political power. Wherever ways of belief change, structures of power change also.

Pull the creed of divine right out from under a monarch, and you have very little left—as we can see wherever that maimed institution endures. Substitute for the ironclad certainty of Marxist dialectic the notion that Karl and Friedrich were just a couple of intellectuals with a few good ideas and a few bad ones, and yet another empire begins to totter.

The American fundamentalists have gotten themselves excessively worked up over the fear that the social order will collapse entirely unless we have a consensus on some absolute truths. If they were right about that, the prospects for pluralist democracy would be very dim indeed. But there is a more limited rule of politics that does apply: wherever you do find such a consensus, a group of people united by a belief system and a conviction that it is reality itself—be the belief Scientology, Marxism, or the American Way of Life—you will find individuals within that group who have built their lives and fortunes on the belief system and who are going to be deeply interested in maintaining it. The collapse of old ways of belief and the coming into being of a new worldview threaten all existing constructions of reality and all power structures attached to them—and a lot of people aren't going to like it. We must understand—and the kindly hordes of liberals, New Agers, and one-worlders who think globalism is the end to all our troubles need to understand—that it is one of the most psychologically and politically threatening events in all of human history.

People of power and position are not the only ones who resist threats to a belief system; so do ordinary people who have internalized that belief system and take it to be absolute reality. The collapse of a belief system can be like the end of the world. It can bring down not only the powerful, but whole systems of social roles and the concepts of personal identity that go with them. Even those who are most oppressed by a belief system often fear the loss of it. People can literally cease to know who they are.

There are many people in the world who have been thus deeply dispossessed. You don't have to have left home to become a refugee. This dispossession does not have to happen, but it can and does—and will—happen in many cases as old belief systems erode, as old bases of personal and social identity change.

These problems are not going to be resolved either by romantic "traditionalism" that seeks to preserve old cultures intact, or by the cheerful globalism that equates interdependency with improvement. They require a postmodern worldview that is aware of the tragedy as well as the promise of the liberation—for that is what it is—from premodern and modern social constructions of reality.

Such a worldview—call it an ideology, call it a new sense of history or a global political culture—is latently present among us, but has yet to discover itself. It lurks in the backs of the minds of fundamentalists who are forced to superhuman acts of denial as they strive to keep from themselves the knowledge of the freedom and choice they regularly exercise in their battle against relativism. It is present in an embryonic way in the thinking of relativists and secular humanists who champion tolerance but have never asked themselves what they are really saying about belief when they say that people of different beliefs can live together.

We can see in many parts of the world signs of a postmodern attitude emerging in a tentative way, as people find it possible to retain some sense of their connection to older traditions and at the same time create new arrangements; the European experiment of link-ing divergent nationalities together into a European Community is one example of such an attitude at work—and a development that seemed utterly impossible only a few decades ago.

In order for the postmodern worldview to emerge fully and mature, it needs, among other things, a better sense of history—an idea of what it is the human species has found out about itself in recent centuries, and what effects that discovery has had on us. It is not hard to find some of that in the public record. The postmodern worldview has been a long time in coming. And in recent decades it has been anything but shy about proclaiming its imminent arrival.

CHAPTER 2

To See the Wizard

The Wizard of Oz is another myth for our time—especially rich in meaning at its conclusion, in which, after a long quest for the great Oz, Dorothy and her friends reach his palace. They are ushered into the throne room and are finally in his mighty presence. Lights flash, and a great voice thunders at them. They are suitably terrified and impressed—until Dorothy's dog Toto pulls away the curtain to reveal that behind the awe-inspiring machinery is nothing but an ordinary human being. The wizard is seen at last. Dorothy, in her disappointment, accuses him of being a very bad man. He replies that he is a very *good* man, but a very bad wizard.

So goes the human quest for the reality beyond human artifice. We like to believe that our constructions of reality come from beyond us—from God, or at the very least from superhuman larger-than-life givers of meaning and truth.

But for centuries the human species has been discovering that it is the creator of its own reality—making the discovery, and retreating from it in disappointment (because the wizard is not what we expected) and in fear (because the freedom the discovery brings is unknown and terrifying).

We have no Columbus of this discovery, no 1492 to mark it—only hints and clues of many occasions when people seem to have glimpsed something of the artifice, transience and fragility of the public worldview. It may well be that the discovery has been made far more times than we can know, in partial and hidden ways.

Probably the discovery has been lingering in the shadows every time people from one culture have come into contact with people from another, throughout human history and well before it began to be recorded. The explorer, the wandering merchant, the far-reaching military conqueror—all encountered different customs, different beliefs, fundamentally different ways of looking at the world and of being in it. They usually missed the significance of such differences, explained away the situation as one in which the other people were simply ignorant and in need of conversion—but there must always have been those who experienced an inner sense of anxiety about their own worldviews (the anxiety we now call culture shock) and suspected that something more was going on here than simply a meeting with a bunch of people who did not have much of a handle on reality.

WHEN WORLDS COLLIDE

Karl Mannheim, an early scholar of the social construction of reality, theorized that it took more than one kind of mobility to bring home the "alarming fact that the same world can appear differently to different observers"—horizontal mobility to send people into strange social settings and vertical mobility to shake up the social orders from which they came and render them more vulnerable to such a discovery. Social stability, Mannheim said, increased the binding power of social constructions of reality and made it possible for people to view other cultures as merely primitive or wrong; but when a soldier or a merchant ventured forth from a society in turmoil, he was more likely to be—whether he knew it or not—in a more relativistic and receptive frame of mind.[1]

By the time Greek civilization emerged into the record of history, many people were beginning to suspect that different worldviews were possible, and were publicly expressing their suspicions in various ways. We can catch a strong hint of such a suspicion in Plato's metaphor of the people in the cave, and in his discussion of the noble lie. Mannheim, staying with his class-based analysis, thought the surge of skepticism in the Athenian democracy was tied up with the increasing social mobility that brought into conflict two classes with two different ways of looking at the world: a dominant but declining nobility whose consciousness was anchored in the ancient myths, and a rising urban artisan class more given to an analytical approach to the world. Out of this came the skepticism of the Sophists and then of Socrates who mastered the technique of raising questions and still more questions until he had—so it seemed at the time—probed to the very core of reality.

Is this perhaps what was going on in New England in the 18th century specifically (Newport)

But the ancient Greeks did not discover the social construction of reality. Their quest was to discover the enduring and perfect truth, not to reveal the extent to which all societies are built on truths that are neither enduring nor perfect. Their work contributed to a new orthodoxy of thought that lasted, if not for all time, at least for several centuries.

Greek philosophy—parts of it, at any rate—became the foundation of medieval Christian society, a monolithic structure of reality that covered an immense territory and endured for a long period of time.

Even that mighty bastion stood on shaky ground. It was nervously on guard against heresies, murderously antagonistic toward them when they arose. Some of its solidity may well have been illusory. Max Weber has argued that there were actually quite different versions of Christianity operating in medieval Europe—an intellectualized one for the priests and scholars, and a much different one, full of folk beliefs and superstitions, for the ordinary people.[2]

At any rate, its authority eroded—partly because increasing social mobility made it possible for more people to find out about the differences between the two versions, partly because the Church itself, the keeper of the faith, was a cesspool of power and greed that failed spectacularly to operate according to Christian principles. It is hard to maintain the facade when you have political incidents such as the schism of the fourteenth century that produced two popes, each of whom excommunicated the followers of the other. The Western world began a long slide away from its faith in the cool, ultimate truths that the Greeks believed could be found and the medieval clerics believed had been revealed by Christian theology.

I am talking here in very general terms about a massive historical transition that took place throughout Western civilization over a period of several centuries, and I do not want to imply that it was a straight march in a single direction. We do know that the reality structure embodied in the medieval Church and the feudal system gradually declined, lost its status as the definer of cosmic truth and the shaper of social order. That decline released many different energies: bursts of creativity as people shook off the old bonds, profound doubts in all reality, searches for new certainties, defenses of the old order. All those energies were parts of the dynamic of the modern age, and all of them are still with us in the postmodern age.

We associate the Renaissance with the bursts of creativity. Scholars argue about whether the Renaissance was more modern or medieval, whether it was really a glorious torrent of freedom or only an overrated creation of recent historians, whether there was any Renaissance at all—but clearly there were modes of thought that would not have been tolerated in the medieval era.[3] We remember the Renaissance for such things as Machiavelli's famous self-help book on how a ruler might pretend to Christian virtue while operating by another set of rules entirely; it took the Middle Ages to produce such behavior, and the Renaissance to produce a book about it. The era brought forth some of the world's greatest artistic creations and also a new humanistic philosophy that took a creative view toward life itself. Pico della Mirandola caught the essence of it in his famous *Oration on the Dignity of Man*, in which he has God say to Adam that "you, being your own free maker and artificer, may fashion yourself into whatever form you choose."

The doubt? It runs like a dark river through the art and thought of the early modern years. *Don Quixote*, the book we hail as the first modern novel and one of the most profound literary works of all time, is an epic of human illusion. The old knight, swathed in the fantasies of the medieval age, goes forth with his equally fantastic sidekick into a new world he does not understand and tries to live out his dreams in it. Cervantes invites the reader to be amused by these ludicrous adventures, but we come away from his entertainment with a disturbing feeling that the "real" world is in the grip of its own illusions, and that every one of us is Don Quixote and/or Sancho Panza.

René Descartes, the philosopher we regard as the father of modern thought, built his life's work on doubt. As Hannah Arendt points out in *The Human Condition*, the famous *cogito ergo sum* ("I think, therefore I am") was closely linked to *dubito ergo sum*. Doubt was for Descartes the primal human experience, the source of whatever wisdom we might be able to gain in the midst of life. "If there was salvation," she writes, "it had to lie in man himself, and if there was a solution to the questions raised by doubting, it had to come from doubting. If everything has become doubtful, then doubt at least was certain and real."[4]

Cartesian doubt was in large part the consequence of an early meeting between the reality of faith and the reality of science—not only science, but science abetted by technology. This was a new kind of culture shock: Copernicus's revolutionary image of the solar system had been working its disturbing way through human consciousness for a century or so by Descartes's time; Galileo preceded Descartes by only a few decades. Galileo's telescope revealed, much more dramatically than Copernicus's theoretical writings had, a solar system that didn't seem to be at all the same as the familiar one people had seen for centuries with the naked eye. Could it be that God did not simply reveal the universe to humanity? Descartes did not doubt that God existed, but he did question all assumptions about how God went about his business. As Arendt puts it: "Only now, when it appeared as though man, if it had not been for the accident of the telescope, might have been deceived forever, did the ways of God really become wholly inscrutable; the more man learned about the universe, the less he could understand the intentions and purposes for which he should have been created."[5]

As the Enlightenment unfolded, Cartesian doubt gave way to scientific debunking mixed with a spirit of social creativity. The idea of progress, of constant betterment of the human condition, took on almost mythic force—and a doctrine of progress produces a different way of looking at things as they are: the thinkers of the Enlightenment believed the world would achieve constant improvement if people would use their rational minds to scrutinize social beliefs mercilessly and throw them away like worn-out shoes when they no longer served. Political revolutionists proclaimed that people should tear down old structures of governance and replace them with new ones more to their liking. The dominant conflict of the time was between faith and reason, with reason—that is, science—on the rise. Doubt was what fueled scientific inquiry, but the product appeared to be certainty: science, for many people in the modern era, merely replaced religion as the source of absolute truth.

In many ways, science had, by the end of the nineteenth century, won the war. But we know that the triumph of a new construction of reality did not produce an era of stability. For one thing, the old reality refused to acknowledge defeat and go away; it was right there, for all the world to see—as obvious as the two popes—that there are different kinds of truth. For another, science itself turned out to be not a single revelation but an ongoing process, continually revising its own truths. Doubt did not go back to wherever it had come from, and neither did the creative/destructive impulses that had been unleashed at the end of the medieval era. And soon there burst upon an astounded world an unprecedented period of improvisation.

BOMBTHROWERS AND MINDBLOWERS

In the later years of the modern era—culminating in Europe in the early twentieth century—a new kind of revolutionary attitude toward social structures of reality began to be expressed, and expressed in a wide variety of ways—destructive, creative, impish, playful, angry, hopeful, philosophical, scientific. People in many segments of society were discovering in different ways that the wizard was only human—and extremely fallible.

In politics the expression took the form of revolutionary and counterrevolutionary ideologies: Marxism, anarchism, nihilism, fascism. The nihilists yearned for the collapse, saw old values and beliefs and the power structures built on them as corrupt beyond redemption, were willing to sweep everything away and take their chances with what comes next. "Our task," said the Russian nihilist leader Sergei Nechayev, "is total, terrible and ultimate destruction." Fascists feared the destructive antiauthoritarian forces that were being unleashed and embarked upon an equally destructive search for new forms of authority. Anarchism was a plunge into freedom; fascism, in Erich Fromm's words, an escape from freedom.

While Nechayev and his colleagues pursued freedom by blowing up prominent citizens, and their fascist enemies sought to preserve order by blowing up nihilists, a new generation of artists pursued freedom on other fronts by ridiculing—and, once in a while, by blowing up—the aesthetic expressions of classical European civilization.

Tristan Tzara, a short, monocled Romanian, burst on the Paris art scene in 1920 as founder of a movement named, with deliberate meaninglessness, dada. Dada was the nihilism of art, aimed at the total, terrible, and ultimate destruction of social reality. As its first public performance, Tzara read a "poem" that was actually an insignificant news item he had clipped at random from a paper. His helpers sounded cowbells and rattles as background music. The audience expressed its appreciation appropriately, by shouting insults and throwing things. Tzara had a terrorist's sense of publicity. He announced that Charlie Chaplin would be present at one of his performances. An overflow audience turned up to see the great *Charlot*, whom Tzara had not invited. They rioted; riots became common features at dada gatherings.

European painters were, like Galileo, inviting people to see the world in new ways. In the early 1900s, Pablo Picasso and Georges Braque had created cubism, a style of painting that they said was based on nature but which fragmented objects into flat surfaces so that the viewer could see different sides of an object simultaneously. They insisted this was not unrealistic, but merely a new view of reality. This influenced sculptors such as Jacques Lipchitz and architects such as Le Corbusier—and influenced the way people looked at the world around them.

Then along came the surrealists. We think of surrealism as an artistic movement, but in Paris in the 1920s the *surréalistes* saw themselves as social activists. Staunchly anti-Catholic, they liked to insult priests and spit on nuns in the streets. Staunchly antiestablishment, they followed the funeral cortege of the immensely popular novelist Anatole France, shouting insults to his memory. (*Un cadavre littéraire*!) New movements and new ideas about art vigorously expressed the growing belief that the old classicism had served only as a straitjacket to creativity. They wanted an art that would be formless, even meaningless according to the older sense of meaning, and would thus plunge deeply into the heart of human experience.

In drama the new sensibility was expressed by Luigi Pirandello in the title of his 1916 play *Right You Are If You Think You Are.* Pirandello became for a time Europe's most eminent playwright, his work based on themes of illusion and reality, of real selves behind social masks. His best-known play, *Six Characters in Search of an Author,* might well be taken as an allegory of modern European society, of individuals wandering in search of meaning.

The loss (or destruction) of old reality, the discovery (or creation) of new—these were the themes that played through European politics and art. Yeats's *The Second Coming* was published in 1921, the same year *Six Characters* was first performed. It revealed a profound, poetically intuitive sense of history, both in its sense of what was happening to European culture (the center cannot hold, mere anarchy is loosed upon the world) and what lay ahead (the rough beast slouching toward Bethlehem—or Berlin—to be born).

Existential philosophy, which soon became a prominent part of the new cultural order that was rapidly replacing the old classical establishment, had its own way of searching for a new sense of reality. Jean-Paul Sartre was easily its most visible and provocative spokesman, and managed to convey some of its ideas to the general public. A created object such as a chair, he would explain, has an essence that precedes its existence. First there is the *idea* of the chair in the mind of its maker, and then there is the chair in reality. But humanity, he insisted, had no such essence. All humanity had was existence. If it wanted to have an essence, it would have to create one for itself. This was Pico della Mirandola in a sidewalk cafe, with God and Adam nowhere to be seen.

And meanwhile, Sigmund Freud and his followers revealed an unconscious stratum of the human psyche—not only unconscious but irrational. Freud talked about the "reality principle," but while he did he made it clear that he considered many social reality structures—definitely including religions and political institutions—to be merely the expressions of irrational needs.

Marx and Freud, whom many regard as the twin pillars of twentieth-century European thought, were both hard on the public reality, although in different ways: Marx called the political order and the worldview that supported it tools of class exploitation and sources of "false consciousness." Freud took them to be shadows cast on the wall of the cave, reflecting unresolved conflicts of childhood and primal memories buried in the unconscious.

A third giant of the century, Einstein, offered to the world a new and disturbing view of the physical universe, and in the process revealed yet another kind of "false consciousness" (although Einstein never used the term) in everyday life. Einstein's challenge to commonsense reality was far greater than Galileo's: he asked us to believe that time and space were not at all as we ordinarily experienced them and *thought* we perceived them to be, that matter and energy were the same, and up and down were merely relative notions.

It was a tough time for absolutes: every road that appeared to lead to certainty had some genius standing in the middle of it with a "wrong way" sign.

Not surprisingly, many people found life most uncomfortable in this climate of thought, and new terms came into the language to define the discontents of the time: alienation, anxiety, anomie, the Cartesian doubts of the man and woman on the street. Each term had something to do with what happens to people when they lose their certainty that social convention is objective and permanent truth. Émile Durkheim, the great French sociologist, had written of anomie as a cause of suicide—people finding themselves in a world with no fixed rules or norms, with "only empty space above them" as he put it, and deciding that life under such conditions was literally not to be endured. These terms became part of the basic vocabulary of new schools of thought that were trying to make sense out of a world losing all its fixed points of reference.

THE SOCIOLOGY OF KNOWLEDGE

Throughout the twentieth century, many scholars have made the social construction of reality their central concern—have taken on with all the sober apparatus of modern rationality the task of comprehending one of life's most mysterious processes.

The anthropologists probably deserve much of the credit—or the blame—for bringing out into clear view the remarkable range of realities that exist in a world that, one would have thought, had but a single reality. The early anthropologists were the true pioneers of the twentieth century, going out in search of culture shock, exposing themselves to it in the same valiantly careless way scientists might expose themselves to disease. They invented "participant observation," a brilliant addition to the human mind's repertoire of ways to make itself uncomfortable. It meant living as closely as possible to the way people of primitive cultures lived.

The anthropologists squatted in the dust of African villages, hunted and feasted on whale blubber with Eskimos, danced in the magical rites of Trobriand Islanders. And they returned with information—not only anecdotes and analyses, but art and sculpture and clothing and tools. Nothing had ever before matched the accumulation of information about different societies that filled the libraries and the museums in Europe and America in the decades after World War I.

People contemplated this and felt something more serious than a mild case of culture shock. Those who really took it in, in all its awesome variety, experienced a deep psychological disturbance that has sometimes been described as the "vertigo of relativity." They saw overwhelming evidence that different peoples had constructed entirely different systems of value and belief, knowledge and myth. Inevitably, those who absorbed this material revised not only their ideas about exotic peoples, but also their ideas about themselves. (Some anthropologists now believe that what happens to the anthropological field-worker is something like what happened to Molière's M. Jourdain when he discovered that he had been speaking prose all his life: the anthropologist discovers that he or she is also living in a culture, not simply in objective reality. "In the act of inventing another culture," writes Roy Wagner, "the anthropologist invents his own, and in fact he reinvents the notion of culture itself.")[6]

And so came into being—appearing in Germany, in the early 1930s—the new academic subdiscipline called the sociology of knowledge: the first intellectual movement devoted to the study of how societies create and perpetuate structures of reality.

Karl Marx is honored as one of the movement's ancestors for having insisted that consciousness is determined by material circumstances. Marx gave the movement some key terms like "false consciousness," by which he meant belief in social reality structures that betray the true (class) interests of the individual.

Sociologists of knowledge like Karl Mannheim borrowed freely from Marx, but turned his own weapons upon him by suggesting that a Marxist's consciousness could be as false as anybody else's. Mannheim said: "It is no longer the exclusive privilege of socialist thinkers to trace bourgeois thought to ideological foundations and thereby to discredit it. Nowadays groups of every standpoint use this weapon against all the rest."[7]

Mannheim escaped from Germany after the Nazis came to power; he taught in England, and the sociology of knowledge became an established school of thought in Europe and the United States, as its practitioners went to work identifying the ways societies create reality.

They talked about how patterns of behavior become institutions. An action is first performed spontaneously among two or more people; it works for them in some way or another, and it is repeated. Repeated over time—and taught to members of the next generation—it becomes an institution.

They talked about the various forms of social control by which societies make sure that people do what an institution requires them to do. They talked about the social roles that form around certain actions, like the spontaneous assumption of leadership in a battle or a ritual that eventually turns into the institutionalized monarchy or priesthood—roles that dominate the people who occupy them. They talked about legitimation devices—myths and theories that build up around an institution to justify and explain it.

They talked about reification—probably the most important single concept in understanding how people create reality. There are all kinds of reification, but for the sociologists of knowledge, the most interesting was the magical game people play when they invent institutions and then forget they have done so. Peter Berger and Thomas Luckmann, whose book *The Social Construction of Reality* is one of the great classics on the subject, describe reification as

> the apprehension of human phenomena as if they were things, that is, in non-human or possibly supra-human terms. Another way of saying this is that reification is the apprehension of the products of human activity *as if* they were something else than human products—such as facts of nature, results of cosmic laws, or manifestations of divine will. Reification implies that man is capable of forgetting his own authorship of the human world, and further, that the dialectic between man, the producer, and his products is lost to consciousness. The reified world is, by definition, a dehumanized world. It is experienced by man as a strange facticity, an *opus alienenum* over which he has no control rather than as the *opus proprium* of his own productive activity.[8]

Reification is often deification—giving institutions like monarchy the sanctity of having been created by God—but it comes in many packages: in America, the popular reverence for the framers of the Constitution is a kind of secular deification, in which a gathering of colonial aristocrats turns into a collective Wizard of Oz.

The sociology of knowledge became an established subdiscipline in the American academic world, and books such as *The Social Construction of Reality* (first published in 1966) undoubtedly contributed in some degree to the remarkable cultural convulsion that gripped the Western world in the 1960s.

GENERAL SEMANTICS

General semantics is another intellectual movement that emerged in the period between the two world wars, another pathway into the postmodern era.

In 1933 Count Alfred Korzybski, a Polish mathematician living in the United States, published *Science and Sanity*, in which he presented what he hoped would become a new science of human communication and the key to a new era in human progress.

Korzybski believed there was a very poor fit between language (at least language as people ordinarily used it) and objective reality—and that this poor fit accounted for most personal psychopathology and produced endless turmoil and unhappiness in societies. He wrote: "Few of us realize the unbelievable traps, some of them of a psychopathological character, which the structure of our language sets before us. . . . We grope by animalistic trial and error, and by equally animalistic strife, wars, revolutions, etc."[9]

At the very core of his indictment of language was one small culprit: "is." He located our most serious semantic problem in the everyday act of naming or describing things: whether we say the earth *is* flat or the earth *is* round, we get ourselves into difficulties that we could avoid by saying that the world *appears* flat or that we now *believe* it to be round.

The word is not the thing, said Korzybski and all the general semanticists who came after him; the map is not the territory. To confuse word and thing is to commit the act of "identification," which in his system became sort of original sin: "Identification is found in all known primitive peoples; in all known forms of 'mental' ills; and in the great majority of personal, national, and international maladjustments."[10]

General semantics was a modern-era movement with a brisk, scientific confidence in facts and rationality, in the possibility of acquiring sure and dependable knowledge. The problem, for

Korzybski, was that the objective world had one structure and language had another; the solution would be to devise language structures that more accurately described the world: "If the structures are similar, then the empirical world becomes 'rational' to a potentially rational being. . ."[11]

Stuart Chase, a writer who popularized general semantics in his 1938 book *The Tyranny of Words*, thought the problem might be solved by a better understanding of the "referent"—the object or situation that a word or label referred to. If people could get clear on what the referent was—and especially if they could agree on what *kind* of a referent it was—then accurate knowledge, rational thought, and good communication might be acheived. People might begin to see that in many cases what they thought was a referent was really only a free-floating label with scarcely any "real world" equivalent at all.

Chase identified three kinds of labels:

1. Labels for common objects, such as "dog," "chair," "pencil." Here difficulty is at a minimum.
2. Labels for clusters and collections of things, such as "mankind," "consumers' goods," "Germany," "the white race," "the courts." These are abstractions of a higher order, and confusion in their use is widespread. There is no entity "white race" outside our heads, but only some millions of individuals with skins of an obvious or dubious whiteness.
3. Labels for essences and qualities, such as "the sublime," "freedom," "individualism," "truth." For such terms, there are no discoverable referents in the outside world, and by mistaking them for substantial entities somewhere at large in the environment, we create a fantastic wonderland. This zone is the especial domain of philosophy, politics, and economics.[12]

Chase, like Korzybski, was an avid philosophy-basher. Korzybski in *Science and Sanity* usually put "philosophy" in quotes to show his contempt for it, and frequently compared it to delusional forms of mental illness. Chase liked to quote philosophical clunkers like this piece of deep thought from Nicholas Berdyaev: "History is the result of a deep interaction between eternity and time; it is the incessant eruption of eternity into time."[13] Where, Chase would want to know, is the referent in such statements?

Chasc's work, and that of other general semanticists, became the basis for a healthy critique of abstract blather in academia and in politics. It set the tone for works like George Orwell's 1946 essay "Politics and the English Language," which argued that sloppy language, sloppy thinking, and dishonest politics are all of a piece. Orwell said: "Political language—and with variations this is true of all political parties, from Conservatives to Anarchists—is designed to make lies sound truthful and murder respectable, and to give an appearance of solidity to pure wind." He did not think this could be changed immediately, but hoped that if people paid attention to the problem they could at least change their own habits, and with luck might together manage to jeer loudly enough to "send some worn-out and useless phrase—some *jackboot, Achilles' Heel, hotbed, melting pot, acid test, veritable inferno* or other lump of verbal refuse—into the dustbin where it belongs."[14]

I don't know that Orwell was directly influenced by general semantics; it would have been impossible for an intellectual of his time to miss it entirely. General semantics was taught in many universities in the United States and Europe, and had (and still has) its own scholarly journal—named *Etc.* in honor of Korzybski's dictum that it would be good to use "etc." whenever one described something, to convey the reminder that it had characteristics other than those mentioned and was not precisely the same as its description. It included among its supporters such eminent thinkers of the time as Bertrand Russell and Bronislaw Malinowski.

Although it started out as an objectivist enterprise—Korzybski wanted to get people to clean up their linguistic act so they could get on with the business of finding facts—general semantics became increasingly constructivist as time went on. The movement drew into its orbit may odd new notions, such as the Sapir-Whorf hypothesis, that were not quite so congenial to a hard-facts view of the world.

Edward Sapir, a linguist at Yale, and Benjamin Lee Whorf, an interdisciplinary explorer who was trained as a chemical engineer and later took up the study of American Indian languages, saw language as not merely a means of communication but a structure of reality. Whorf wrote:

> The forms of a person's thought are controlled by inexorable laws of pattern of which he is unconscious. These patterns are the unper-

ceived intricate systematizations of his own language.... every language is a vast pattern-system, different from others, in which are culturally ordained the forms and categories by which the personality not only communicates, but also analyzes nature, notices or neglects types of relationships and phenomena, channels his reasoning, and builds the house of his consciousness.[15]

Although their ideas were in a way close to Korzybski's and were enthusiastically endorsed by him, they suggested realms of experience far more complex and mysterious. They described languages such as the Hopi that reflected entirely different ways of experiencing time and space and causality—ways that could not simply be dismissed as bad maps.

If one took the Sapir-Whorf hypothesis and went far enough with it—which, as time went on, many people were inclined to do—one could imagine that other cultural/linguistic heritages contained other modes of consciousness, other realities. There might be any number of such realities, and who could say which was the map that fit the territory?

With the map/territory identity thus deeply in question, with the "is" dethroned and referents on the run, anything was possible.

THE SIXTIES: COUNTERCULTURE AND COUNTERREALITY

One might have thought that with all those upheavals during the first half of the twentieth century—assaults on cultural tradition and convention, two world wars, intellectual movements that saw into and through the social construction of reality—the institutions and reifications of the modern era would have simply collapsed in a heap.

Certainly the death of society as everyone had known it was reported frequently enough. But the reports—such as Scott Fitzgerald's proclamation that his generation had returned from World War I to find all gods dead and all wars fought—turned out to be somehow premature. Throughout World War II America appeared to be a nation with all its gods, all its myths, all its old beliefs and symbols still in excellent condition. The media of mass communications did their part to grind out vivid symbols of the wartime drama, and showed what a powerful force entertainment could be. The war was—as wars are meant to be—a great restorer of cultural unity.

Soon afterward, however, that same cultural unity revealed a surprising weakness, and the society turned quickly to control mechanisms such as loyalty oaths: enforcement rather than entertainment. In the 1950s, America became insanely anxious about loyalty. We had a national witch-hunt born of the fear of internal Communist subversion, a modern inquisition that sought to frighten the dissident elements of society into conformity to its central beliefs. The tools of the new inquisition were loyalty oaths, investigations, newsletters, and blacklists identifying supposed subversives; the inquisitors were ambitious politicians like Joseph McCarthy and Richard Nixon, who established public reputations as Communist-hunters. It was a troubled time, yet still recognizably part of the modern era. There was, after all, nothing essentially new about one society, threatened by a rival belief system, coercing its citizens into conspicuous public acceptance of the official reality. The center seemed to be holding.

And one might have thought that it would hold forever, Yeats or no Yeats—and then in the 1960s everything went up for grabs. America (and much of the Western world) passed through an unprecedented social upheaval. The cultural nihilism of the early part of the century flourished again and appeared to be on the verge of sweeping all before it.

The 1960s were the true beginning of the postmodern era. The decade brought forth audacious critiques of the modern worldview, attacks on all belief systems. Strange new ideas about such matters as consciousness and sanity and objective truth entered the public dialogue. The public may not have fully understood them—the people who were throwing them around probably did not fully understand them—but nevertheless we began to grapple more resolutely than we ever had before with open challenges to social reality. Social reality, the *concept* of social reality, became more visible than it had ever been. By the end of the decade we had all been persuaded that we were in possession of something called a worldview—or that it was in possession of us. The worldview itself became something to worry about, defend, change, or, as seemed preferable to many, utterly demolish with whatever weapons were handy.

Theodore Roszak, whose *Making of a Counter Culture* was (and is) the best guide to avant-garde thought of the 1960s, characterized the events of the time as a revolt against the established culture—which he described as built on "the myth of objective consciousness"—and a project of creating a new culture to replace it. He named among the leaders of the counterculture such iconoclasts as Timothy Leary, who sang the praises of drug-aided liberation from the modern worldview, and Alan Watts, who popularized a new Zen Buddhism with curious ideas about the illusory nature of social reality.[16]

Leary first came to the public attention in the early 1960s when he and his colleague Richard Alpert got thrown out of Harvard for giving psilocybin, a synthetic form of mescaline, to various volunteers including maximum-security prison inmates and Harvard undergraduates. He went on to a better drug—LSD—and bigger times. The newspapers often called him the "high priest" of LSD, and it was an apt description; in Leary's gospel, LSD became a kind of chemical messiah that would lead us all into the Kingdom of Heaven. He staged public events—I attended one in Santa Monica Civic Auditorium—that were countercultural versions of Billy Graham revival meetings. Leary appeared on the stage in white robes, surrounded by white-robed followers, and urged one and all to tune in, turn on, drop out, take some dope, and blast through the walls of social reality into True Experience.

Alan Watts also "worked with the psychedelics," as he put it, and in his 1962 book *The Joyous Cosmology* (written with a foreword by Leary and Alpert), he described his experiences with drugs as having produced insights very close to mystic enlightenment.[17] However, as time went on, he took some distance from Leary's view that LSD was the straight ticket to liberation and wisdom. His main gift to the counterculture was Zen. He had published his first book on the subject in London when he was only twenty years old. Later, in San Francisco, he became the priest of Zen to the Beat writers of the 1950s—Jack Kerouac, Allen Ginsberg, and Gary Snyder—and thus to Zen's diffusion into American culture. Watts *was* a priest, an ordained minister of the Episcopal church who had at one time been chaplain at Northwestern University before he got into trouble with his superiors for being a bit too creative with the liturgy and advocating (and practicing) free love. In the 1960s, he expanded his ideas about the meaning of Zen to incorporate new influences: psychedelic experience, radical psychotherapists such as Wilhelm Reich and Frederick Perls, and general semantics. His mysticism echoed what was rapidly becoming the cry of the time: that social reality is both illusory and oppressive. In *Psychotherapy East and West*, he described therapy and spiritual teaching as different paths to freedom from that oppression:

> The psychotherapist must realize that his science, or art, is misnamed, for he is dealing with something far more extensive than a psyche and its private troubles. This is just what so many psychotherapists are recognizing and what, at the same time, makes the Eastern ways of liberation so pertinent to their work. For they are dealing with people whose distress arises from what may be termed *maya*, to use the Hindu-Buddhist word whose exact meaning is not merely "illusion" but the entire world-conception of a culture, considered as illusion in the strict etymological sense of a play (Latin, *ludere*). The aim of a way of liberation is not the destruction of *maya* but seeing it for what it is, or seeing through it. Play is not to be taken seriously, or, in other words, ideas of the world and of oneself which are social conventions and institutions are not to be confused with reality. The rules of communication are not necessarily the rules of the universe.[18]

When I attended one of Watts's seminars in 1967, he recommended various books by psychotherapists as background reading. Among them was *The Book of the It* by George Groddeck, and *The Politics of Experience* by R. D. Laing. Groddeck was a renegade Freudian who said a human being does not so much live as be lived by a larger and not altogether civilized force he called the "it"; his book never quite made it into the counterculture library of classics, but Laing's certainly did.

It was inevitable that an assault on culture would challenge prevailing ideas about what is sane and what isn't. It is very hard, in a world with many realities, to maintain the position that satisfactory adjustment to one reality is equivalent to mental health, and that unsatisfactory adjustment is a form of illness. Laing exploited that fallacy with a vengeance: "Our sanity is not 'true' sanity. Their madness is not 'true' madness. . . . Let no one suppose that we meet 'true' madness any more than we are truly sane."[19] Instead of calling schizophrenia a failure of human adaptation, he said, we can as reasonably call it "a successful attempt not to adapt to pseudo-social realities."[20] Under the assaults of Laing and other counterpsychiatrists, it became a rather common item of 1960s thought that society, afflicted by its constructions of reality, was crazier than anybody in the mental hospitals. *One Flew Over the Cukoo's Nest,* the popular 1962 novel by Ken Kesey—leader of the acid-tripping Merry Pranksters—gave the world a vivid expression of this view in his story about lovable mental hospital inmates battling a demented system.

Leary, Watts, Laing, Zen, and acid represented one wing of what was sometimes called "the movement." There was also a more recognizably political wing. Its theorists were people like Herbert Marcuse, a link to Marx, and Paul Goodman, who aimed his critiques at institutions of power such as the military-industrial complex and the educational establishment. Its activists were the young revolutionaries of Students for a Democratic Society, the ever-growing ranks of protesters against the Vietnam War, the blacks demanding civil rights. Some people said there were two movements, but actually there were any number of them: the civil rights movement, the peace movement, the women's movement, the human potential movement, the sexual freedom movement, the hippie movement, the drug scene, rock music, and new religions. They surged and eddied in all directions, sometimes overlapped and came together, sometimes battled each other. "Somethin's happenin' here," sang Buffalo Springfield, "what it is ain't exactly clear."

Running through all the movements was an idea of reality, of worldviews, of something in the realm of *thought* that could be changed. Even the political revolutionaries, for all their contempt of Leary and Watts, considered themselves to be at war against a "false consciousness" that propped up unjust political structures. The women's movement pioneered the technique of consciousness-raising to enable women to break free of male-dominated worldviews. In the civil rights movement, minorities demanded not only legal rights but a new construction of reality in which they would be *seen* and understood in a fundamentally different way. Before the eyes of the world, black activists dismantled the pickaninny-Aunt Jemima fiction that had for so long shaped the reality of their lives.

The sixties left a legacy of doubt about the public reality—about all public realities—that has not been dispelled by later retreats into familiar beliefs and behavior. It was a time of transition from which there is no turning back. The revolutionaries with their talk of "the politics of consciousness" were, like all revolutionaries, unclear about what might come after the revolution. They massively underestimated the staying power of cultural myths and institutions, the ability of such myths to live on in new ways long after having been abandoned as living beliefs. Most of all, they underestimated the complexity of the very thing they professed to comprehend better than the rest of us—human consciousness. They did not guess at the multidimensional nature of our personalities, our ability to drop beliefs and yet appear (even to ourselves) to retain them. They challenged the entire modern worldview, and thought it advisable to "drop out" of it forthwith into—well, they never made it too clear what you dropped into when you dropped out. They assumed that if you developed enough contempt for your old socially adapted self, a new True Self, unsullied by any conformity, would magically appear, that a True Culture and a True Politics likewise stood in the wings—and that, when they appeared, they would not have to coexist with old selves, old cultures, old politics. Things didn't work out the way they expected, at all. Todd Gitlin in his history of the 1960s says: "Anybody who went to sleep in 1968, with Eldridge Cleaver's *Soul on Ice* leading the best-seller list and *The Graduate* first at the box office, and woke up in 1985 to behold *Iacocca* and *Rambo*, and Cleaver as an apostle of the fire-breathing anti-Communist Unification Church, would be entitled to some astonishment."[21]

Because the nature of the revolution was so muddily understood at the time—because the stories we told about it were so simplistic—we are left wondering if it ever happened at all. But it happened: in a way we *have* all dropped out—not out of the modern worldview completely, but out of the simple acceptance of it that once prevailed, and certainly out of the innocent belief that there are no alternatives.

NIHILIST CHIC

One reason it is so hard to tell when true cultural revolutions have occurred is that societies are terribly good at co-opting their opponents; something that starts out to destroy the prevailing social construction of reality ends up being a part of it. Culture and counterculture overlap and merge in countless ways. And the hostility toward established social constructions of reality that produced strikingly new movements and behaviors in the early decades of this century, and peaked in the 1960s, is now a familiar part of the cultural scene. Destruction itself becomes institutionalized.

Take as an early example the case of the French writer of the 1930s, Antonin Artaud, who hoped that artists—particularly dramatists—could serve a social role as protesters, disturbers of the peace, destroyers of the idolatry of classical art, destroyers of *all* artifacts of past creativity. "The library at Alexandria can be burnt down," he wrote hopefully in his 1938 book *The Theater and Its Double*. Artaud called for an end to masterpieces:

> One of the reasons for the asphyxiating atmosphere in which we live . . . is our respect for what has been written, formulated, or painted, what has been given form, as if all expression were not at last exhausted, were not at a point where things must break apart if they are to start anew and begin afresh.[22]

Let there be no more Shakespeares, Artaud pleaded; instead, let there be a "theater of cruelty" to force its audience into confronting the primal reality of life, beyond all social convention. "In the true theater," he wrote, "a play disturbs the senses' repose, frees the repressed unconscious, incites a kind of virtual revolt. . . . " Artaud spent nine years confined in insane asylums. In his last years, he was lauded as one of the great thinkers of France. In the 1960s, his work was promoted in the United States by Susan Sontag, who pointed out its influence on Peter Weiss's *Marat/Sade*, a play-about-a-play in which the inmates of the asylum at Charenton—directed by the Marquis de Sade—take the parts of the leaders of the French Revolution, and in the end attack the audience.

The spirit of Artaud—and that of Tristan Tzara and the *surréalistes* and all the other pioneers of cultural nihilism—live on today in punk. Punk is our contemporary nihilism, and it suffers the cultural nihilist's occupational disease of teetering always on the verge of respectability.

Certainly the destructive urge is alive and well in the punk subculture. Here is Greil Marcus, author of a laudatory book on punk, describing the music of Johnny Rotten and the Sex Pistols:

> Damning God and the state, work and leisure, home and family, sex and play, the audience and itself, the music briefly made it possible to experience all those things as if they were not natural facts but ideological constructs: things that had been made and therefore could be altered, or done away with altogether. It became possible to see those things as bad jokes, and for the music to come forth as a better joke. The music came forth as a no that became a yes, then a no again, then again a yes: nothing is true except our conviction that the world we are asked to accept is false. If nothing was true, everything was possible.[23]

The punk world shows, at times, a lucid postmodern awareness that ordinary reality is socially created, and shows also in vivid colors the naively romantic faith that so often comes with such an awareness: the belief that (a) since public reality is a sort of fiction, it can easily be destroyed, and (b) when it is destroyed, something of great beauty, something "natural," will immediately break through. The punk rockers seek to break through in acts of brutality, violence, and outrageously bad taste. Punk concerts have the flavor of a dada event, or of *Marat/Sade's* climax, in which the performers attack the audience. Marcus in his chronicles of punk mentions the tradition of performers spitting on audiences and vice versa, so that at a Sex Pistols concert in San Francisco the band was greeted "with a curtain of gob." He recounts other sundry assaults, including the time a man wearing a football helmet "butted his way through the crowd, smashed a paraplegic out of his wheelchair, and was himself beaten to the floor."[24] All this in search of reality, *real* reality beyond the "social facts" that the music was meant to destroy.

But for whom are the social facts destroyed? And when is a fact not social? Obviously quite a number of people have never heard Johnny Rotten's music or, if they did, couldn't understand what he said or were unmoved by it. If you did hear and were moved, were all your society's values and beliefs then purged from your brain?

Of course not. The beliefs-about-beliefs of the punk culture are shot through with grandiose notions of the power of its rituals to purge social reality, and of the promised land that lies beyond.

Punk, carrying on the nihilistic tradition, becomes its own social reality. Its adherents are eloquent in their alienation, dedicated to their anomie. "I belong to the Blank Generation," a young woman told another writer researching the punk world. "The Blank Generation" was a punk rock song. (The woman was, at the time of being interviewed, in bed with another woman and a male photographer.) She said: "I have no beliefs. I belong to no community, tradition, or anything like that. I'm lost in this vast, vast world. I belong nowhere. I have absolutely no identity."[25]

She was right in a way, and wrong in a way. The punk subculture provides community, tradition, belongingness, and identity. The denial of worldview becomes its own worldview. The young woman was stuck with being *some*body, a representative of a tradition—even an authority on it. The pastime of the twentieth century is shopping for meaning and personal identity, and punk becomes yet another packaged life-style.

Many of its artists know this and fight valiantly against it, because they believe in their quest; but they find themselves eternally running to keep ahead of socially created realities—including their own:

> That was punk: a load of old ideas sensationalized into new feelings almost instantly turned into new cliches, but set forth with such momentum that the whole blew up its equations day by day. For every fake novelty, there was a real one. For every third-hand pose, there was a fourth-hand pose that turned into a real motive.[26]

Punk belongs to the postmodern era, but this does not mean the postmodern era belongs to punk. The punk rock subculture gives a true statement of the postmodern condition—of the quest to see the wizard and the flight from the human face behind the curtain. That it is present among us as a fixture of society shows where we have come to, and that its representatives understand so little and flail with such futility against the "social facts" shows how far we have to go if we are to have a civilization on this side of the sixties, a world that is ready for freedom from the kind of believing that dominated premodern and modern minds.

Whatever freedom we are ultimately able to achieve will be gained not merely by shouting naughty words at social constructions of reality—not merely by unlearning, but also by learning about why we think and behave and believe as we do, and why and how we create realities. Such learning is possible; much is being discovered, in many fields, and none of it is secret.

PART TWO

POSTMODERN VISIONS

CHAPTER 3

Science and the Creative Brain

Today men and women in many different intellectual disciplines are thinking about social reality: how we create it, how we live with it, what it does. This is not a single intellectual movement but a *zeitgeist*, a stirring of excitement and doubt and discovery in many fields. Occasionally reports of their work trickle into the popular press, but on the whole the public is less exposed to such ideas than it was to the psychedelic philosophizing of the 1960s.

In this chapter and the next, we will take an exploratory tour through some of the more interesting corridors of postmodern thought—not the whole field, of course, but enough to get a sense of what it is trying to tell us about what kind of animal we are and how we make our worlds. Postmodern revolutions are well under way in the world of science and the world of the humanities; one bridge across the gap between the famous "two cultures" is that people in both of them are taking a new look at what they mean by reality. In chapter 4, we will see what is happening in the literary culture. Here we note what is happening as science looks at the human mind, and as human minds look at science. We begin with cognitive science, with the brain.

COGNITION AND CREATION

The subject of the experiments is a pleasant boy, fifteen years old. He is undergoing a series of psychological tests, working in a mobile unit parked outside his house. He is talkative and curious and amiable, and if you met him casually you would not suspect that he is quite different from you and me.

The researcher, a neuroscientist, has an optical device that makes it possible to flash visual messages in such a way that a message reaches only one hemisphere of the brain.

He flashes to the boy's right hemisphere the command, "Smile." The boys smiles. He flashes, "Tap." The boy taps his fingers on the table. This is of great interest to the experimenter because it reveals something about the right hemisphere: even though it is the half of the brain that is *not* verbally dominant, it can receive and act on a verbal message.

And something more interesting yet is going on here, because the two halves of the boy's brain have been forever separated from one another. He is an epileptic, and has undergone what the doctors call "full callosal surgery" to relieve the violent seizures that were once a regular part of his life—a brutal procedure, and yet apparently effective. The seizures have abated, and the boy seems to have the same personality and the same abilities he had before—but his left brain literally does not know what his right brain is thinking, and vice versa. Just now, even while receiving and acting upon the visual message, he said he didn't see anything at all.

Now the researcher flashes to the boy's right brain the command, "Walk." The boy accommodatingly pushes his chair back and starts to leave the testing area. The researcher asks *why* he is doing this.

This a verbal inquiry, and therefore it is processed by the verbally dominant left hemisphere—the one that didn't get the command and doesn't know why the boy is getting up. But an answer is provided, a perfectly good reason: "Going into my house to get a Coke." It is a perfectly good reason, but quite unrelated to the reason that prompted the action.[1]

Michael Gazzaniga, the researcher in the above experiment and one of the pioneers in cognitive neuroscience, sees the human mind as a many-sided "modular" organ with several relatively independent functioning units. A key player in this system is the unit he calls the "left brain interpreter module." It is the talker, the explainer, the maker of narrative meaning—the storyteller. It performs a function that answers one of the human organism's deepest needs—the need for coherent explanations of causes and effects, for orientation in a world of sequential events. And it appears to be quite capable of creating good stories on skimpy resources. It will use any material available, and fill in the blanks whenever a little imagination is necessary to make a story hold together.

In experiments such as these, the neuroscientists are developing an ever more sophisticated understanding of how the human brain works—how the billions of neurons and ganglia packed into that astounding organ (or group of organs) function to produce human thought. Neuroscience is part of a larger intellectual movement, cognitive science—a field of inquiry whose practitioners include psychologists, computer scientists, mathematicians, philosophers, anthropologists, linguists, and probably a few other academic affiliations that I have neglected to mention. It has created a full-fledged revolution in psychology.

For some decades—say, from the late 1920s to the late 1960s—research in psychology was dominated by the behaviorists.[2] You remember them: the people with the rats in the mazes, the pigeons eternally pecking away in search of food pellets. Behaviorism seemed, in the latter years of the modern era, to be the only way to study human thought scientifically. Introspection had been a widely accepted approach in the nineteenth and early twentieth centuries, but how could you replicate someone else's introspective discoveries—prove them right, prove them wrong, do any of the things with thoughts that the practitioners of the "hard sciences" were doing so productively with things like molecules of matter? The behaviorists hit upon the looney but surprisingly successful idea of declaring that psychology should pay no attention to thought at all, but instead deal only with measurable physical behaviors. As John B. Watson put it:

> They saw their brother-scientists making progress in medicine, in chemistry, in physics. Every new discovery in those fields was of prime importance; every new element isolated in one laboratory could be isolated in some other laboratory; each new element was immediately taken up in the warp and woof of science as a whole. . . .
>
> In his first efforts to get uniformity in subject matter and in methods the behaviorist began his own formulation of the problem of psychology by sweeping aside all medieval conceptions. He dropped from his scientific vocabulary all subjective terms such as sensation, perception, image, desire, purpose, and even thinking and emotion as they were subjectively defined.
>
> The behaviorist asks: Why don't we make what we can *observe* the real field of psychology? Let us limit ourselves to things that can be observed, and formulate laws concerning only those things.[3]

Under this influence, talk of the mind became suspect, researchers produced tons of data on animal adventures in mazes and cages, and Harvard's B. F. Skinner brought forth the blandest utopian novel in the history of literature, *Walden Two*—an account of a society in which the people were perfectly happy because their behavior was benevolently controlled by a wise scientist who had a remarkable resemblance to B. F. Skinner.

The cognitive revolution began quietly in the 1950s, while behaviorism was at its zenith, and gained momentum rapidly in the following decades as researchers in several fields found new ways of studying human thought systematically. "Mind" again became a respectable subject of scientific inquiry; you could not only admit you had one, but entertain the possibility of using yours systematically to understand minds in general.

Advances in neuroscience had a lot to do with making the mind again a valid subject of scientific inquiry. So did the work of a new generation of linguists led by Noam Chomsky, whose work was based on the now-familiar idea that language is basically a system of cognition rather than a mere window on the objective world. In a premodern reality, words are describers of the things they represent—that is what makes magical incantation possible, manipulating nature by manipulating its names. Modern views of language, informed by the work of anthropologists, came more and more toward understanding it as the tool with which a culture creates its reality. This in turn opened up a vast range of questions about how language affects the cognitive operations of individuals.

The real ground breakers of the new cognitive revolution were the computer scientists: the scholars of artificial intelligence, cybernetics, computation. For the first time it became possible to construct "thinking machines" that modeled some of the operations of human cognition, and to study these operations apart from the astoundingly complex—and persistently unscientific—conditions of lived human experience.

Some people not too familiar with cognitive science fear that such an approach must lead inevitably to a mechanistic and therefore dehumanized psychology: the mind of a Socrates or an Einstein seen as only quantitatively different from the latest item out of Apple or IBM. Such fretful humanists will probably be relieved to hear that the general result of the use of computers is an increasing body of proof that the human mind's thought processes are most uncomputerlike. We think in ways that might generously be described as "rational," but we do not plod in linear fashion from point to point, nor do we—even when solving logical problems—hold to the rules of that supreme human invention, logic. We seem to employ models, use intuition, play games, sometimes deliberately *ignore* logic.

In one set of experiments, a couple of cognitive scientists made up a biographical description of a woman: the fictitious character was named Linda; she was thirty-one years old, bright, and outspoken, had been a philosophy major and an antinuclear activist in college. Research subjects were asked to read a series of statements about Linda and then to rank them in order of probability. The statements included, "Linda is a psychiatric social worker," "Linda is a bank teller," "Linda is a bank teller and is active in the feminist movement." Now, anybody with the slightest smattering of statistics or logic knows that the probability of one independent event is higher than the probability of two independent events combined. Yet over 80 percent of the research subjects, many of them with statistical training, gave a higher ranking to the statement that Linda is a bank teller and a feminist than to the statement that Linda is a bank teller; the second fit better with the cold odds, but the first fit better with the image of Linda, and with all the images of the known world that a human mind contains.[4]

Such findings do not of course eliminate all computerlike views of the brain or all attempts to design brainlike computers—indeed, progress in cognitive science keeps sending the artificial intelligence experts back to the drawing boards with new ideas about ways to design computers—but they serve to reassure us that cognitive science is not simply nuts-and-bolts reductionism.

In fact, the cognitive revolution has breathed new life into philosophy, stimulated dialogue between scientists and philosophers of a sort that would have seemed utterly impossible in the days of the behaviorist boom. Contemporary cognitive scientists are much interested in some of the classic issues of philosophy, and are exploring those same concerns with new methods.

Immanuel Kant's name is often mentioned in relation to cognitive science, for a couple of good reasons: one, because he said it would never exist; two, because some of his work is highly relevant to it.

Kant was certain that a science of psychology was not possible, and never would be. One cannot, he said, have a scientific approach to the mind, which is affected while studying itself. Furthermore, he said, it has no spatial extension to make experimentation possible, and there is no way of quantifying thought. He put his finger on the very problems that the behaviorists tried to outflank in the twentieth century.

His work in the late eighteenth century began with a problem that was as divisive in its time as the objectivist-constructivist one is in ours—in this case, a conflict between the British empiricists such as Locke and Hume, who saw thought as merely an instrument for understanding or using "real world" experience, and the Continental philosophers such as Descartes and Leibniz, who saw the mind as the supreme organizer and discoverer of all reality.[5] This was not a postmodern debate, of course; all parties assumed that people could apprehend unchanging and universal truth. The question was how to do it, and the conflict between science and the humanities, two rival approaches, was already heating up. Kant's attempt to resolve the conflict was his own contribution to the search for "foundational" knowledge of reality—beyond historical and cultural relativism—but it pointed toward a view of the mind as a *creator* of reality, and some people hold him responsible for opening the door to postmodern thought.

Kant described the mind as an active organ that orders and forms the raw data of experience—imposing upon them its own structure. It was not Locke's blank tablet, but neither could it make anything without external stimuli. A safe middle-of-the-road position, you might say, but the subversive part of Kant's thought lay in his assertion that we do not experience "things in themselves" but rather representations of them: phenomena, not noumena; appearances, sensations structured by human thought, not the actual events of what he saw as the unknowable external world. Working in the old-fashioned philosophical way, with introspection and reason and words, he came to the basic question of cognitive science: how does the mind "represent" the external world to itself?

Contemporary cognitive scientists divide into two camps according to their answer.

To those of the objectivist persuasion, the mind (or, as many would prefer to identify it, the brain) is the "mirror of nature" that has evolved for the specific purpose of enabling the organism to get good information about its physical environment.

But other cognitive scientists have a different idea of what the brain does, and in the process offer an entirely new way of thinking about the Kantian question. For example, Marvin Minsky, one of the founders of artificial intelligence, addresses the question in terms of modularity. Kant had seen the mind as a single entity; Minsky describes the brain as a number of organs, each with slightly different functions, and points out that only a portion of the brain is involved in direct perception—those parts associated with the vision, touch, and hearing systems, for example. "But most parts of the brain," he points out, "are connected not to the outer world but to other parts of the brain—and their realities are the states of those other brain parts." For this reason, he believes that "we have to abandon the idea that the mind looks out on the world."[6]

The brain massages raw perceptual data through an enormous amount of material, including socially inculcated values and beliefs. And clearly much creativity is involved in the stories it tells about what is going on in the world. Consider Dr. Gazzaniga's young research subject, who found himself in the situation of being asked to explain why he was getting up and walking away from the table. He (or, to be more precise, the part of him that heard questions and composed answers to them) didn't know why, but he effortlessly worked backward from effect to a reasonable cause—in the same way that Creation myths do on a larger scale—and produced a story that made life make sense.

Minsky breezily kicks away one of the props of the Western worldview—the self—with his pronouncement that it is really only a part of the mind that feels like all of it. He finds it quite understandable that we have developed and used this "single-agent image," but we shouldn't let it get in the way of developing greater understanding of ourselves. He writes:

> [There are] compelling reasons why it helps to see ourselves as singletons. Still, each of us must also learn not only that different people have their own identities, but that the same person can entertain different beliefs, plans, and dispositions at the same time. For finding good ideas about psychology, the single-agent image has become a

grave impediment. To comprehend the human mind is surely one of the hardest tasks any mind can face. The legend of the single Self can only divert us from the target of that inquiry.[7]

So, without great fanfare, two basic elements of what we might call commonsense reality—the idea of the mind as mirror of the external world, the idea of the self as single agent—are challenged by leading figures in cognitive science.

And, in other research, equally serious damage is done to the commonsense assumption that the world is naturally divided into distinct categories of things.

CATEGORIES

Jorge Luis Borges, the great Argentine explorer of the far reaches of human imagination, described a taxonomy of the animal kingdom found in an ancient Chinese encyclopedia:

> On those remote pages it is written that animals are divided into (a) those that belong to the Emperor, (b) embalmed ones, (c) those that are trained, (d) suckling pigs, (e) mermaids, (f) fabulous ones, (g) stray dogs, (h) those that are included in this classification, (i) those that tremble as if they were mad, (j) innumerable ones, (k) those drawn with a very fine camel's hair brush, (l) others, (m) those that have just broken a flower vase, (n) those that resemble flies from a distance.[8]

An odd and fanciful categorization, surely a long way from what we learned in our biology classes, but a passage that often turns up in books about cognitive science. Because categorization is an essential part of cognition. One of the things the human mind must do in order to make sense of its environment is to put things into sets. Our symbolic systems—most of language, all of mathematics—are essentially ways of describing and managing categories. So the study of classification has become an important subdiscipline among linguists and anthropologists.

And in those circles, the objectivist-constructivist debate takes the form of a debate over whether categories reflect the properties of the things categorized—and are therefore merely reflections of the external world—or are social constructions of reality, so idiosyncratic that a classification that seems to one group of people to be merely the way things are naturally arranged may seem to another as bizarre as the contents of Borges's fantastic encyclopedia.

Objectivists point out that we do, after all, get around in our environments pretty well—we must be getting *something* right—and they propose, reasonably enough, that the human brain evolved as an instrument capable of aiding the organism to survive by accurately learning the properties of things it encounters in the world. A person sees a scorpion, notes that it is in the class of poisonous insects rather than in the class of edible fruits, and acts accordingly. Objectivists search for (and sometimes find) evidence of human classifying experiences that are structured according to what is "out there" in the physical environment rather than "in here" in the forms prefabricated by social tradition or language.

The work of Berkeley anthropologists Brent Berlin and Paul Kay is frequently cited as such evidence. Berlin and Kay did some thorough and impressive research on how people respond to color and found that, although different cultures have vastly different ways of naming colors, and different ideas about how many basic colors there are (the Dani of New Guinea have two color words, one for bright/warm and one for dark/cool), people from all cultures would pick the same hues out of a color spectrum as a "good blue" or a "good green."[9] In other research, Berlin found that people from different cultures shared a hierarchical view of nature, tended to group plants and animals in ways that resemble our concept of the genus.[10]

Such findings appear to support a view that conceptual structures merely reflect the properties of objects, and in fact you can find them cited in popular books on cognitive science as evidence for an objectivist view of cognition.[11]

But wait a minute: have you located the meaning of a category for people, a reality *they* experience, when you have found some commonality such as a primary color? Marshall Sahlins, an anthropologist at the University of Chicago, criticized the Berlin-Kay study for its lack of attention to the "cultural significance" of colors as codes of social, economic, and ritual value. He insisted that the *meaning* of colors had nothing to do with how people responded to sample chips (a Western technological gimmick anyway) but lay in their relation to concepts such as life and death, noble and common, pure and impure—the sorts of things we communicate by calling a person green or yellow or black-hearted, a day golden or a song blue.[12]

And Berkeley linguist George Lakoff, in his marvelously entitled book *Women, Fire, and Dangerous Things*, accepted his colleague Berlin's findings without criticism and then used them to demolish the objectivist view of categorization. Lakoff argued, first of all, that the locus of the color identification is as much in the human nervous system as in the color chips (the distinctions are not there for someone who is color-blind) and, secondly, that the only classifications that can be identified cross-culturally are primitive "basic level" classifications that, as people mature, become part of much more complex systems—different stories—that include "higher" levels of generalization, specific propositions about individual members of types, and all kinds of cultural embroidery.

Lakoff tells about the Dyirbal, an Australian aboriginal tribe whose language divides all known objects into four categories. One of these, *balan*, includes women, bandicoots, dogs, platypuses, echidnas, some fishes, most birds, fireflies, scorpions, crickets, the hairy mary grub, anything connected with water or fire, sun and stars, shields, some spears, some trees, and so forth.[13] At first glance the system seems almost as bizarre as Borges's, but there is a logic to it—a logic based on Dyirbal life and culture. The main item in the *balan* group is women, and many other items are in the same group because they are believed to be similar in some way: the sun is regarded as female (the moon is in the category with men), and fire is in the group because it is like the sun. Birds are in the group because they are believed to be the spirits of dead women. The hairy mary grub is in the group because its sting feels like sunburn. And so it goes throughout the system, items linked because of various kinds of associations, from the physical to the mythic.

We can smile at the primitive worldview of the Dyirbal, because we have a scientific way of grouping and classifying living beings—the system of genera and species—and we know it is an objective description of the way things are. But is it?

Stephen Jay Gould once wrote a nice essay about this. It was entitled, "What, If Anything, Is a Zebra?" He pointed out that biology has its own intellectual disputes. One of them is between the cladists and the pheneticists, two schools of thought about how to classify living beings. Pheneticists focus on overall similarity in form, function, and biological role; cladists categorize according to "family tree" information based on the branching order in the course of evolution. The two approaches converge most of the time, but diverge in the case of the zebra. There are three species of zebra: Burchell's, Grevey's, and the mountain zebra. The first two appear to have the same evolutionary ancestry, but the mountain zebra, despite its stripes, turns out to be genealogically more closely related to ordinary horses than to other zebras; by cladistic criteria, there is no true biological category that includes all zebras and only zebras. Gould goes on to say:

> Some of our most common and comforting groups no longer exist if classifications must be based on cladograms (evolutionary branching diagrams).... I regret to report that there is surely no such thing as a fish. About 20,000 species of vertebrates have scales and fins and live in water, but they do not form a coherent cladistic group. Some—the lungfish and the coelacanth in particular—are genealogically close to the creatures that crawled out on land to become amphibians, reptiles, birds, and mammals. In a cladistic ordering of trout, lungfish, and any bird or mammal, the lungfish must form a sister group with the sparrow or elephant, leaving the trout in its stream. The characters that form our vernacular concept of "fish" are all shared primitives and do not therefore specify cladistic groups.[14]

Other elements in our "natural" taxonomy, such as the definition of species in terms of the ability of its individual members to interbreed within, but not beyond, species boundaries, also break down under close scrutiny. We are left with a taxonomy that is more a set of highly sophisticated stories about other living beings—and about how we perceive them—than an objective reflection of the conditions of nonhuman life.

Does it matter? It matters, of course, to the biologists, who keep looking for new and better descriptive systems—gene mapping and sequencing is the current cutting edge—and it matters to the rest of us if we become concerned about social or political issues involving nonhuman life-forms. The fuzziness of species boundaries makes the pronouncements of those who would legislate the integrity of species—make it illegal to mix the genes of one with the genes of another—look equally fuzzy. Ideological stances based on what is "natural" are very hard to defend. It matters also, of course, to anybody involved in the seemingly endless American Armageddon between evolutionists and creationists. A defender of evolutionary biology can make a very good argument that the scientific story is a much more useful one than the Creation story and fits with much more of the available evidence, but he or she cannot get very far by saying that it is the one and only and perfect representation of the cosmic facts.

And our taxonomy of life-forms is only one of many intellectual structures that turn out to be, on closer examination, social constructions of reality. Lakoff believes that the systematic study of categories leads inevitably to the need to discard many familiar ideas. Here is his list of propositions he is willing to leave behind:

- Meaning is based on truth and reference; it concerns the relationship between symbols and things in the world.
- Biological species are natural kinds, defined by common essential properties.
- The mind is separate from, and independent of, the body.
- Emotion has no conceptual content.
- Grammar is a matter of pure form.
- Reason is transcendental, in that it transcends—goes beyond—the way human beings, or any other kinds of beings, happen to think. It concerns the inferential relationships among all possible concepts in this universe or any other. Mathematics is a form of transcendental realism.
- There is a correct, God's eye view of the world—a single correct way of understanding what is and is not true.
- All people think using the same conceptual system.[15]

Lakoff likes the term "experientialist" rather than "constructivist" as a general term for his way of looking at things. He is particularly interested in calling attention to the "bodily nature of thinking beings," the importance of physical experience in the mind's acts of creation. But his work is very much in the mainstream of constructivist thought.

CONSTRUCTING A WORLD, AND MAKING IT FIT

Constructivism is more a momentum than a movement. It includes not only the many people who identify themselves as constructivists, but also "experientialist" linguists, sociologists of knowledge, social construction psychologists such as Kenneth Gergen of Swarthmore College, and symbolic anthropologists such as Clifford Geertz who have studied the way worlds are created in non-Western cultures.[16] It is both a philosophy and a science.

As philosophy, it is a departure from a long, long tradition of what is usually called "metaphysical realism." Philosopher-historian Hilary Putnam writes: "It is impossible to find a philosopher before Kant (and after the pre-Socratics) who was not a metaphysical realist, at least about what he took to be *basic* or unreducible assertions."[17] Philosophers disagreed about what was true, but they shared a common and usually unexamined assumption about truth itself—which was that truth meant objective, permanent, superhuman validity. (Actually, there may have been exceptions: Giambattista Vico, whose work preceded Kant's by more than half a century, is being resurrected these days as a sort of early constructivist for whom philosophy meant fabricating systems of thought rather than discovering ultimate cosmic structures. Vico said: "As God's truth is what God comes to know as he creates and assembles it, so human truth is what man comes to know as he builds it, shaping it by his actions."[18]

As a science, constructivism is a departure from behaviorism; it studies not only the processes of thought, but the processes of reality-creation. It maintains, in Ernst von Glasersfeld's words, "that the operations by which we assemble our experiential world can be explored, and that an awareness of this operating . . . can help us do it differently and, perhaps, better."[19]

Constructivist scientists are interested in all the operations that our brains perform in every nanosecond of our lives, as we take in sensory experience, interpret it, compare it to other experiences, name it, evaluate it, relate it to our self-concepts and goals of action, and assemble it into ever-changing patterns of reality.

Much of their research focuses on the individual's thought process, but nobody in the field thinks we construct the world all by ourselves. The brain/mind is not only a constellation of organs but also a repository of language, myth, memories, social norms, cultural values and beliefs, idealized images of who we are and what we would like to be. Evolution and human history speak through each of us as we assemble each second's reality, and the ghosts of millions of others are with us in our most private moments. The brain may be studied as a part of an individual human being, but the mind is not, as the Chilean neuroscientists Humberto Maturana and Francisco Varela put it, simply something that is within the brain: "Consciousness and mind," they write, "belong to the realm of social coupling. That is the locus of their dynamics."[20]

Constructivists generally follow Minsky's reluctance to regard the individual as an individual, and are equally reluctant to describe a reality-construct as a single "thing" that a person "has," like a house or a left foot. Reality-construction is process, and although some constructs may be tenacious they are still only temporary manifestations of a dynamic flow of thought that no philosophy or science has yet been able to map or describe in its entirety. Cognition, insists cyberneticist Heinz von Foerster, is a process of computing *a* reality—not *the* reality.[21] And it appears that we construct not just one reality, but realities and realities and realities, and that they overlap and enclose one another and sometimes conflict. We have large-scale images of the universe and metabeliefs and concepts of space and time, and we have mid-range norms and values and beliefs and customs that shape our social experience, and we have personal images of the self and identities and stories about the courses of our individual lives: multiple realities even within ourselves, and changing ideas about what reality is. We know how to reconstruct some realities, not others; some we do not experience as constructs at all.

Here is a little anecdote that Rupert Riedl, the Austrian anthropologist and biologist, recounted in a paper on causal thinking. He used it as an illustration of how we make up causes to fit effects; I want to use it to illustrate a couple of other points about the constructivist view of experience processing:

> People are getting on a streetcar in Vienna. Among the passengers is a working-class woman with her young son. The boy has an enormous bandage wrapped around his head. (How dreadful! What happened

> to him?) People give up their seats to the afflicted pair. The bandaging is not a professional job, it was obviously done at home and in a hurry; they must be on their way to the hospital (people secretly search the child's face for an explanation, and the bandage for traces of blood). The little boy whines and fusses (signs of sympathy from everyone). The mother seems unconcerned (how inappropriate!); she even shows signs of impatience (that is amazing). The little one begins to fidget; his mother pushes him back in his seat. The passengers' mood turns to open confrontation. The mother is criticized, but for her part rejects all interference. Now she is criticized again and more openly. Thereupon she tells them to mind their own business and questions the competence of all those who criticized her. (That is too much! An outrage to human decency!) Emotions run high, and things get noisy and turbulent. The child is bawling; his mother, red-faced and furious, declares she is going to show us what is the matter and begins (to everyone's horror) tearing off the whole bandage. What appears is a metal chamber pot that the little Don Quixote has pushed so tightly on his head that it is stuck; they are on their way to get help from the nearest plumber. People get off the streetcar in great embarrassment.[22]

Riedl directs our attention to the way people infer causes, and notes that those who assume there has been a serious accident ignore various indications that do not fit that construction.

But this is a very busy streetcar, and a lot of reality-construction activity is going on:

For one thing, the situation becomes a *drama* in which different people have roles. The streetcar passengers get to be the defenders of a mistreated child, a satisfying role. The mother gets to be the heavy, and obviously doesn't like it much.

Then we see another development: she removes the bandage, and everybody's reality-construct changes. We are reminded that the brain not only constructs patterns, but continually reconstructs them, and is capable of substituting one reality for another in a second, creating a whole new story.

We may note that when the story changes, so do the roles; the meddlesome passengers are now the heavies, and the long-suffering mother gets to make them all feel guilty—one of the great pleasures of civilized life.

Note also that the change is confined to interpretations of the mother-and-child situation: nothing in the anecdote tells us that any of the passengers experience an inversion of up and down, an altered sense of time, a loss of personal identity, a sudden religious conversion, or any of the other large-scale transformations of reality that are known to be possible. They merely change their opinions, and some of them probably change streetcars.

Note that the anecdote is itself a story, presumably about something that really happened once on a Viennese streetcar, and that like all stories it offers a neatened-up version of the events. Did the passengers criticize the mother with such unanimity? Were they all embarrassed when they got off the streetcar? Probably not. But even when we are narrating real events in order to make points about reality, we are *creating* something out of the complex and chaotic raw material of experience.

And let us note, finally, that although the anecdote is a constructivist parable, trying to illustrate in a very simple way something about how we build our stories about the world, it very definitely is not trying to persuade us that one story is as good as another. The story that the boy stuck his head in a chamber pot looks considerably better to us, when we have read to the end of the anecdote, than the story that a heartless mother is riding around on the streetcar with a horribly injured child. (But further developments might call for still better stories: what if two kids wearing chamber pots get on the streetcar at the next stop?) We are being shown that human reality does not equate with objective, ultimate reality, but not being asked to believe that any old reality will do. Yet people commonly assume that to let go of "metaphysical realism" is to ooze into a world of unchecked relativism, in which anything goes. There are some radical relativists who see things that way—it is definitely a part of the postmodern scene, but it is not constructivism.

Constructivists do have ways of evaluating stories and reality-structures. The whole movement is a search for ways that people can make sensible choices about such things in a world of multiple realities. But they use a different set of scales.

Von Glasersfeld proposes a test of "fit" rather than "match." The quest for truth has been dominated by an idea of a perfect "match" between cosmic reality and human understanding of it. The idea of a "fit" leads to a more pragmatic way of looking at things. A philosophical system, a scientific theory, a religion, or even a personal identity does not have to be a precise mirror of ultimate reality as long as it works more or less well in its context. He uses the metaphor of a key and a lock: a key fits if it opens a lock, but we know from our experience with burglars' tools and passkeys that a number of different keys may work. This is a first-step metaphor that suggests only one test—the key fits or it doesn't. But the "fit" concept goes far beyond that, in directions that amplify our understanding of evolution and of what we mean, in the postmodern world, when we talk of scientific truth.

CREATING SCIENTIFIC TRUTH

Although Darwin's theory of evolution is sometimes described as "survival of the fittest," natural selection does not necessarily call forth the perfectly fit species; it only eliminates the unfit. Darwinian evolution is (as Gregory Bateson once put it) based on the principle of constraints, not on the principle of cause and effect. A given environment does not *require* that a certain organism evolve to inhabit it; many keys may fit the lock. And evolution's creativity is so great that the variety of organisms, the variety of their survival strategies, is wondrously wide. But the game is not exactly "anything goes," either: The number of mutations that do not survive is astronomically higher than the number of those that do. And the species that survive must not only "fit" the environment, but coexist with one another.

Constructivists believe that the evolution of social reality operates under similar rules. Many social constructions of reality (which I'll refer to merely as SCR's) may fit sufficiently well within the constraints of the environment to survive—at least for a while. There may even be room for diametrically opposing beliefs based on essentially the same raw material: Riedl points out that in some Indian tribes, pregnant women are forbidden to eat squirrels because squirrels tend to disappear into dark burrows and a woman is supposed to bring a body out into the light; but the Hopi women are encouraged to eat squirrels because squirrels also are nimble at finding their way *out* of dark burrows.[23] The relativists who say one SCR is about as good as another can point for evidence to the obvious multitude of realities available: with so many around, who is to say which is best? SCRs have survival capabilities that plants and animals do not. One reason there are so many around is that we have so many ways of believing; another is that we have so many subcultures of belief. In various ways we find room for philosophies, ideologies, and religions that are no longer taken as seriously as they once were. In the evolution of ideas, the dinosaurs do not always disappear when they become extinct.

Science is an attempt to develop a system for the evolution of constructions of reality, and to permit a graceful exit for the dinosaurs.

Science began, as if anticipating constructivism, with the recognition that the human mind is a tireless and not altogether careful fabricator of stories about everything, infinitely inventive at making up connections between events and creating causes to fit effects. Scientists—or "experimental philosophers," to use an earlier term—devised ways to test stories to see if they could find some that fit better than others.

And they did, of course, with spectacular results. The successes of science were so impressive, its superiority over traditional philosophy and religion so clearly proven in the minds of many people, that science became the new metaphysical realism: the source of ultimate and objective truth. There were always more moderate voices: David Hume in the eighteenth century told us we never know the real connection between cause and effect, that to observe something happening a thousand times does not guarantee it will happen the one-thousand-and-first time. Karl Popper in the twentieth century told us we can prove a hypothesis is false but can never prove it is true—only that it is the best we happen to have at the moment. These represented the constructivist minority report; the prevailing view of science, in the mind of some scientists and a large portion of the general public, was the mystique of the scientific fact—scientism, it is sometimes called. It is a mechanistic view that wants nothing to do with creativity or intuition—indeed, with any aspect of human thought that is not pure computation. Clark Hull, an eminent behaviorist, warned against contaminating science with what he called "anthropomorphic subjectivism," and said: "A genuinely scientific theory no more needs the anthropomorphic intuition of the theorist to eke out the deduction of its implications than an automatic calculating machine needs the intuitions of the operator in the determination of a quotient, once the keys representing the dividend and the divisor have been depressed."[24]

Thomas Kuhn's *The Structure of Scientific Revolutions* was a major step toward a postmodern view of science. Kuhn offered a different view of how scientific progress takes place: he said scientists do not make their progress by adding one fact to another in a mechanistic, objective sort of way, but rather lurch ahead from time to time in sudden creative bursts he called paradigm shifts. A paradigm is a social construction of reality, a belief system that prevails in a certain scientific community.

Those belief systems, according to Kuhn, never quite manage to explain all the facts. Researchers keep coming across anomalies, findings the prevailing theory can't account for. But for a while the theory prevails anyway (partly because some researchers ignore findings that don't fit it), and as research proceeds, more anomalies accumulate. Eventually somebody comes up with a new explanatory system that replaces the old one. The eighteenth-century French chemist Lavoisier, for example, performed experiments that produced results incompatible with the prevailing idea that the atmosphere was composed of a substance called phlogiston. Eventually his work led him to discover oxygen as a main component of the atmosphere and the active ingredient in combustion—and that led to a vast reformulation of all of chemistry, a true scientific revolution.

The Structure of Scientific Revolutions is a twentieth-century landmark in the philosophy of science, but it could as easily be called a work on the psychology of science. Kuhn identifies as major influences on his own thinking Jean Piaget's work on the cognitive stages of human development, various Gestalt psychologists, and Benjamin Whorf's work on the role of language in thought.[25]

Kuhn describes a major scientific paradigm shift as a leap into a new cognitive pattern, into a different worldview. As he puts it:

> When paradigms change, the world itself changes with them. Led by a new paradigm, scientists adopt new instruments and look in new places. Even more important, during revolutions scientists see new and different things when looking with familiar instruments in places they have looked before. It is rather as if the professional community had been suddenly transported to another planet where familiar objects are seen in a different light and are joined by unfamiliar ones as well. Of course, nothing of quite that sort does occur: there is no geographical transplantation; outside the laboratory everyday affairs usually continue as before. Nevertheless, para-

digm changes do cause scientists to see the world of their research-engagement differently.[26]

A paradigm shift is a little bit like what happened to the people on the Viennese streetcar when the lady unwrapped her son's head: they revised their perception of that particular reality, but the rest of the world remained the same. Kuhn illustrated the psychology of paradigm change with examples from Gestalt psychology, such as the drawings in which one can see a drawing of a box in different ways, as if from above or below.

In Kuhn's account, paradigm shifts are social, not individual; there is no such thing as a paradigm without a community. Paradigm shifts take place within communities, and sometimes help create them: by adopting a paradigm, a loosely constituted network of scholars may begin to turn into a profession or a discipline.

Although Kuhn's work has been enormously influential, it is not the only story about science. Some people think it's far too relativistic, because it does not regard any paradigm as the final and perfect truth. Others think it's not relativistic enough. Kuhn's colleague Paul Feyerabend, much more radically postmodern, sees all our learning as the production of different realities that coexist in a sort of global tower of Babel. "Knowledge," says Feyerabend, "is not a series of self-consistent theories that converges toward an ideal view; it is rather an ever increasing *ocean of mutually incompatible (and perhaps even incommensurable)* alternatives, each single theory, each fairy tale, each myth that is part of the collection forcing the others into greater articulation and all of them contributing, via this process of competition, to the development of our consciousness."[27]

Compared to Feyerabend's ideas about our knowledge of reality, Kuhn's seem downright conservative. Kuhn is quite reassuring about the possibility of evaluating different theories, finding some better than others. He mentions criteria such as accuracy of prediction, number of problems solved, simplicity, compatibility with other specialties. All these are criteria of "fit" and pragmatic usefulness, and they are criteria by which he judges later scientific theories to be better than earlier ones. "That," he declares, "is not a relativist's position, and it displays the sense in which I am a convinced believer in scientific progress."[28]

So in day-to-day work, a postmodern/constructivist philosophy of science such as Kuhn's uses theories and facts much the same way a modern/objectivist one does. It is not a "whatever turns you on" proposition. But neither is it a simple view of science as getting closer and closer to The Truth, a truth that is not somebody's story about the truth. There is, as Kuhn puts, it, "no theory-independent way to reconstruct phrases like 'really there'; the notion of a match between the ontology of a theory and its 'real' counterpart in nature now seems to me illusive in principle."[29]

Constructivist ideas such as Kuhn's have become rather quickly the mainstream view among philosophers and historians of science, and seem to be replacing or at least joining objectivist ideas in the popular image of science as well. I imagine a poll would show that most people still think of science as a way of getting The Truth, or think they think that. But so many ideas about science are circulating now and so many scientific ideas are flashing through the daily news—chaos, nonlinear mathematics, alternative universes, antimatter—that there really can't be too many people around who think science is simply a lot of objective "facts" about cosmic reality.

An old joke about three umpires summarizes the range of viewpoints. They are sitting around over a beer, and one says, "There's balls and there's strikes, and I call 'em the way they are." Another says, "There's balls and there's strikes, and I call 'em the way I see 'em." The third says, "There's balls and there's strikes, and they ain't *nothin'* until I call 'em." Here we have an objectivist and two kinds of constructivists. The second ump is what I would call a mainstream constructivist, the third a postmodern radical.

For the mainstream constructivists, the cosmos—a real, one might even say an objective, cosmos—is always present, a tantalizing step or two (or perhaps an infinite distance) beyond what we know about it. Most would agree with Albert Einstein's description: "Out yonder . . . this huge world, which exists independent of us human beings and which stands before us like a great, eternal riddle, at least partially accessible to our inspection and thinking."[30] The "out there" and "in here" concepts are basic to constructivist thinking—I have used them frequently—and they are about the best the language gives us for that purpose. They presume that an objective universe still exists and has its own properties. Thus

Heinz von Foerster says: "'out there' there is no light and no color, there are only electromagnetic waves; 'out there' there is no sound and no music, there are only periodic variations of the air pressure; 'out there' there is no heat and no cold, there are only moving molecules with more or less mean kinetic energy, and so on. Finally, for sure, 'out there' there is no pain."[31]

Von Foerster thus crisply states the constructivist point that the *meaning* of the things we experience is created out of the raw material from "out there." But, others inquire, don't we also create the raw material? Aren't electromagnetic waves, air pressure, and kinetic energy also constructs? And, since we are admitting that anything we say about "out there" is a construct, don't we create "out there" also? Why assume that there is such a thing as an objective cosmos?

This is where postmodern science gets really interesting—and, some would say, really weird. Some constructivist philosophers—Nelson Goodman most effectively—insist that *versions* of the world are all there is. He writes: "When I say that worlds are made, I mean it literally."[32] Goodman represents the third umpire.

Cosmologists, people who make it their profession to try to figure out what the whole universe is like, have been having a good time in recent years with various ideas about the relationship between the "in here" and the "out there," or the identity of the two, or the nonexistence of the two.

Could it be that the universe has labored all these billions of years toward the goal of bringing forth a species that could understand and appreciate it? Or, to put a much less outrageous question that is still in the same philosophical neighborhood, could it be that it takes a universe about like the one we've got to produce intelligent life? Such questions, and others like them, are being asked regularly and with great seriousness by theoretical physicists. The dialogue has brought forth a number of different notions with names like the Weak Anthropic Principle (WAP), the Strong Anthropic Principle (SAP), and the Final Anthropic Principle (FAP). The Final Anthropic Principle suggests that, once intelligent life is created, it will continue forever, becoming more and more knowledgeable and shaping the universe to its purposes. Martin Gardner, one of our leading professional skeptics, thought the FAP should be called the CRAP—Completely Ridiculous Anthropic Principle.[33]

The most science-fiction-ish of all the "athropocist" cosmologies is the idea of parallel universes—that each act of construction of reality by intelligent life creates a new universe, which then separates from other universes that have been constructed differently by someone else; an infinity of realities spin off and never touch one another again.

All these notions are true science, serious work by brilliant people daring to ask the kinds of questions that the postmodern world makes possible. Some of these principles are not testable by any method we now know, not even falsifiable; others are being explored more deeply to see if they can generate tests, or if they lead to other theories that can be tested.

Testing, experimentation, replication, methodology, and all the apparatus of modern science are just as important in the postmodern world as they ever were. Science is judged, possible explanations compete. Proposed theories are tested for their ability to "fit" with other theories, with intuitive feelings about reality—and also for their ability to fit with any kind of data that can be generated by observation and measurement.

Yet something is different, and that something is an increasing recognition that the foundation of scientific truth is ultimately a social foundation, a human foundation. The Duhem-Quine thesis holds that an experiment cannot test a theoretical prediction in any final way, because the test itself depends on the validity of the various theories that support the experiment.[34] Any instrument, any machine, even any clever artificial intelligence that might be sufficiently nonhuman to meet Clark Hull's standard of how scientific thinking ought to be done rests ultimately on a network of theory, opinion, ideas, words, tradition, and culture.

So we still have science, laboratories and all, but we have science with a human face. And we have ahead great projects—not only projects of scientific discovery, but also projects of discovery about science involving psychology, philosophy, sociology, history, and anthropology. We seek different knowledge about our own knowing. As Jerome Bruner, one of the leaders of the cognitive revolution, put it:

> The moment one abandons the idea that "the world" is there once for all and immutably, and substitutes for it the idea that what we take as

the world is itself no more nor less than a stipulation couched in a symbol system, then the shape of the discipline (of psychology) alters radically. And we are, at last, in a position to deal with the myriad forms that reality can take—including the realities created by story, as well as those created by science.[35]

CHAPTER 4

The Meanings of Literature

While the cognitive scientists search for new understanding of how the brain/mind works—and in the process revise our ideas about reality—another postmodern revolution is going on in the world of literature.

Literature no longer occupies a central role in our society the way it did a hundred years ago, when Walt Whitman could say confidently that "in the civilization of today it is undeniable that, over all the arts, literature dominates. . . ." It is no longer clearly dominant in the arts, or even as a medium of communication—any number of futurists will tell you the written word is already over the hill—yet we can scarcely imagine a civilization without it; we rely heavily on written works as containers of meaning, as repositories of social reality. And when people begin to question the ability of written works to contain or communicate reality, they are asking questions about reality itself.

Those are precisely the kinds of questions that postmodern literary critics are asking. And paradoxically enough, the dialogue they have begun is doing two things that might seem mutually exclusive: eroding the very foundations of the written word at the same time that it is bringing literature again back to a central place in society.

THE CENTER DOES NOT HOLD

Throughout the nineteenth century, while literacy increased and more things to read became available—and while monarchs lost some of their magic as symbols of national identity—literature assumed great importance in the Western world not merely as an art form and a means of communicating information, but as the stuff out of which nations (and empires and civilizations) were made.

It was quite a revolution when the English began to take their own literature seriously as an academic discipline. The tradition—an old and deeply entrenched one—had been to regard a good education as a deep immersion in the "greats" of classical Greece and Rome, and to regard English literature as more akin to entertainment and journalism. But this changed dramatically: poems and plays, novels and stories and essays—at least, some of them—began to take on a new role, to be regarded as the very heart and soul of English civilization. These gradually formed the canon of great works that every man and woman who aspired to be recognized as an educated person in the English-speaking world—the one on which the sun never set—was expected to process through his or her neurons; the canon became the storehouse of England's national reality. Other civilizations—the French, for example—had their own canons. Each canon drew on works from other languages, but literary nationalism was rampant.

And in the shade of the canons of literature sprouted canons of interpretation. The whole literary-culture enterprise was built on the assumption that the great works contained great ideas, messages of value and meaning that could be communicated from mind to mind—but only if the person on the receiving end put in some hard work. If you were a student of literature around the turn of the century (and if you were getting a formal education you became a student of literature, like it or not), you had to learn about the lives of great writers, and about the historical conditions under which they did their writing. You had to try to "get into" the writer's world, and thus prepare yourself to receive the true and correct meaning that the writer had intended. Literary experts like Matthew Arnold, the George Washington of English criticism, supported their interpretive writings with prodigious amounts of historical scholarship. Different scholars might have different opinions about the true meaning of a work—how mad was Hamlet?—but the arguments were the arguments of the modern era, based on the belief-about-belief that *some* certain meaning, intended by the author, was there to be found.

The first signal of an approaching doom for this state of things came in the 1930s, in the form of an intellectual movement that came to be known as the New Criticism.[1] The New Critics were not a bunch of postmodern troublemakers, and at first their movement appeared to be more a reformation than a revolution. In fact, it was remarkably similar in spirit to the earlier Reformation of the Catholic church in which dissidents such as Luther had insisted that every person could relate directly to God, without necessarily having a priestly middleman. The New Criticism was an effort to get the scholars off the reader's back, and make possible a simpler, more direct appreciation of literature.

They said to the reader: the poem is yours. Read it. Read it *closely*, and find its meaning right there, in the poet's own words. And the critics and professors of this school took on the work of helping the reader in this interpretive effort. That meant staying close to the text—sometimes chewing through it word by word, thought by thought—rather than straying too far into history or biography.

And you know what happened: close reading became a new kind of scholarship.

When I was taught the poems of T. S. Eliot as an undergraduate in the New-Crit 1950s, the experience reminded me of the hours I had passed in the previous decade with a Captain Midnight decoder. When I was about ten, I had hovered by my radio listening to the strange garbled messages that were given out by the announcer at the end of each day's episode of the serial, and with the help of my trusty decoder had turned them into perfectly understandable previews of the next day's story. Later, at age twenty or so in a Berkeley classroom, I followed the instructor as he took us line by line through Mr. Eliot's symbolic gobbledygook and transformed the various allusions and mythical images into clear pronouncements about the emptiness of modern life. These we understood to be the *real* meanings, the things Mr. Eliot would have told us himself if he had been a man of less monumental talent and had just gone ahead and said what was bothering him.

New Criticism at that time was the voice of modernism, and of liberalism. It stood for the rigorous, almost scientific explication of texts for the purpose of making the meaning accessible to many people. Leaders of the movement such as Cleanth Brooks spoke eloquently of their desire to democratize literature, to grant more people membership in society's literate center. They saw society's construction of reality—its beliefs, and also its values—as embodied in literature and thus available in its fullness only to those who could read and understand. Brooks said the critic's social job was "keeping open the lines of communication with the realm of value . . . exercising to health the now half-atrophied faculties by which man apprehends value."[2]

The New Criticism was not an assault on meaning or an invitation to create meanings that weren't already in the text. Its advocates were strongly—and as time went on, almost fanatically—committed to the idea that the meanings were right *there* in the text, locked up like little prisoners, and that it was the reader's task to set them free. But, as often happens, the reformation turned into a revolution. New Criticism produced not only a new kind of scholarship, as it was taken up by the universities, but also a growing willingness to challenge the faith in absolute meaning. As close readings and new interpretations proliferated, some students of literature began to give themselves permission to find anything in the text they damn well pleased.[3]

This erosion of literature's authority was hastened along by new schools of thought that questioned whether the authors of the great works had known exactly what they meant anyhow. Marxist critics, for example, said that many of our "great writers" had been unwitting tools of the bourgeoisie, victims and dispensers of false consciousness. Freudian critics said that works of literature were disguised and rationalized products of the writer's unconscious.

In the 1950s, we read Ernest Jones's ground-breaking study *Hamlet and Oedipus*, and encountered the novel idea that a literary critic might *psychoanalyze* a fictional character (and, indirectly, an author) and in the process find meanings the author had never consciously intended. Who could have thought that you could find a whole new interpretation of Hamlet, already the most analyzed character in all of literature? Hamlet had always seemed so mysterious and contradictory—powerful and decisive at some points, paralyzed at others, sometimes seemingly mad—and Jones offered, with magisterial authority, an explanation for all this: the prince is *neurotic*. He is not merely an intellectual vacillator, the perennial graduate student, but a man torn by powerful unconscious drives—among them, repressed guilt about having secretly wished for the death of the father whose murder he is supposed to avenge, and a carnal lust for the mother who is now incestuously entertaining his uncle. The play is a projection of the Oedipus complex—Hamlet's, and Shakespeare's.

Jones's interpretation breathed new life into the play for twentieth-century audiences, inspired exciting new productions, and set the precedent for a vast new outpouring of literary criticism. And although Freud had always called psychoanalysis a science, his science led readily to endless new and different and unprovable (and, more to the point, un*dis*provable) interpretations of literature. Many scholars took note that Dr. Freud had established his reputation as one of the leading thinkers of the century by making astounding pronouncements that were supported by no tangible evidence whatever—and proceeded enthusiastically along the same lines: endless villains turned out to have been the products of faulty toilet training, and the strange lightning flashing along the ship's mast in *Moby Dick* symbolized orgasms, and the mast—well, you know what the mast symbolized.

Theories of literature grew richly and wildly in academia, and in graduate seminars it became common for instructors to teach a half-dozen or so different ways of interpreting a work. And some of these, notably "reader response" theory, were out-of-the-closet subjectivistic: they located meaning, without apology, in the experience of the reader, made the reader the true creator of the reality of a literary work.

Conservatives began to scream in protest, of course—all kinds of conservatives. By the mid-1970s, literary versions of the objectivist-subjectivist controversy were going strong in departments of English everywhere—and there were different factions on both sides.

Most of the objectivists were moderates who simply wanted people to keep faith in the central principle of the New Criticism—the sanctity of the text. William Wimsatt and Monroe Beardsley, speaking for this point of view, warned their colleagues against two dread fallacies that had come to haunt literary interpretation: they called these the "intentional fallacy" and the "affective fallacy." The first, they said, was a mistaken attempt to discover the precise intention of the author, as the old-school critics had tried to do—an impossible task. The second was to rely excessively on the subjective response of the reader, as some of the newer approaches were beginning to do. The latter, they said, confuses what the poem *is* with what it *does*. It ends in "impressionism and relativism." And "the poem itself, as an object of specifically critical judgment, tends to disappear."[4]

Then there were the "stylisticians," the mad scientists of the literary world, with another version of objectivism: they wanted to overcome the rampant impressionism in criticism and get down to the "real meanings." They proposed to do this by breaking literary works down into their component parts—something like the way a chemist might analyze a compound. Some of them did this by running texts through computer programs. One stylistician, for example, studied the works of Swift and produced tables with titles like "Percentage of Initial Connectives in 2000-Sentence Samples of Addison, Johnson, Macaulay and Swift."[5] Another, having discovered certain recurrent sentence structures in Faulkner's work, theorized that "a writer whose style is so largely based on just these three semantically related transformations demonstrates in that style a certain conceptual orientation, a preferred way of organizing experience."[6] What this meant was that the mind of Faulkner could be read (but not by the ordinary human reader, of course) in quantifiable patterns of syntax.

A third conservative voice, probably the one best known outside of academia, was that of E. D. Hirsch. Yes, this is the same Professor Hirsch who became familiar to newspaper and magazine readers in the late 1980s as the author of lists of things that every American ought to know. Hirsch, speaking for an old-school trust in enduring meanings, defined a text as "an entity which always remains the same from one moment to the next," and called for a return to some kind of textual interpretation that would be, as he put it, more a discipline than a playground.[7] Hirsch, more than anyone else, defined the difference between modern and postmodern approaches to criticism; he called his opponents "cognitive atheists."[8] And he knew that the battle was not merely literary/academic; he knew he was defending the reality of civilization's common store of values and beliefs.

WHAT'S THE TEXT HERE?

As the conflict between modern and postmodern approaches became more acrimonious—and more clearly defined—students of literature found themselves buffeted between the two, and they naturally tried to figure out which reality they were being exposed to at any given time so they could get a good grade in the course.

Stanley Fish, who teaches English at Johns Hopkins, tells the story of a student who approached a professor at the beginning of a term and asked, "Is there a text in this class?" The professor replied that there was—the *Norton Anthology of Literature.* The student said, "No, no. I mean in this class do we believe in poems and things, or is it just us?"[9]

In such exchanges—and there are lots of them, in all kinds of situations—people manage to orient themselves to the shifting realities of the contemporary world. Some people decide to be in the classroom where there are (more or less) permanent meanings, and some other people decide to be in the classroom where there aren't. And everybody knows there are other rooms.

Fish believes that there *is* a text in this class—which may not be the same as the one next door—and he also believes that the transition into a new way of looking at literary meaning doesn't necessarily begin a free-fall into the bottomless depths of right-you-are-if-you-think-you-are. Fish is a postmodernist, his name up near the top of Hirsch's cultural atheists list. He was at first identified with "reader response" theory, a radically subjective approach in which (as he described it) "the reader was now given joint responsibility for the production of a meaning that was itself redefined as an event rather than an entity.[10] Then, in his later work, he went on to a more complex, more socially grounded explanation of what goes on between a reader and a piece of literature.

In his later theorizing he argued that whenever a work is read, it is read not by a solitary isolated person but by an individual who is a member of a community—an "interpretive community," he calls it—and that such communities are engaged in ongoing projects of reality-construction

He said, for example, that one kind of construction project is going on whenever people tacitly agree to grant to a piece of writing the status of a great work of literature—or even, for that matter, the status of literature:

> Paying a certain kind of attention (as defined by what literature is understood to be) results in the emergence into noticeability of the properties we know in advance to be literary. The conclusion is that while literature is still a category, it is an open category, not definable by fictionality, or by a disregard of propositional truth, or by a pre-

> dominance of tropes and figures, but simply by what we decide to put into it. And the conclusion to that conclusion is that it is the reader who "makes" literature. This sounds like the rankest subjectivism, but it is qualified almost immediately when the reader is identified not as a free agent, making literature in any old way, but as a member of a community whose assumptions about literature determine the kind of attention he pays and thus the kind of literature "he" makes.[11]

This kind of talk would probably not make Matthew Arnold's day, but it is still not quite the utter self-indulgent anarchy that objectivists fear—and that Fish is often accused of fomenting. He means that some SCR is always in place; it may change as the reader's understanding changes or as fashions change, but still the reader is a social animal embedded within systems of value and belief. In the literary experience as he describes it, writing, reading, studying, and criticizing are all parts of a dynamic social process. That process is one of ever-changing creation of values and understandings and norms; it is creative, not nihilistic: "There is never a moment when one believes nothing," he says. He argues rather that at any point, however much things may be changing, people do believe in the meaning of a written work—and when they do, "they do so confidently rather than provisionally (they are not relativists)" and furthermore, "those beliefs are not individual—specific or idiosyncratic but communal and conventional (they are not solipsists)."

Although Fish is frequently attacked by conservative critics, neither his early reader response theory nor his later affective community theory is all that far-out. In fact, I'm afraid they're not far-out enough. The first is solidly in the Kantian tradition, the second is basic social psychology; there is nothing particularly radical about the notion that people shape their beliefs according to what they perceive to be the beliefs of groups they belong to or aspire to belong to.

But such ideas are troubling—and not only troubling to the old guard. William E. Cain, an eminently reasonable critic, can't quite make out the state of mind that Fish is trying to describe: "It is a queer kind of belief," he observes, "that is already informed by the possibility of unbelief."[12]

Queer indeed, but such belief may well be the only game in the postmodern town. It takes a superhuman kind of faith—or monumental pigheadedness—to entertain a belief with the unshakeable conviction that no evidence or persuasion will ever change it. To consider any possibility of change is indeed to be "informed" by that possibility and quite likely to have secretly flirted with it. To avoid being invaded by the possibility of unbelief is somewhat akin to the children's game of not thinking about a white elephant.

It would be hard to find an interpretive community left in the academic/literary world whose members don't have some idea about interpretive communities—don't understand in some general way that their belief systems are social constructions. Even Hirsch (who is, after all, not merely a conservative but an intelligent conservative in a postmodern era) occasionally slips into subversively relativistic notions that seem to belie his opposition to them; he says, for example, that there is a difference between *meaning* (what the author intended, and which doesn't change) and *significance* (what a work means to people in a certain historical period, and which does change). Surely if you let such thoughts enter your consciousness, you are continually in the presence of the possibility of unbelief. And your belief is likely to be, whether you want it to be or not, provisional. That's what I mean about Fish not being far-out enough.

Ideas of provisional, socially based belief are difficult enough to get used to, but they are not by any means the most disturbing ideas running through the halls of ivy. Deconstruction, the assault on meaning imported from Europe in the 1970s, goes well beyond the theory of interpretive communities, and well beyond right-you-are-if-you-think-you-are. Its message is closer to wrong you are whatever you think, unless you think you're wrong, in which case you may be right—but you don't really mean what you think you do anyway.

THE DECONSTRUCTION DERBY

Henry David Thoreau would seem to be the most straightforward of writers, an honest American who struggled through the falseness of civilization toward something simpler and quieter, whose work has the effect of a calming encounter with the bone-deep certainties of nature. Not all people have seen him so—Emerson said it made him "nervous and wretched" to read Thoreau's work, it was so full of contradictions—but Thoreau's popular image, nevertheless, is that of a direct and uncomplicated guy who said what he meant and meant what he said.

Walter Michaels, a critic from the deconstructionist school, finds something else entirely. Peaceful Walden, subjected to his analysis, becomes a maddening morass of conflicted meanings, symbolic of the futility of any search for certainty.

Take this oft-quoted passage in the second chapter of *Walden*, in which Thoreau writes:

> Let us settle ourselves, and work and wedge our feet downward through the mud and slush of opinion, and prejudice, and tradition, and delusion, and appearance, that alluvion which covers the globe, . . . through church and state, through poetry and philosophy and religion, till we come to a hard bottom and rocks in place, which we can call *reality*, and say, This is it, and no mistake. . . . [13]

Judging from this, Thoreau appears to be a patriarch of old-fashioned positivism, strongly committed to the search for bed-rock truth. But then Michaels draws our attention to a passage in chapter 18 where, in what starts out to be another commercial for solid ground, Thoreau recounts an anecdote about a traveler who asks a boy if the swamp just ahead has a hard bottom. The boy says it does; the traveler rides into it, and soon his horse has sunk in up to the girths. The traveler says to the boy, "I thought you said that this bog had a hard bottom." The boy replies, "So it has. But you have not got halfway to it yet." And Thoreau concludes that it is the same way with the bogs and quicksands of society—"but he is an old boy that knows it."

These passages might seem at first to be quite harmonious, but Michaels observes that a deep ambiguity is revealed to the close reader: although both point to the contrast between hard bottoms and the mud and slush above, the message about what to do is actually quite different. In the first, the wise man works his way down through the ooze to get to the bottom; in the second, he knows enough to ride clear of such places, and thus escape the fate of the foolish traveler.

Elsewhere, Thoreau talks about plumbing the depths of Walden Pond, and mentions with some contempt the many gullible people who have accepted the legend that it is bottomless. "It is remarkable," Thoreau says, "how long men will believe in the bottomless-ness of a pond without taking the trouble to sound it." And he tells how, with no great difficulty, he personally ascertained the greatest depth to be precisely 102 feet. Here Thoreau condemns all the people who lacked the scientific curiosity to do what he did and celebrates his own tenacity in getting (literally) to the bottom of things. Then he proceeds to say:

> This is a remarkable depth for so small an area; yet not an inch of it can be spared by the imagination. What if all ponds were shallow? Would it not react on the minds of men? I am thankful that this pond was made pure and deep for a symbol. While men believe in the infinite some pond will be thought to be bottomless.[14]

Well, there you go again, Thoreau: first congratulating yourself for dispelling the mystery, then telling us we need mysteries.

Michaels—whose essay is entitled "*Walden*'s False Bottoms"—is not merely engaged in catching Thoreau out in a couple of contradictions. That is small game: contradictions abound in literature. The New Critics were fond of pointing out the paradoxes and "creative stresses" that could be found in great works, but that nevertheless (as they saw it) served to enhance the power of the central meaning. Michaels rather finds Thoreau to be ambiguous about truth itself—as though slipping and sliding back and forth between a modern and a postmodern view of reality—and finds *Walden* to lack any central meaning whatever.[15]

Deconstruction is a lot easier to approach in essays such as Michael's than in the works of its originator, Jacques Derrida. Derrida, a professor of the history of philosophy at the École Normale Supérieure in Paris, writes with a Continental intellectual's conviction that nothing you want people to regard as profound should ever be expressed clearly. His style of writing is to drift mysteriously about the subject, wandering off into inscrutable digressions and refusing utterly to give the reader anything so square as one of those "in this essay I shall attempt to demonstrate—" introductions. He fastens on details and on obscure turns of phrase, and gradually manages to sort of pull apart the work under review—showing that it is not a group of subthemes organized around a central message, but rather a play of meanings going in all directions, full of gaps and "otherness."

He deconstructs the work, in short. Over the course of his career, he has deconstructed (with great impartiality) classical philosophy, structuralism, and Marxism. He deconstructed psychoanalysis. And I imagine that if Freud were alive, he would in turn psychoanalyze deconstruction, find Derrida the victim of a Hamlet-like ambivalence toward authority—in this case, the authority of texts—born, no doubt, out of unresolved Oedipal conflicts.

Deconstruction has become a great growth industry in the academic world. It is a new critical technique that gives scholars an opportunity to go back over all the works that have already been interpreted according to various theories and interpret them all over again in the manner of Derrida: deconstruct them. Some critics deconstruct the interpretations of prior critics. Some deconstruct the works of other decontructionists, and a good time is had by all. Some writers attack ideas they do not like and use deconstruction as a form of refutation. It has become quite commonplace in intellectual discourse for writers to say that they have "deconstructed" someone else's position whenever they have argued with it or managed to find some logical weaknesses in it.

But deconstruction is neither a method of interpretation nor a debating device. It is a serious critique of representation itself. If you read Derrida and other deconstructionists with patience (and believe me you will need it), you discover in their work a subtle and important discussion of how difficult it is to tell the truth.

The deconstructionists are not after any writer or message in particular. A work successfully deconstructed has not been revealed as an inferior piece of literature, only a typical one. Deconstruction is about language, about the impossibility of representation. It is an assault upon "logocentrism"—the idea that there is anything *beyond* the human symbolic system that a written work can refer to so it can be an authentic statement from one person to another *about* something. The British critic Terry Eagleton says in his exposition of Derrida that Western philosophy has always been logocentric, and thus objectivistic—

> committed to a belief in some ultimate "word," presence, essence, truth or reality which will act as the foundation of all our thought, language and experience. It has yearned for the sign which will give meaning to all others—the "transcendental signifier"—and for the

> anchoring, unquestionable meaning to which all our signs can be seen to point (the "transcendental signified"). A great number of candidates for this role—God, the Idea, the World Spirit, the Self, substance, matter and so on—have thrust themselves forward from time to time. Since each of these concepts hopes to *found* our whole system of thought and language, it must itself be beyond that system, untainted by its play of linguistic differences. It cannot be implicated in the very languages which it attempts to order and anchor. . . .[16]

Deconstructionists say no written work is held by such an anchor. Literature has no extralinguistic referent, no place for Archimedes to stand so he can move the earth. Whenever a writer attempts to construct such a referent, be it Walden's bedrock nature or Freud's pleasure principle, the construction is inevitably a *fiction* (the word *fiction* means literally a thing modeled or created), and the substance out of which it is created is—words. The "first principle" thus created is a system of symbols, not propped up by anything outside language, and (since first principles are commonly defined by what they exclude) the thing excluded tends to lurk somewhere in the written work's dark corners, threatening to dart out at any moment and pull down the whole structure. A deconstructionist merely points out the things in the dark corners. Deconstruction is, as one of its practitioners (J. Hillis Miller) puts it, "a demonstration that the text has already dismantled itself."

There are, as I suppose is appropriate, many paradoxes about deconstruction.

One is that it is rather dogmatic about the truth of its *own* first principle, which comes through with a consistency that ought to cheer up any old-fashioned believer in the written word. There are few surprises about deconstruction: a deconstructionist critic always seems to find what he or she is looking for. (I suspect that many aspiring deconstructionists have set to work on certain texts and given it up when they could not find what they were looking for—but we will never know.)

Another is that deconstruction has in a way done what generations of earnest New Critics never managed to do: it has set literature again at the center of civilization. All written work—definitely including history, philosophy, and the law—is now regarded as literature, and thus as fair game for "close reading" and deconstruction. Critical studies programs that have developed as outposts of postmodernism in many universities are not just about literature as traditionally defined, but about language as a social institution. And deconstruction-inspired analyses mount absolutely devastating critiques of the written foundations of modern society. History becomes, instead of discernible patterns of human action, "indeterminate"—any meaning imposed upon events by a historian is mere fiction, made of other fictions. The law becomes another jumble of words going in all directions, and lots of luck to anybody who tries to get the precise "legislative intent" of a law to serve as a sure guideline to its meaning.

It is easy to find faults in deconstruction, and people have found them with a vengeance. Some have jeered at its trendiness, some have reacted angrily against its apparent assertion that there really are no clear values and beliefs held publicly in any modern society, and some have concentrated on attacking the deconstructionists. Deconstruction's enemies have made much of the news that came out after the death of Paul de Man (the leading exponent of deconstruction in the United States)—that he had been an enthusiastic and frequent contributor to an anti-Semitic pro-Nazi journal as a young man in Belgium.

No doubt much *should* be made of that, and particularly of de Man's long concealment of it (the joke about it that became popular in the academic world said de Man had forgotten as a result of a severe case of "Waldheimer's disease"). But some critics have publicly expressed their hope that the incident would do what nothing else had succeeded in doing so far—discredit and finally deconstruct deconstruction. Poet David Lehman wrote of how "poetically just it would be if so antibiographical a theory of literature should be vanquished by the discovery of a ruinous biographical fact."[17]

The de Man scandal does not appear to have blown deconstruction away, and I don't think anything else will. It has taken up residence among us as yet another postmodern vision, another dissenter against the modern view of meaning.

It is more nihilistic than the constructivist thought we explored in the previous chapter, which at least does have a concept of a provisional and limited kind of knowledge, and it is less hopeful about literature than the reader response and interpretive community approaches to criticism. But it is not quite as bleak as some deconstructionists (and some opponents of deconstruction) paint it, and it is not the antihumanistic "ideology of despair" that one critic recently accused it of being.[18] It is a serious critique of language (revealing it to be a flawed and sometimes paradoxical symbolic system, as Gödel revealed mathematics to be), and it is yet another blow to objectivistic ideas of representation. Yet we cannot help observing that all the works that have been deconstructed are still around, and still sending out their messages. Freud's work—which had already been revealed to be full of contradictions and plain hokum before Derrida took it on and which never had the scientific credibility Freud claimed—remains a useful and brilliant contribution to our far-from-perfect understanding of our own minds. And Derrida's work deserves precisely the same status.

Deconstruction does not render written works meaning-less, but meaning-full—perhaps more so than their authors intended. I don't see why we need to get particularly upset by the news that any work of literature has its dark side, its deep paradoxes, its hidden contrariness, even that it fails to make a single clear statement—unless we are incapable of living with the same news about ourselves. Depth psychologists such as the Jungians have been saying for a long time that every personality has its shadow side—perhaps many shadow sides—and cognitive scientists such as Minsky have more recently been describing the human mind as a veritable factory of meanings, and a not particularly centralized one at that.

DECONSTRUCTING LAW

Of all the fields that have been affected by the shock waves traveling outward from the postmodern deconstruction of literary meaning, the law seems to be the one that is taking it the hardest—and this may be, also, the area in which the critical studies movement has its greatest social impact.

Is the law merely literature, with all that has come to mean in terms of ambiguity, internal conflict, lack of anchor to anything outside itself? Doesn't the law have a special status because of its connection to social norms, tradition, society's aspiration to justice? Can it, too, be deconstructed?

Clare Dalton, a member of the critical legal studies group at Harvard Law School, wrote a paper that answered two of those questions in its first sentence. She began, "Law, like every other cultural institution, is a place where we tell one another stories about our relationships with ourselves, one another, and authority." The paper's title had already answered the third question. It was "An Essay on the Deconstruction of Contract Doctrine."[19]

The battle between modernism and postmodernism became particularly bitter at Harvard Law School, and turned that eminent institution into what a departing professor called "the Beirut of legal education." One of the central figures in the troubles there was Ms. Dalton, who was denied tenure.

The issues in this battle are, as one might expect of a conflict among legal scholars, astoundingly complex—a few years ago the *Stanford Law Review* put out a six-hundred-page special issue on it—but the central theme is one we have already seen elsewhere: a collapse of modern-era belief. Since before the turn of the century, the study of law at Harvard (and at all the law schools that followed its lead) had been based on a method, sometimes called the doctrinal approach, which looked on the law as something like a science—or at least something like what nonscientists believed science to be: that is, an objective body of logical truth from which the correct answer to any question could be deduced.[20] Proponents of the doctrinal approach taught that the study of cases would lead to the discovery of the proper principle—and that the principles themselves, embodying the fundamental structure of the society, were something more than matters of mere human opinion.

Then, in the 1920s and 1930s, along came a movement known as legal realism. Legal realism was not a postmodern revolution in law any more than the New Criticism was in literature, but it has a similar place in history as a preview of coming attractions. The legal realists merely pointed out that judges could find all kinds of precedents, and the one that decided a given case was likely to have been chosen because of human (and relative) reasons such as the judge's personal opinion, his politics, or what he thought his friends down at the club might say. The legal realists believed that court decisions reflect the social values of the time more than permanent and objective legal principles.

Legal realism and other approaches to the study of law—approaches based more on twentieth-century modes of analysis than on older philosophical styles—impacted schools of law everywhere. They do not, however, appear to have shaken Harvard much. Even the 1960s did not shake Harvard Law School much; Calvin Trillin, in his account of the events there, says, "The style of the faculty of that period is sometimes spoken of as 'mandarin,' although 'stifling' is also a word I've heard applied to it."[21]

The troubles at Harvard started in the 1970s, with the arrival of young faculty members who represented the approach called Critical Legal Studies, C.L.S. for short—a mixture of legal realism, 1960s New Left radicalism, and postmodern critical theory. The "crits," as they came to be called, mounted an attack on traditional legal scholarship that challenged not only its methods but its view of reality. This included any number of diverting pieces of campus politics—demonstrations, sit-ins, an attempt to get the school's janitors pay equal to that of its faculty—and an enormous amount of intellectual discourse.

Chief theoretician of the crits is Roberto Mangabeira Ungar, who argues that the conditions of the current era are such that it is necessary to see the law as a structure of artifacts that serve to protect and perpetuate all kinds of hierarchies of economic power and unjust social distinctions. Sounding at times like Antonin Artaud, he pleads for a new era of "creative negativity" to dismantle those old structures and bring an entirely new social order into being.[22]

The Critical Legal Studies movement and the outraged reaction to it has now gone far beyond Harvard; it is a central issue in what one scholar calls "the collapse of traditional liberal jurisprudence and of constitutional education in our time."[23]

The crits and their allies adopt a postmodern stance toward any prop under the law that looks like an absolute verity: Sanford Levinson, professor of constitutional law at the University of Texas at Austin, has written with enthusiasm about the impotence of "timeless moral norms," "the persuasive force of detached reason," the thoughts or intentions of the Constitution writers, and thus of constitutionalism itself as we have known it. "The death of 'constitutionalism,'" he says, "may be the central event of our time, just as the death of God was that of the past century (and for much the same reason)."[24]

Like Ungar, Levinson sees this disintegration of belief as a creative opportunity, with "political truths" being replaced by "political visions," and the future constructed out of the visions that are most persuasive. And—just as Dostoyevski acknowledged that, without God, anything is possible—Levinson acknowledges that, without the old-fashioned constitutionalism that contains permanent moral truths, anything is politically possible if the people want it: fascism definitely included.

Some people are (as is not surprising) deeply offended by such statements, and highly suspicious of critical legal studies. Levinson's book, said a reviewer, "should be for all of us an alarm bell ringing in the night. Something ominous is afoot in the teaching of the law of this land."[25] Some legal scholars react as though the law were a religion and not the highly rational (and/or pragmatically political) body of thought the modern era took it to be: Paul D. Carrington, dean of the Duke University Law School, said all C.L.S. law teachers were morally bound to resign, because it is immoral to teach a subject in which one does not believe. Is it appropriate, he asked, for an atheist to teach religion?[26]

In a way, the Critical Legal Studies movement is most unrevolutionary. A good sociologist of knowledge fifty years ago, confronted with the declaration that constitutions and the norms and principles underlying them are all social constructions of reality, would have said, "So what else is new?" Yet something important is happening; both the crits and their enemies recognize that. And it is happening as part of a growing willingness of many people to think new thoughts about written words—definitely including the ones in the law books.

Judge Robert Bork, the Reagan nominee to the Supreme Court who was denied confirmation by the Senate after a bitter political battle that focused on his conservative legal views, wrote a book in which he describes himself as a casualty of a much larger conflict, a conflict over *meaning*. He says:

> The clash over my nomination was simply one battle in this long-running war for control of our legal culture. There may be legitimate differences about that nomination, but, in the larger war for control of the law, there are only two sides. Either the Constitution and statutes are law, which means that their principles are known and control judges, or they are malleable texts that judges may rewrite to see that particular groups or political causes win. Until recently, the American people were largely unaware of the struggle for dominance in

> law, because it was waged, in explicit form, only in the law schools. Now it is coming into the open.[27]

The conflict, he says, is essentially a "clash of law and politics"—law represented by those who stand behind a solid Matthew Arnold-style reliance on the intent of the framers of the Constitution, and politics by those more inclined to follow the agendas and ideas of the times. He traces the origins of this war back beyond the 1960s, even beyond the liberals of the Warren Court—back to the law professors.

He thinks the Warren Court took unpardonable liberties with the Constitution in some of its major decisions involving racial segregation, poll taxes and privacy rights—engaged in jurisprudence that was "not law but social engineering from the bench." And the real cause of its errors was not so much the chief justice as the philosophy of legal realism:

> Other Courts had certainly made policy that was not theirs to make, but the Warren Court so far surpassed the others as to be different in kind. Nor is this entirely, or even primarily, attributable to Earl Warren himself. The groundwork had been laid by a generation of legal scholars, the "legal realists" . . .[28]

Bork describes the damage wrought by the legal realists as bad enough, yet mild compared to what may happen when the courts begin to be taken over by a new generation of jurists trained in the current intellectual climate of the universities, where the "mindless form of leftist politics," the "crude anti-intellectualism" of critical legal studies are tolerated.[29]

The sole bulwark against complete deterioration of the "shared values and moral first principles" of society, he thinks, is a return to an "original understanding" doctrine of law based on the intent of the authors of the Constitution: "The interpretation of the Constitution according to the original understanding . . . is the only method that can preserve the Constitution, the separation of powers, and the liberties of the people." The foundation of such a doctrine would be the intent of the framers; in an attempt to make this even more solidly objective he says that we should not be concerned about their "subjective intentions" but rather general public understanding as to what those intentions were: "All that counts is how the words used in the Constitution would have been understood at the time."[30]

Although the conflict he describes is certainly going on, I don't think the picture is as black-and-white as he paints it. We are not faced with a choice between return to governance in the mode of Judge Bork and his friends at the American Enterprise Institute, or a blind leap forward to governance in the mode of deconstructionist law professors—and I think it's a mighty good thing we're not. The conservatives do not appear to know that their rock-of-ages understanding of the Constitution is a social construction of reality, and many of the crits are in the grip of a punkish fantasy that they can sweep away all SCRs, all rules entirely, and achieve a political order based on "natural harmony."

Instead of either of those extremes—but with both of them very much parts of the dialogue—we are likely to see a long period of postmodern engagement with the serious question of how much a society *needs* reification—or some kind of "constitutional faith"—in order to hold itself together. It has been no secret that the Constitution's public support rests more on a vague reverence for it than on what is actually in it. Most people have only the vaguest idea of what is in it, and some polls suggest disturbingly that most people are not at all sure about some of those rights when presented with them out of their sanctified context.

Does that mean that constitutionalism is dead? I don't think so. I note that even Professor Levinson says he is willing to make a "limited affirmaton" of faith in the Constitution. It is one of the things that holds American society together. The country has not yet reached the time when it can do without one, and I suspect it is well past the time when it could create a new one. If we had the new constitutional convention that some desire, bringing together a nationally representative group of framers, could they create an organic document? I seriously doubt it. I doubt that we could even get one out of a smaller gathering—I doubt, in fact, that you could get a decent bill of rights out of the Harvard law faculty.

So our government continues to be based (perhaps loosely) on the old Constitution, and sometimes when judges are in doubt about how to apply it they make up stories about what the people who wrote it (or read it) had in mind. It all comes down to words, and interpretations of them. But who would have thought that, on the eve of the twenty-first century, the world's most advanced post-modern society would be so concerned about a work of literature?

THE END AND BEGINNING OF STORIES

Throughout the twentieth century, as the modern era's construction of reality collapsed and a new consciousness emerged, literature revealed what was happening. In fiction, poetry, literary criticism, and theater, people encountered not only new stories and ways of telling them, but also new ideas about the role of story in life, and new challenges to the belief in a clear boundary between fiction and reality.

As we become aware of the social construction of reality—consciously, *publicly* aware—the boundary erodes between the kind of fiction we call art or literature and the kind of fiction we call reality. History becomes another kind of storytelling, personal and social life becomes another kind of drama, and it becomes possible for Paul de Man to say (in a sentence much more meaningful to us now than when he first wrote it), "It is always possible to face up to any experience (to excuse any guilt), because the experience always exists simultaneously as fictional discourse and as empirical event, and it is never possible to decide which one of the two possibilities is the right one."[31]

We begin to get self-consciously postmodernist literature that refuses to play the old game of pretending to be a representation of "real life." Susan Sontag saw this coming in the 1960s when she wrote her celebrated essay about "camp," which was, as she put it, "a way of seeing the world as an aesthetic phenomenon," the love of "things-being-what-they-are-not," a sensibility that "sees everything in quotation marks."[32] When an artist creates in the mode of camp it is to mock the medium, the artist, the audience, and art itself—the only failure is to appear to be taking oneself seriously.

And, of course, camp recognizes no boundary between art and life. If you do not happen to be a professional performer, you can perform in your behavior, in your choice of clothes—camp has roots in homosexuality, and the campy cross-dresser is playing the game in life. I thought of camp one year when I was running in San Francisco's famous Bay to Breakers race (a pretty campy event anyway) and a young man passed me wearing a white wedding dress, skirts daintily held high as he ran to reveal muscled hairy calves and size-twelve running shoes.

A similar playfulness is evident in much of postmodern*ist* literature (I want to emphasize the "ist" at this point), which impishly calls attention to its fictionality—makes visible its story-creating, world-making machinery. A leading critical writer on the genre, Brian McHale, says, "The workings of *all* postmodernist world-making machines are visible, in one way or another, to one degree or another; this, precisely, is what makes them postmodernist."[33] Even so mainstream a novelist as John Fowles comes out from behind the curtains in *The French Lieutenant's Woman* and tells us, "This story I am telling is all imagination. These characters I create never existed outside my own mind." And when the novel is made into a movie (with a screenplay by Harold Pinter), we see at the end a scene in which all the actors, in modern dress, are *actors* at a garden party.

Postmodernist fiction plays much more complex games: games of *trompe l'oeil*, of stories within stories, of realities revealed to be unrealities and vice versa, of recursive structures and what Douglas Hofstadter calls "strange loops" or tangled hierarchies of meaning: in a Julio Cortázar short story, a man is reading a novel in which a killer approaches a house in which he plans to murder his lover's husband—who is the man reading the novel.[34]

Whatever became of the sanctity of illusion, the old belief that the audience must *believe* in the story? How quickly it faded in the postmodern light. When I was an earnest young reporter for *TV Guide* magazine in the last, last years of the modern era, I was supposed to make the rounds of the Hollywood TV studios and find material for picture features about how special effects were created. This part of my job turned out to be "Mission Impossible," because most of the TV studios had firm policies about *not* allowing such things to be photographed. "We want to protect the illusion" a publicist at Warner Bros. told me. I was stunned by this. Was there anybody out there in the world who really believed that Troy Donahue was a private detective? Anyway, such was the studio policy in the early 1960s. Yet, just a few years later, when the word from Susan Sontag trickled down to television, Warner Bros. produced the first camp TV series, *Batman*. Nobody was expected to believe in Batman and Robin; they played it for laughs—and on we went into the late 1960s, illusions crumbling behind us.

Postmodern*ist* fiction—which is cerebral and usually campy and seems to have been written for (if not by) critics—is quite self-conscious in showing its awareness of the social construction of reality, calls our attention to the games it plays with the conventions of literature. Postmodern fiction—which is simply anything written in the postmodern era—reveals its own awareness of the social construction of reality in different, and sometimes more interesting, ways.

McHale thinks the detective novel was the epitome of modernist fiction: detective fiction is about knowing and not knowing, about a quest for truth and certainty—and it typically ends with the discovery of the *facts* and the story that pulls them together. And he thinks science fiction is "postmodernism's noncanonized or 'low art' double, its sister-genre in the same sense that the popular detective thriller is modernist fiction's sister-genre."[35] Where the detective story searches for (and usually finds) the one "real truth" that solves the mystery, the science-fiction story explores otherness—other worlds, other realities—and is more likely to lead the reader into a state of culture shock than into secure possession of certainty: "Science fiction, by staging 'close encounters' between different worlds, placing them in confrontation, foregrounds their respective structures and the disparities between them. It thus obeys the same underlying principles of ontological poetics as postmodernist fiction."[36]

While giving all due credit to science fiction as an entertaining education in postmodern consciousness, I would like to nominate another genre as equally typical of our time: the spy novel.

In the hands of a first-rate practitioner such as John Le Carré, the spy novel is yet another kind of close encounter between different worlds. It can be more unsettling because it is set in the contemporary "real" world—and because, even more than the detective novel or the science-fiction novel, it keeps us in a continual state of uncertainty about who is who, what is happening, what is real, and what is staged in order to entrap or deceive somebody. Charlie, the aspiring actress in *The Little Drummer Girl*, is lured into playing a role in an elaborate intrigue; Magnus Pym, the British agent in *A Perfect Spy*, appears to be "running" a Czech double agent but is actually a double agent himself, being "run" by the Czech.

If we take spy novels at all seriously, we are likely to wonder if people and events in the real world around us are exactly what they appear to be. And how can we not take them seriously, when the newspapers, our main source of nonfiction, report to us regularly about agents and double agents and disinformation campaigns, about "sting" operations that create staged stories for unsuspecting individuals who suddenly discover—surprise!—that the man who has enticed them to commit a crime is actually working for the FBI. One is impressed, too, by the extent to which the people who run our government's actual cloak-and-dagger operations seem to be living out fantasies of themselves as characters in spy novels—or even James Bond movies.

So, whether you get your literature from deconstructionist critics and university-press novelists, or from the latest item in the airport bookstore, or from the daily news, you are likely to get a similar subtext about the human condition: a message that life is a matter of telling ourselves stories about life, and of savoring stories about life told by others, and of living our lives according to such stories, and of creating ever-new and more complex stories about stories—and that this story making is not just about human life, but is human life.

PART THREE

THE THEATER OF REALITY

CHAPTER 5

Making Beliefs and Making Believe

In the 1950s, the British novelist Nigel Dennis wrote a funny, bizarre book entitled *Cards of Identity* that was both a work of comic fiction and yet another indicator of movement along the road to postmodernism.

In the novel—set in an English village any reader of novels would immediately recognize—a strange trio, who *seem* to be a wealthy middle-aged gentleman, his attractive second wife, and his son, perform a sort of psychological kidnapping of a dreary brother and sister who live nearby. The two—first the brother, then the sister who comes looking for him—are welcomed into the manor house, drawn into conversations that make them somewhat muddled about what is going on, and then given to understand that *they are not the people they thought they were.* The docile pair begin to forget who they were and to respond warmly to the new identities that are now skillfully woven around them by the words and responses of the kidnappers. The brother becomes the butler, Jellicoe, a hardworking man with a raffish past. The sister becomes the faithful and beloved housekeeper, Florrie.

Where the identities of the brother and sister had before been wispy and unsatisfying, the new ones are meaningful and emotionally nourishing. The two now have rich, almost Dickensian, personalities; the family *cares* about them. As the story unfolds, the mysterious trio proceed to shanghai more anomic locals into the household, and we learn that they are members of an organization called the Identity Club, whose purpose is to compensate for the psychological uncertainty of modern life by creating entirely new structures of reality. They are manufacturers and entrepreneurs of reality. At one point in the book, in a manifesto that takes a satiric shot in the general direction of Marxists, Freudians, Christians, and other seekers after converts to the prevailing SCRs of the time, a leader of the club says:

> We are . . . the idea behind the idea, the theory at the root of theory. And what we like about ourselves is the frank way we go about our work. Other clubs stubbornly deny that they try to supply their patients with new identities. They insist that they merely reveal an identity which has been pushed out of sight. Thank God, gentlemen, we shall never be like them! We are proud to know that we are in the very van of modern development, that we can transform any unknown quantity into a fixed self, and that we need never fall back on the hypocrisy of pretending that we are mere uncoverers.[1]

Just a few years earlier, Jean-Paul Sartre had written a short story entitled "Childhood of a Leader" that played with the identity theme in a somewhat more conventional—and more explicitly political—way. Its hero is a Parisian student named Lucien who lives an ordinary adolescent life: his main activity is a dishonest and unconsummated romance with a lower-class girl. He feels unhappy with "this small existence, sad and vague," which is his own. He thinks he should be more like another student he knows, Lemordant; Lemordant is very impressive, seems like a "man with convictions," and hates Jews. Gradually Lucien decides he too will be anti-Semitic—not because he cares the least about Jews, one way or another, but because the social role of the anti-Semite obviously has some clout. After a few tentative ventures in this direction, he becomes recognized as someone with a violent hatred for Jews. His parents and his friends seem to respect him for his newfound force of character. His girlfriend submits to him sexually. In the glow of these experiences, he has a sort of political epiphany in which he comprehends his place in the system. He becomes aware of his life as "an enormous bouquet of responsibilities and rights" including a social position that will give him workers to command and a married life with a woman of his own class. He is a man, a leader. As the story ends, he decides to grow a mustache.[2]

In such playful tales the light of human intelligence flickers about the dark corners of the subject of personal reality constructs—a subject that, while central to our being as political animals, is also one that most of us really do not want to think too much about, nor know how to think about. Yet it is the master theme—the theory behind the theory—that weaves through the other themes such as brainwashing, cults, terrorism, and propaganda that describe the political life of the twentieth century. A politician in California said once that money is the mother's milk of politics. He was widely quoted, because he was expressing a notion quite popular in America—a two-dimensional SCR that makes us think we understand more than we do—but he was wrong: the real fount of political power, the source of all loyalty and all independence, is the reality-creating process by which we decide who we are and what we think is happening.

In this chapter and the two that follow, we look at the twin themes of personal reality and politics. We begin with some basic observations about social life in the postmodern world. We then investigate two problems that confront us in this world: in chapter 6, the problem of making a personal identity; in chapter 7, the problem of governing responsibly in a society in which realities are created irresponsibly.

IN OUR TIME

These are some of the givens of life in the early postmodern era:

1. The society itself is a social construction of reality. All the things that identify and define a "people"—such as its boundaries, its culture, its political institutions—are the (usually reified) products of earlier inventions.
2. Individual identity is also a social construction of reality, and the concept of a "self" is different in different societies and at different stages of history.
3. We regard the collective beliefs of individuals (rather than the mind of God or the laws of history) as the ultimate repository of social reality (what is true is defined by what we all believe), and we know that beliefs can be modified.
4. Consequently, all sectors of society are deeply interested in finding out what people believe (public opinion) and modifying those beliefs (advertising, propaganda, brainwashing, public relations, and so forth).

5. In a postmodern society we perceive life as drama, and our major issues involve the definition of personal roles and the fabrication of stories that give purpose and shape to social existence.
6. Public happenings have the quality of scenes created or stage-managed for public consumption. They are what Daniel Boorstin called pseudoevents.

Let us look more closely at each of these.

Making a People

One of the fundamental fictions of politics is the fiction of a "people"—an aggregation of human beings distinguishable from other aggregations of human beings and therefore capable of being organized into a political unit; an "us" that can be identified as separate from "them." Unless you have created that fiction you cannot proceed to any of the other activities—such as drawing boundaries, fighting wars, and singing songs about the inherent superiority of your people—that are so much a part of politics as we have known and loved it.

But it is always hard work to keep such a fiction going: societies, like other categories, are fuzzy around the edges, while the fiction demands a certain neatness. Freud observed a kind of behavior he called "the narcissism of minor differences," in which people who lived near a national boundary would go to great pains to distinguish themselves from the people who lived just across the border. Socrates had to devise a noble lie to give the guardians of his ideal republic a strong sense of their identity as citizens of it. Only occasionally and with massive exceptions are "peoples" linked by the ties of blood that the fiction usually celebrates; an old European saying describes a nation as a group of people united by a common mistake about their ancestry and a common dislike of their neighbors.

The origins of most "people" are not known, but here and there we can find accounts of people-making activities that have taken place in the modern era. One historian, Hugh Trevor-Roper, has documented various inventions of the traditions that symbolize Scotland's distinct identity, all of which took place much more recently than most of us would imagine—after, not before, the union with England. Until late in the seventeenth century, the Scottish highlanders were not a distinct people but merely an overflow population from Ireland and linked to the Irish racially, culturally, and politically. The lowlands were populated by other racial groups including Picts and Saxons. Then there began a deliberate "cultural revolt" against Ireland, which combined a good deal of creativity with a good deal of plagiarism. Trevor-Roper credits the work of two men, James Macpherson and the Reverend John Macpherson (not related), who between them invented an ancient Celtic literature for Scotland and a history to go with it. He writes:

> The sheer effrontery of the Macphersons must excite admiration. James Macpherson picked up Irish ballads in Scotland, wrote an "epic" in which he transferred the whole scenario from Ireland to Scotland, and then dismissed the genuine ballads thus maltreated as debased modern compositions and the real Irish literature which they reflected as a mere reflection of them. The minister of Sleat then wrote a *Critical Dissertation* in which he provided the necessary context for "the Celtic Homer" whom his namesake had "discovered": he placed Irish-speaking Celts in Scotland four centuries before their historical arrival and explained away the genuine, native Irish literature as having been stolen, in the Dark Ages, by the unscrupulous Irish, from the innocent Scots. To complete the picture, James Macpherson himself, using the minister's papers, wrote an "independent" *Introduction to the History of Great Britain and Ireland* (1771) repeating the minister's assertions.[3]

Scottish national dress was also being invented at about the same time. Until the seventeenth century, the highlanders had dressed much the same as their Irish relatives; then gradually a cloak, belted around the waist and forming a kind of skirt below the waist, had come into wide use. This was called a "belted plaid." Around 1730 a Quaker industrialist named Thomas Rawlinson, who considered the belted plaid a "cumbrous, unwieldy habit," hired a tailer to design a new garment for his workmen: the pleated kilt. This innovation, said a historian of the time, "was found so handy and convenient that in the shortest space of use it became frequent in all the Highland countries and in many of the Northern Lowland countries also."[4] Later still came the invention of the "clan tartan." At the time of the rebellion against England in 1745, highland clan identities were vague, and people who wore tartans at all wore whatever pattern suited them or was available. After the rebellion, the British Parliament (doing what national governments have often done) tried to erase highland culture entirely and outlawed the wearing of all highland costume. Men took to wearing the ordinary trousers of the time, and travelers to the highlands reported no sign of kilts or plaids.

And that was pretty much how it remained, for the lower classes. But among the upper classes, the wearing of kilts at home became fashionable as a defiant statement of Scottish nationality. In 1778 the Highland Society was formed in London, dedicated to preserving highland traditions, and a few years later its members managed to get the prohibition against highland dress repealed. After that, kilts and tartans became standard dress wear for Scottish aristocrats, and uniforms for Scottish regiments. In the ensuing plaid boom an enterprising cloth manufacturer, William Watson and Son of Bannockburn, came up with the idea of marketing distinctive clan tartans. This proved quite successful, and the highland dress became popular in the lowlands as well. In 1820 a Celtic Society was formed in Edinburgh; its president was Sir Walter Scott, a lowlander. Members of this society dined together regularly: "kilted and bonneted in the old fashion," Scott wrote, "and armed to the teeth."[5] Although some lowlanders vainly protested this takeover of their identity by the styles of the backward hillbillies, the job had been done: highland culture, most of it a recent creation, had become the proud emblem of Scotland's nationality.

Nationalism, the predominant form of political identity in the modern era, was itself created out of heroic efforts at mythmaking: myths of the divinity of kings and, in the early postmonarchical years of revolutionary nations such as France, myths and symbols of *la patrie*. Nationalism is a relatively recent construction of reality wherever it appears, and the builders of nation-states have always had to overcome other identities: ethnic or tribal or religious loyalties that dilute allegiance to the motherland or fatherland. This often calls for something stronger than mythmaking—everything from mild repressions such as outlawing the use of a dialect to all-out genocide. Even now, national governments that have endured for centuries are still fighting rearguard actions against separatist movements. Scarcely any major nation-state in the world is free from such problems—persistent efforts of dissident tribes or nationalities to reject the identity fictions handed down from Madrid or Moscow or Beijing.

Much symbolism is pressed into service to help the cause of the nation-state. If you should happen to attend some ritual celebration based on national identity, such as the Olympic Games, you might be inclined to believe that nationalism is in fine shape. Such events reinforce the SCR that is portrayed by a map of the world in which the nations of the world are divided from one another by neat black boundaries and are colored differently so you can tell them apart at a glance. But nationalism has never been a roaring success, despite all the flags and all the songs and all the people who have died for it. Most nation-states have never yet managed to overcome the competing loyalties, managed to persuade their citizens that they are indeed a *nation*—consider the meaning of the word—of a people united by something more than symbolism. The United Kingdom has survived at the cost of many bloody battles with Irish, Welsh, and Scottish separatist movements, and still has trouble staying united.

All nation-states are in trouble to some extent—even Japan, the one that comes closest to the ideal of ethnic and cultural unity, is increasingly occupied with its minority groups—and nationalism itself is a threatened ideology. Among liberal intellectuals, it is definitely not trendy. What is now trendy is devolution, the idea that the world is (or should be) devolving—getting nation-states off its back and decentralizing into smaller political units of Estonians, Basques, Tamils. These are identified by proponents of devolution as natural "peoples" or "nations." Bernard Nietschmann, in an article written for *Cultural Survival Quarterly*, defines a nation this way:

> Nations are geographically bounded territories of a common people. A nation is made up of communities of people who see themselves as one people on the basis of common ancestry, history, society, institutions, ideology, language, territory, and (often) religion. Nation peoples clearly distinguish themselves and their countries from other people and countries—both adjacent and distant. The existence of nations is ancient.
>
> Today there are between three thousand and five thousand nations in the world.[6]

This rather generous definition of nations includes large groups such as the Oromo in East Africa (with more than 20 million people), the Irish, the Catalans, American Indian tribes, the Kurds, and any number of others.

The devolution ideology is based on belief in the naturalness of these groups as opposed to the unnaturalness of nation-states. "The Sri Lankan nation-state," wrote Thomas S. Martin in the *Progressive Review,* "which like so many others is founded on accidents of history and geography rather than on the self-identity of its people, is brutally suppressing the separatist movement that threatens its existence and the power of its ruling elite." Elsewhere in the same article he says, "When people cease to be passive subjects and begin to participate in government, they invariably reject artificial political boundaries and seek to regroup into more natural ethnic, linguistic, religious, or cultural domains."[7]

In a way, nationalism—and I mean nation-state nationalism—is in better shape than devolution. At least the nation-builders know they are constructing a reality. The devolutionists, whose thinking is at the core no different from that of the fundamentalists who want the Bible to tell us how to govern, are looking for a simple principle to take care of all the thorny problems of who is who, where the boudaries are, and who had the right to do what. Tribes or nationalities seem to be "natural" peoples whose identity was not created out of any such "accidents of history and geography," or indeed created at all. This requires overlooking a lot of history, including the history of how the natural peoples and their cultures and their traditions came to be in the first place.

It also requires overlooking the escalating population growth, mobility, urbanization, and cultural change going on in our time, which make traditions so ephemeral and boundaries so indistinct. We are in a world of many cultures, and in such a world any identity—including that of "natural" peoples—involves choice and creation. Many choices can be made, but they are all choices. And—this may be the hardest lesson of all for protectors of "indigenous peoples" to learn—you do not choose to be natural. You do not choose to be premodern. If you choose, you are at least modern. If you know you are choosing, you are postmodern.

Obviously those who want to help indigenous peoples to preserve their cultures approach the effort with commendable goodwill, but they show amazing insensitivity, in their reverence for those cultures, to the difference between merely living in a tradition and *trying* to live in a tradition. I read recently about a man who went down to Arizona to teach Navajo children about their heritage, to help them gain their self-respect. He did various things including showing them videotapes of the television programs in which Bill Moyers interviewed Joseph Campbell about myths. I am pretty sure that, whatever the consciousness of the ancient Navajos was, it wasn't the same as what you get from watching a couple of Anglo intellectuals discuss the world's myths. You may well learn something about your tradition from such experiences, but what it is ain't exactly clear. It is something invented out of ideas about the past, the way the Scots invented their ancient highland heritage.

What is clear is that it becomes necessary to persuade people to choose "natural" or "primitive" identities and cultures as well as to persuade them to choose "national" or "artificial" identities. All are social creations of reality.

The Birth of the Self

The modern era created the modern self, which became the ideological battleground of modern and postmodern politics, the canvas upon which nationalists and traditionalists paint their visions of society.

Personal identity as we know it is a fairly recent social invention. Medieval Christians regarded the individual human's life on earth as only a pale reflection of the cosmic struggle of good and evil. Such noble modern notions as the uniqueness of individuals and the belief that every person has some special destiny to work out in his or her lifetime can scarcely be found anywhere in the record of medieval culture. Insofar as a person had an identity, it was inseparable from occupation, social class, and other designations that most people could neither choose nor change.

Even then, a new consciousness was in the making. Christian thought was beginning to place a greater emphasis on the individual's sins, the individual's chances for redemption to heaven. The Western world was lumbering slowly into an era in which people began to suspect that they were something special, all by themselves—but were not at all sure what.

Modern identity was forged out of several converging trends:

(1) A new concept of an inner or hidden self, symbolized by increasing preoccupation with dissembling—the contrast between people as they *seemed* and people as they *were*. We can see this kind of dissembling dramatically displayed in Machiavelli's advice to the prince and in Shakespearean characters such as Iago. (2) A sense of individuality expressed in the writing of biographies and autobiographies such as Benvenuto Cellini's, in the gradual decline of vendetta justice (all members of a person's family being held accountable for his offenses) in favor of a growing sense of *personal* guilt and retribution. (3) A taste for privacy, reflected in changing styles of architecture—corridors, separate bedrooms, parlors and dining rooms designated as places to receive guests—and in the beginning of separation between public and private domains of life. Norbert Elias says in *The Civilizing Process* that the sight of totally naked people was quite unremarkable in Germany and elsewhere until the sixteenth century.[8] (4) A growing cultural emphasis on the importance of death as a delineator of personal life. (5) A basic change in family formation marked by an increase in the practice of personally choosing a mate. (6) The "discovery of childhood" in which new customs and institutions of child rearing were created in response to the perceived need to prepare the young for the personal responsibilities and choices that would be required in adulthood.[9]

But the flowering of individualism did not end human dependence on socially created reality. That is the great illusion of the modern age. The newborn "modern individual" still internalized values and beliefs, still reified, still structured the world within the language and the myths of his or her civilization, still depended on others to know who he or she really was. The wan ghosts seduced so easily into new lives in *Cards of Identity* were products of centuries of individualizing trends.

Yet clearly something did change. The individual personality born out of the collapse of the medieval monolith must *choose* and keep choosing, whether or not he or she knows it or wants such freedom: must determine who to be, what to believe in, how to live. The individual in search of self-identity becomes a consumer of reality. Some of us go at this with great seriousness, shop in some rather fancy boutiques, fashion our roles and self-images like works of art. The great majority, of course, settle for the ready-to-wear. There are many ironies and paradoxes involved, especially in

America where individualism is a social norm and the most conventional person is the most faithfully rugged individualist. It takes a most unconventional American to think of himself or herself as an inseparable part of society, and to know that its culture is an internalized part of his or her personal psyche.

Political institutions can help us create ourselves and contribute to the re-creation of our societies, or they can exploit our urges toward self-creation. The individual's need for a personal identity and for a social context that supports it is the basis upon which are built ideologies of the left and the right, causes both noble and despicable; it is the stuff out of which are made dictators and patriots, martyrs and assassins, presidents and PR men.

Public Opinion

The same modernizing forces that created individual identity as we know it also created public opinion.

Public opinion is a collective expression of the opinions of individuals. That sounds like a tautology, but it isn't. To have public opinion as we know it, you must have individuals, and furthermore individuals who think they are (or should be) somebodies and not just faceless carriers of social roles. Without selfhood and the new hunger for social meaning that comes with it, there is little room for personal quirkiness, and opinion has no connotation of choice or change. Modern selfhood is what gave rise to the Marxists' worries about "false consciousness." That kind of individualism is what gets people started taking on ideas that express their own characters—or what, in the search for identity, they decide to pretend their characters to be—and not merely their class status.

Earlier monolithic societies recognized only one official reality, and had little or no concern about the opinions of the public. Kings occasionally felt the need to rally support of the masses, especially when they were planning to ask the citizens to sacrifice their lives in battles against other kings, but this was a long way from entertaining any genuine interest in what the people might have been thinking, or even from seriously considering whether they were thinking at all. Public opinion is a democratic idea, and also a constructivist one. It implies that different realities can exist in the same environment—that people can come to different conclusions from the same data.

Whenever governments become more democratic—and especially when they become mass democracies—then groups seeking power take a strong interest in manipulating opinion, and the reality-constructing process goes public. The PR expert does not think of public opinion as some solid shining object waiting to be discovered, like Rousseau's "general will," but as something to be *created.* The great games of modern politics, the by-products of democracy that often threaten to destroy everything democracy was meant to be, are the games of opinion molding: propaganda, brainwashing, programming and deprogramming, advertising, and public relations. Games of reality making.

The word *propaganda* came into general use in the twentieth century, and coincided with the emergence of totalitarianism.

A totalitarian state is a modern-going-on-postmodern phenomenon, an attempt to create a monolithic reality structure in a pluralistic world. And although we think of totalitarianism as the antithesis of democracy, it is actually sprung from the same roots: both democracy and totalitarianism are ways of dealing with a relativistic world in which different views of reality are commonplace. Both recognize individualism and public opinion as sources of power. And both express a creative, revolutionary impulse, a late-modern readiness to smash old structures of reality and start over again.

Totalitarian leaders like to think of themselves as heroes, and indeed there is something inherently heroic in their ambition: to maintain a stable and separate structure of social reality in a world being transformed by globalism and cultural change is by no means an easy thing to do. In the final analysis it may be an impossible thing to do, a gargantuan consumer of political energy. The totalitarian state is constantly at war: at war against the enemies of the regime, at war against its own populace, at war against the modernizing and internationalist forces of history that constantly threaten to undermine it.

Totalitarianism feeds on the modern need for a personal identity, and on public opinion. It uses both of those, and subverts them. The identity problem is resolved by giving the individual a prefabricated self-respect based on the grandeur and transcendent purpose of the state. Public opinion is first manipulated—the aspiring dictator has to be an effective demagogue—then repressed.

Adolf Hitler's accomplishments along these lines make *Cards of Identity* seem far less like fantasy. He took a dispirited people—humiliated by military defeat and economic collapse, bewildered by ideological conflict that tugged their allegiances in all directions—and offered them a simple, dramatic new story: they were the master race, builders of a superstate that would be the wonder of the modern world. Like the leaders of the Identity Club, Hitler did not create out of nothing. Where they used the stereotypes of English literary culture, he used bits and pieces of the German heritage: Hegel's concept of the state as the instrument of God's will, Nietzsche's ideas of the superman rising above the horde, Wagner's stirring music of Teutonic heroes and heroines.

But the story played out in Nazi Germany was from its beginning a far more bleak and brutal one than Nigel Dennis's whimsical fantasy. Hitler never thought persuasion was enough. He supplemented propaganda liberally with physical force and the terror of it, used the power of the state to prevent people from expressing subversive thoughts. And he plunged the nation into war because the best way to keep an audience from seeing the weakness in any plot is to step up the sense of menace; the maxim of hack screenwriters is that when things get slow you put a bear on the beach.

In his speeches Hitler railed against all internationalist movements, against anything that might subvert the grandeur of the Reich. He made the state the great new unifying force to serve as the vehicle for the psychological needs of all its members; to be a German was to be someone to be reckoned with. And German identity had to be made clear, not capable of being confused with anything else. German boundaries marked the line between the hero and his inferiors. All that was of value had to be totally *German*—not international, not universal. The new German reality became a barricade against the uncertainties of membership in the international community. The Nazi regime rejected international law with the declaration that legality was simply that which did the German *volk* good, and eventually proclaimed the belief that there was a distinct German mathematics and a distinct German medicine, and that German meat was nutritionally superior to meat from other countries. And it focused the people's hatred on the Jews, an international race with a non-German identity.

In a rather short time, as we know, this mad exercise ran its bloody course through genocide and war to a dismal collapse that left the nation defeated and divided, that brought Hitler to suicide in a cramped little concrete bunker beneath the ruins of his capital. The German adventure is in some ways like the experience of an unstable person who finds some new religion or style of therapy and is propelled by the discovery into a euphoric bender of inflated self-satisfaction, imagining he or she is capable of everything—until at some point the person bumps up against a part of the world that rudely refuses to share the delusion, and then he or she collapses in a despondent heap. Suicide is often the end of such adventures, and the recurrent pattern bears out Durkheim's analysis: desperate flights into new belief systems are desperate defenses against anomie, and their failure can leave life truly and literally meaningless.

Because so many totalitarian adventures have been such spectacular failures, it would be comforting to conclude that totalitarianism itself simply does not *work*, that any such enterprises are predestined to fail. I think this is true in the long run—that the forces of globalism and postmodernism will ultimately defeat any attempt to corral people into a single narrow reality system—but I would not counsel complacency. The forces that give rise to totalitarianism are latently present in all societies, in all cultures and subcultures, and the payoffs for the successful totalitarian adventurer are high enough to make the effort seem worth the risk. One reason to expect that totalitarian projects will be launched again and again is that the social construction of reality is increasingly an open secret. There is ample evidence before us, now, that belief systems can be altered by restructuring reality within the psyche of the individual, and political operators of all persuasions are becoming audacious about creating new realities for the world.

One of the major advances in this direction was the discovery of brainwashing, the stunning piece of psychological technology that has contributed so much to the emergence of postmodern politics.

In the early 1950s, shortly after the Communist victory in China, an American journalist coined the term *brainwashing* from the Chinese colloquialism *hsi nao* ("wash brain"). The word referred to a form of political indoctrination that the Chinese Communists were using with foreigners and enemies of the revolution, and that seemed to be capable of rooting out from the mind an entire belief system and replacing it with a new one.

The word soon became as widely and carelessly used as any other piece of political rhetoric. People of all persuasions enthusiastically accused their opponents of brainwashing. And it fed into a growing American paranoia about communism: if you didn't watch out, they would sneak it right into your head. But behind the hysteria was disturbing evidence that new and effective techniques of political indoctrination *were* being used. Refugees from China told startling tales of long periods of imprisonment in which they had been subjected to constant physical and psychological harrassment until they made massive changes in their values and beliefs—changes that they felt they *wanted* to make. Robert Lifton, who wrote the classic psychological study of brainwashing, identified a prescribed sequence of steps in the process. It began with an "assault upon reality" in the Nigel Dennis mode. One subject was told that he was not a missionary, but a spy. It ended, after months or years of physical pain and endless browbeating, with a "rebirth"—total conversion to the cause of Chinese communism. Some of the subjects who returned to the West lost their new faith, but others remained converts.[10]

In the Korean War, which broke out soon after the communist takeover in China, Americans were confronted with even more troubling news: for the first time in the country's history, soldiers captured by the enemy (twenty-one in all) decided to *remain* with the enemy, because, they said, they preferred the enemy's form of government. Even worse, it became known after the war that almost one out of three American prisoners in Korea has been guilty of some degree of collaboration with the enemy. Furthermore, not a single prisoner had escaped from a permanent prison camp and returned to American lines.[11] This had not resulted from the classic brainwashing Lifton described: the Koreans had not used much physical cruelty, but they had developed a technique that effectively combined leniency and pressure. The news from Korea undoubtedly contributed to the wave of anticommunism that was bringing America dangerously close to its own form of totalitarianism.

Brainwashing itself was not an utter novelty. The Spanish Inquisition was certainly a forerunner of it, and so were other forms of religious indoctrination. In fact, a Catholic priest who had been subject to brainwashing by the Chinese told Lifton that he was struck by how much it resembled the methods and terminology of the conversion techniques used by his own church—a declaration that probably did not gain him any friends in Rome. But, whether brainwashing was new or not, our enemies appeared to be doing it with frightening psychological expertise; many people began to fear that mind molding on a vast scale might well be possible.

The fears of brainwashing were to some extent exaggerated, the news somewhat distorted—yet what took place is enough to disturb anyone. The personal sense of identity *can* be shaken and reshaped for political ends; an entire belief system *can* be destroyed and replaced with its very opposite. The message of brainwashing became for many people the discovery of socially constructed reality. It made political leaders take a new interest in winning not only battles, but hearts and minds.

Getting Into the Act

One of the brainwashing subjects who was interviewed by Lifton reported that he began to understand the experience he was undergoing as "something of a contrived drama, by no means completely artificial." He was, incidentally, one of the more successful subjects—successful in getting through it without losing his grip on the reality of his prior life, his sense of who he was and what he had believed. By the device of seeing the brainwashing experience as a drama, he managed to keep it somehow compartmentalized in his consciousness. He also happened upon one of the most common ways that people come to grips with the idea of the social construction of reality: they see the world as theater. And when they see it that way, they seem to be not so much disturbed by the discovery as anxious to get into the act.

This has to do with a deep political need, one that becomes an increasingly important part of the dynamics of postmodern life but that we tend to overlook in our belief that political action is motivated only by conventional drives such as power and national identity. To get acquainted with it, let us look back to the early decades of the century, when postmodernism was just beginning to peek through the cracks in the old order.

In Vienna in the period between the two world wars—about the same time that the dadaists and surrealists were doing their deconstructive thing in Paris—a young psychiatrist named J. L. Moreno founded an artistic enterprise called the *Stegreiftheater*, or "spontaneity theater." This was an improvisational theater group, and like much of the guerrilla theater of later decades it had a definite political tilt. It grew out of the increasing sense that people had of being a part of a larger social arena, something beyond the village or the town, in which interesting and important events were taking place. One of its most popular presentations was called the Living Newspaper: in these skits, the actors would make up and dramatize plays about what was happening in the great world, the things people were hearing about and reading about in the newspapers. Often members of the audience would take part in the productions. Moreno believed that people had a great need to *act out* things, to throw themselves as performers into the events that were unfolding around them, and that this need was completely unmet in their humdrum daily lives. They were, in a sense, emotionally disenfranchised.

Out of Moreno's early theatrical experimentations came psychodrama (the first group therapy) and a lesser-known invention called sociodrama. You can still find sociodrama practiced in a few places. It is a theatrical and therapeutic improvisational form, somewhat like the Living Newspaper, in which people play social roles, debate issues, and often take the parts of world political leaders to act out their thoughts and feelings. (I participated in sociodramas during the Vietnam War and the civil rights conflicts of the 1960s, and movies still look dull by comparison.)

Moreno recognized that people could discover themselves—*create* themselves—in such activities. He discovered accidentally that there is another dimension to politics—a dramatic dimension. The media and the increasing mobility of life had created an expanded social space, a theater, and the big shots were having all the fun in it. Ordinary people also wanted to participate in the unfolding historical dramas of the time—not just vote, but participate *emotionally*. His discovery could be summed up in Jimmy Durante's favorite line: "Everybody wants to get into the act."

To get into the act: anyone old enough to remember the assassination of John F. Kennedy and all the events that attended it—the assassination of the assassin on network television, the sudden explosion into public consciousness of a bizarre cast of new characters, the subsequent furious activity of conspiracy theorists seeking to come up with new explanations of what had happened—knows that such events do not boil down to the standard power-and-money wisdom by which we pretend to understand politics, nor to Freudian psychodynamics either. The person I especially remember from that national psychodrama is Lee Harvey Oswald's mother, a woman whose great achievement in life was to have given birth to a man who killed a president. She was sought out by the reporters, and for a while she enjoyed a considerable amount of publicity. And I mean she enjoyed it. She told the press: "I am also an important person. I will be remembered."

Mrs. Oswald was not trying to get any laws passed, and she was not crazy. She knew exactly what she wanted. She wanted to get into the act. She knew that once she was a part of the immense story that was unfolding on millions of TV screens, that people all over the world were talking about, she would be *real*. She would have met the requirement the modern era imposed on us all—the demand that we be somebody. And she understood that the more people there are who think you are somebody, the more somebody you are. She had decided, as many people do, that the surest currency of personal value is fame.

When people talk about politics as theater, they tend to speak as though political events become less real when they come more closely to resemble drama. Which is precisely what does not happen. Politics is the theater of reality. The "political arena," as we sometimes call it, is a stage upon which dramas are improvised while real people succeed, suffer, fail, or die—and upon which real people create their conceptions of who and what they are.

Adolf Hitler made his mark on the world not as a political theorist, certainly not as a military tactitian, but as a dramatist. He was a story-maker. Other story-makers were in business in the German-speaking society at the same time: Freudians, existentialists, theologians, scientists, and ideologues of all kinds were offering their own versions of what was happening. Hitler outdid them all, at least for a while, and did it because he was able to place the German people in an awesome story that thundered through their blood and bones.

Political theater is inseparable from political life. Every day little dramas are staged for the public, complete with the advice of wardrobe and property departments. President Jimmy Carter donned a sweater and sat before the fireplace to talk about energy conservation. President Ronald Reagan, that old cowhand from Pacific Palisades, had his picture taken in western gear, chopping wood at the ranch. TV reporters write their stories in their offices and then are hauled off with the camera crew to broadcast from in front of the White House or the Capitol. Terrorists perform before worldwide audiences. Third World mobs obligingly shake their fists at TV cameras. Everyone who gets into the act contributes a little piece to the construction of social reality, and gets from it a definition of his or her personal identity.

In some respects, we of the late twentieth century are still not so far from our ancestors who had no concept of themselves apart from their social roles or class; the difference is that we have egos before we have roles and are able to choose, improvise, define, and if necessary redefine ourselves by moving into new roles. The young man who joins the military to resolve an adolescent identity crisis, the woman who "finds herself" in feminist activism, the Christian who discovers a new sense of purpose as a result of taking part in a demonstration against abortion, the successful businessman who decides to take a run at the U. S. Senate—all are using the political order as a source of personal self-definition. And terrorism is not only drama for the spectator—it is drama for the terrorist, who comes out of an emotionally impoverished social setting in which there are few ways to get into the act and becomes a player on the world stage.

Because we do not take the theatrical dimension of political life seriously, we fail to recognize that when people act politically they are trying to define themselves. When we do recognize it, we tend to disapprove. People are not supposed to get that kind of emotional gratification and personal assistance out of political behavior, we say; they are supposed to be doing things to affect political outcomes. We dismiss their activism as mere "self-therapy."

In the 1960s Nat Hentoff wrote an essay entitled "Them and Us: Are Peace Protests Self-Therapy?" in which he cited a particular act of protest—not particularly unusual for the times—in which twenty-three people stood up during a high mass at St. Patrick's

Cathedral in New York City and unfurled posters showing a maimed Vietnamese child. Hentoff was a journalist of the Left, strongly in support of their cause—yet he found himself suspecting "that their act's essential effect was to make *them* feel relevant, to make *them* feel that some of their guilt as Americans had been atoned for by this witness." He suspected that it was "self-therapy" and added: "I am all for self-therapy, but if that's what it is, let us call it that." He wondered whom the demonstrators were talking to, and, if it was the people attending the mass, whether there might not be some better way of talking to them.[12]

The demonstration was an act of political theater, and the other people in the cathedral were really the dress extras more than the audience. The newspapers and TV covered the event, and that larger public—the media millions—was the one the demonstrators had in mind. In the play, the demonstrators were the good guys, and the other people got to play the role of uncaring and self-indulgent Americans who went about their routines while children suffered. We have no way at all of knowing what was the political impact of the demonstration, whether any opinions changed as a result. We can make a pretty good guess at the emotional impact: the demonstrators felt better, the other people in the cathedral felt worse.

Should people *not* feel better as a result of their political actions? I submit that emotional gratification is a decent reward, and that we would have a mighty hard time anyway preventing people from engaging in political activities that meet their psychological needs.

But something here needs to be sorted out, inquired into, and learned through over time. There is a difference, albeit a subtle one, between a political pose and a political position. Pose taking is done in the political theater, and it has a lot to do with being the hero/heroine and relatively little to do with communicating an opinion—much less having an opinion communicated back. It also has to do with fame: maybe not big-time fame, but at least a bit of reassurance, if you take part in a public demonstration or do something that gets reported or (best of all) shown on television, that you—you in person—exist and are doing something. This was what Hentoff was concerned about: that certain kinds of action create "them and us" situations replete with the drama of political righteousness but devoid of dialogue. We all live now in the political theater, but we have no ethic for it and little real understanding of what we can accomplish in it or what it does to us. And all we know for sure about our leaders—left, right, or center—is that they have managed to get good speaking parts.

Pseudoevents and Real Life

Some years back, Daniel Boorstin wrote a satirical study of contemporary American life in which he talked about pseudoevents. According to Boorstin, a pseudoevent is a happening that (1) is not spontaneous, but comes about because someone planned, planted, or incited it; (2) is planted primarily for the purpose of being reported or reproduced; (3) has an ambiguous relation to the underlying reality of the subject, so that press and public may speculate freely about what it really means; and (4) is usually intended to be a self-fulfilling prophecy—the restaurant mentioned as "popular" in some fabricated item in a gossip column actually becomes popular. Typical pseudoevents are the press release, the interview, and the celebration designed to call attention to a person or a business enterprise.[13]

Boorstin's book was a brilliant piece of work, and the only part of it I would quibble with is its assumption that there is a boundary between event and pseudoevent. If there ever was one, it has disappeared. In the postmodern world, pseudoevents commonly become real life.

A good example of this—and also one of the more successful productions of political theater in recent decades—was the U. S. government's Grenada expedition in 1983. Operation Urgent Fury, they called it. That was a hell of a title, created by somebody with a sure sense of schlock; Sidney Sheldon couldn't have done better. The operation, in case you have forgotten, was a military intervention against a Marxist government on that Caribbean island-state, the smallest nation in the Western hemisphere. Grenada's importance to the American public, measured by any of the traditional standards of objective realpolitik, was none whatsoever. It would have made utterly no difference to the average American whether Grenada were Marxist, Mormon, Green, or Libertarian. Most Americans had no idea of where Grenada was, or even that it existed, before it suddenly became announced as a matter of national concern. When it did surface, it seemed to many people to be important. The American public had been frustrated for years by international conflicts that started out to be simple good-guy dramas and then turned into confusing debacles. A new story formed, with Grenada as its locale. Here, finally, was a clear victory.

The Grenada invasion was real, and it was also a pseudoevent. It was orchestrated by a public-relations operation at least as big as the military one. Reporters were kept away from the action so that the news could be more effectively managed. The government's primary purpose was not to get new rulers in place in Grenada, although in fact it did that: its primary purpose was to give the American public a "win," to flex the muscles of the Reagan administration, to allow Americans to (in the phrase current at the time) "feel good about themselves." It was political therapy, and real theater. And it served its political purpose in the presidential election that followed. Just as Margaret Thatcher had ridden the euphoria of her victory over Argentina in the Falklands to a second term as prime minister of Great Britain, Ronald Reagan now made the most of his new image as a military leader. The Republican admen proclaimed, "America is back—standing tall."

Most acts of terrorism are also "real theater," global publicity stunts. A psychiatrist who specializes in terrorism caught the essence of this nicely when, testifying in congressional hearings, he said:

> Terrorism ultimately aims at the spectator. The victim is secondary. Death, destruction of property, the flamboyant or dangerous use of technological devices, deprivation of liberty, are not ends of terrorism. They are means by which to terrorize—to make an impression on the spectator.[14]

But, of course, in the process of making an impression on the spectator—that is, the global audience—the terrorist does kill, destroy, imprison. The fictions created in the political theater are the realities of our time.

There is a curious reciprocity between personal experience and the media. The media provide the theater in which people experience political life and define their identities, and in turn the experiences of people—all kinds of experiences, from the romances of movie stars to the conflicts of world leaders—become the merchandise of the media. The media take the raw material of experience and fashion it into stories; they retell the stories to us, and we call them reality.

Turn on the television, pick up a newspaper, and the construction of reality is going on right there, before your eyes. And if you look closely, especially if you look closely at the way a given event is interpreted in several different media, you cannot fail to notice that many different realities are being constructed. If there were two versions of Christianity in the Middle Ages, one for the intellectuals and one for the common people, there are at least that many versions of the events of our times, the reality we inhabit, in the information media.

The general rule is, the larger the audience, the simpler the story.

Everybody who takes in information about the events of the time from social media of communications—anything from the satellite news to gossip over the back fence—gets fiction. Forget about the objective reporter who only gives the facts. Some of those fictions are produced by people who have gone to immense trouble to get close to the raw material out of which their stories are created, have made every effort to understand the circumstances surrounding the event and to feel their way into the reality of the people who experienced it, and have invested much passion and intellect in making the material mean something. And, although the myth of objectivity pervades all kinds of journalism, the best of it is produced by reporters who let their feelings, their interpretations, and their subjective biases be present and visible. In the mass media, particularly on network television, the public is more likely to get postmodern creativity frosted with modern objectivity.

Mass journalism has as much reality/unreality ambiguity as postmodern literature, without any of the fancy theorizing that lets the public in on the game. The news is supposed to be "the facts," and consequently there is a constant rumble of concern among media critics about "dramatic enactments" or "dramatic reconstructions" in which staged scenes are mixed in with historical narrative and actual documentary film footage, and incidents such as the ABC news broadcast in August 1989 that showed a "reenactment" of alleged spy Felix Bloch handing a briefcase to an alleged KGB agent. (This was identified as a reenactment in captions in some areas where the news program was broadcast, but the caption was inadvertently omitted in others.)

A somewhat-cynical local TV writer, refusing to get upset about the flap that resulted from this, asked,

> Are we really supposed to believe that the use of actors renders the news any more "staged" than it already is? Are we supposed not to know that news programs already employ scripts and actors (presenters) and center on staged events known days, weeks, sometimes months ahead of time? Should we pretend not to notice that TV news continually poses the day's events in terms of "stories" told as morality tales, which use recurring characters (politicians, celebs, monsters from various evil empires) structured around beginnings, middles, and endings that are as predictable as a fairy story?
>
> . . . the overt presence of the scandal of staging in TV news must be seen as a marvelous development. . . . Every time news and documentary acknowledges its use of fictional conventions it undermines its authority and frees the viewer from the illusion of objectivity.[15]

Experience, "real-life experience," is processed—almost instantly—into documentary-style entertainment. Whenever an incident—a political fracas, a sex scandal, a child trapped in a well, a major disaster, a horrible crime—heaves up into public view, it becomes a commodity—and the more interesting and laden with the things that make good fiction (sex, violence, money, power, conflict, intrigue), the more potentially marketable and the more likely to be packaged and repackaged in many forms for public consumption. Writers get busy on books, publishers get busy signing up the people involved to write their own books, producers of TV movies get busy signing up rights. The event becomes another kind of pseudoevent.

The movie-for-television is usually the lowest common denominator of manufactured reality, the story created with the least amount of integrity and aimed for the largest audience. Currently, as I write, the trial of Lt. Col. Oliver North on charges arising out of the Iran-Contra weapons sale is going on, and CBS has just broadcast a drama entitled *Guts and Glory: The Rise and Fall of Oliver North.* The film, a pretentious turkey, was watched by tens of millions of people who presumably took it to be a source of insight into the character of Colonel North and into the events surrounding the Iran-Contra affair.

But the film gave no new information—its sources were congressional transcripts of the Iran-Contra hearings and a biography of North—and revealed nothing about the arms sales or the cover-up.

Nor did it give a strongly felt personal viewpoint: some of the people who made the film were liberals who didn't like North; the actor who portrayed him was a gung-ho admirer. It gave, in fact, nothing, nor was it meant to; it was meant to take, to exploit a hot subject.

Whenever an event moves into the stage of being represented on mass television, it has moved into a strange never-never land in which there is no longer any serious attempt to bring forth some genuine understanding of it or feeling for it. It has become McReality, experience turned into fast food.

F. Scott Fitzgerald once wrote an essay, about the kind of fiction we call fiction, entitled "How to Waste Material." His argument, a conviction that he held passionately and that I have never seen another writer express in quite the same way, was that there is only a limited amount of material around—and that anybody who appropriates it for the purposes of turning it into art has an obligation to it. He was, at the time, complaining about the platoons of "realistic" novelists who were rushing off here and there about the world to soak up a few impressions about how some appropriately colorful bunch of people lived, and then hurriedly turning that material—"raw and undigested," he thought—into novels that had nothing to do with anything they had ever experienced or even entered into with their full powers of imagination.[16]

Fitzgerald was searching for a critical principle, a basis for aesthetic judgment of literature; I am searching for a principle for judging the curious fiction-fact cocktails that are such a large part of the public life, the shared reality, of a mass society. It is not enough simply to apply the naive objectivist criteria of the modern era and expect everything offered as a newspaper story, a magazine article, a nonfiction book, or a TV docudrama to be based on hard facts. We all know better than that by this time. But as we enter fully a postmodern world in which even the most uncritical couch potato in front of the TV set knows that the show is some kind of a fantasy, even while the show is supposed to be a representation of recent or current history, we really need to begin to search for some standards—and they may turn out to be very like the standards of good art that Fitzgerald was searching for when he wrote his essay in 1926. I don't mean that we should abandon research for unfettered artiness; I mean that we are entitled to work that represents a deep investment of both thought and feeling, and strives for meaning as well as sensation.

Put the matter another way: when we begin to understand that the media's business is not only the retailing of entertainment but the construction of social reality, we will demand something better than *Guts and Glory*.

CHAPTER 6

Being Someone: The Construction of Personal Reality

A hit song of the late 1980s was Tracy Chapman's "Fast Car," with its poignant lyric about a young black girl joyriding with her boyfriend:

> City lights lay out before us
> And your arm felt nice wrapped 'round my shoulder
> And I had a feeling that I belonged
> And I had feeling I could be someone, be someone, be someone.[1]

To be someone, be someone—one of the deep urges of the human heart; perhaps, if we knew how to reckon such things with finality, the deepest of all.

It is a need that becomes more intensely felt—and also more difficult to satisfy—as the course of history carries us all further away from the old realities that structured our identities and life experiences for us. As we become possessors of individual selves, we become more free, and in another sense unbearably burdened: each of us has this thing, this life, and society seems to be telling us that we have to determine for ourselves what shape it takes—create our identities, create our experiences. Be somebody. Be somebody good. Be happy. Be yourself.

In the film *The Dead Poets' Society*, the teacher played by Robin Williams takes his students out into a courtyard and tells them to walk around. Don't just walk like everybody else, he tells them: find your own way to walk. Be an *individual*. And that is one of our society's main messages, blared at us from all directions. I do not mean to come down too heavily on *Dead Poets*, which I thought was a rather good movie. It just happens to be a convenient example of a very common piece of programming we all get constantly. I could have easily picked on Frank Sinatra singing "I did it my way," or on any of thousands of other exhortations to be somebody that are expressed in our popular culture.

The more we heed those exhortations, the more we try to conform to our society's norm and become individuals, the more choices we are required to make. We do not, as I have already pointed out, have the choice about whether or not to make choices. The best you can do if you want to avoid choice making is to live your life within a cult or a fundamentalist religion or a traditional society and try to persuade yourself you have not chosen that. Yet obviously we do not have complete freedom, either, to choose who to be and how to feel. Life is not an equal opportunity employer. We are all commanded to make our own lives—but some of us do everything possible to pretend we didn't hear; others accept the challenge joyfully and then discover that not all doors are open, or that society doesn't like the way we walk after all.

The ethos of the personally created life is probably strongest in America, land of the self-made man. It was memorably expressed in *The Great Gatsby*, Scott Fitzgerald's mythic novel about Jimmy Gatz, an American Don Quixote who succeeded—at least for a while—in making a world commensurate with his fantasies. But the drift of cultural change is in the direction of forcing everyone to be free, requiring everyone to create personal identity and experience, however sparse the resources. The struggle to be someone is a global struggle now.

Every morning billions of pairs of eyes open, and billions of societies of mind set forth on the adventures of selfhood. For many, the adventure only rarely rises above the level of a struggle to keep the body alive, but even the most miserable among us also hear the aspirations of the self—the "me" craving reassurance that (a) it exists and (b) it is good; the modern "me" that pursues happiness and believes that whatever happiness it finds will be what it has taken or created and not what has been handed down by fate.

Symbolic aspirations, symbolic needs. Abraham Maslow's famous catalog of human needs is top-heavy with cravings that can only be satisfied in the symbolic universe. People, he said, seek safety (social structure, freedom from anxiety and chaos); belongingness (a place in a group or family); esteem ("a stable, firmly based, usually high evaluation of themselves"); and ultimately self-actualization, the fullest expression of potentialities.[2]

The self's adventure is a game of symbols, and yet it is deeply, desperately real. Ernest Becker put it well when he wrote of

> the utter vitality of our social fictions, and the deadly seriousness of our efforts to sustain and reinforce them. The world of human aspiration is largely fictitious, and if we do not understand this we understand nothing about man. It is a largely symbolic creation by an ego-controlled animal that permits action in a psychological world, a symbolic-behavioral world removed from the boundness of the present moment, from the immediate stimuli which enslave all lower organisms. Man's freedom is a fabricated freedom, and he pays a price for it. He must at all times *defend the utter fragility of his delicately constituted fiction, deny its artificiality*. . . . There is no cynicism implied here, nor derision, nor any pity. We must realize simply that this is how *this* animal must act if he is to function as *this* animal. Man's fictions are not superfluous creations that could be "put aside" so that the "more serious" business of life could continue.[3]

An eloquent description of the human condition, but the human condition does not remain the same: the pressure to be an individual, to create one's own identity and experience, is a product of the modern era. And the postmodern era is changing the rules again; the artificiality of the fiction is no longer denied. We come to see individual life as gamelike, dramalike. We become more explicit about personal reality-construction, even to the point of creating schools of psychotherapy based on it. Some of us—indeed most of us in one way or another—play the dangerous game of ingesting drugs that modify our reality.

We are still driven to be someone, to be happy, to be good, but we find new ways of playing the game, and of understanding it.

PLAYING THE GAME

Visitors from outer space to late-twentieth-century earth could hardly fail to be impressed by our monumental preoccupation with games and dramas: the vast amounts of money that cities happily splurge on athletic stadia, the adulation and wealth we heap on sports heroes, the emotional energy audiences work up over soccer matches in Buenos Aires or Liverpool, over Super Bowls in Miami or New Orleans; and then the movie palaces, the take-out videocassette shops, the TV sets installed like shrines in every home, the exquisite electronic technology that carries Hollywood's vapid dreams around the world.

Games and dramas, dramas and games; no clear line to draw between them, as sports events compete with dramas for TV time and ticket dollars, and as sports heroes—the newer generations of John Waynes and Sonja Henies—logically move on in their careers from one form of show business to another. Great fame and fortune are won in both, and of all kinds of fame the greatest is the fame of actors and actresses. They become, as so many people have pointed out, the natural royalty of mass-media society. Curiously, the people who are in a way the least "real"—who spend their professional lives playing the parts of others—are the ones we regard as more real than ourselves, of godlike dimensions. We put them at the forefront of causes, accept them as authorities on complex political issues—Meryl Streep will speak to us this week on pesticides—and have even been known to elect them to high political office.

Several centuries have passed since a Shakespearean character declared that all the world's a stage, nearly two since the Duke of Wellington made his famous comment that the battle of Waterloo was won on the playing fields of Eton. We have seen, during that time, the emergence of a global civilization linked as much by its entertainments as by its economics and politics, the consciousness of its younger members saturated by the images of the playing fields and the sports news, the TV and movie screens. The influence of game and drama has gone beyond metaphor.

Contemporary civilization without ball games and movies would be as incomprehensible as medieval civilization without the Church. Our social reality is shaped by those myths and structures, our personal lives informed and sometimes inspired by them.

In 1959, sociologist Erving Goffman revealed, with the publication of his book *The Presentation of Self in Everyday Life,* some of the obvious-yet-little-noticed behaviors by which people manage their lives in gamelike, dramalike ways: he pointed out how we play roles to impress others; how, following unspoken rules, groups of people in business and other situations form "teams" to cooperate in role playing; how we arrange our environments into "front" regions, where we perform for our customers or our guests, and "backstage" regions, such as the bedrooms of more formal homes, where we dress and put on our makeup and perhaps gossip a bit about the audience as we prepare to go on stage.

Goffman was searching not only for ways to understand social behavior but also for a better understanding of the self. Like Minsky and the cognitive scientists, he suspected we are something far more complex than the simple "I" of everyday convenience. Where Minsky (and others) described our complexity in terms of parts (or functions) of the brain, Goffman described it in social and theatrical terms: each of us is a performer—a "harried fabricator of impressions"—and also a character (or characters) representing what we think we are or want the audience to believe we are. And he said:

> In analyzing the self then we are drawn from its possessor, from the person who will profit or lose most by it, for he and his body merely provide the peg on which something of collaborative manufacture will be hung for a time. And the means for producing and maintaining selves do not rest inside the peg; in fact these means are often bolted down in social establishments. There will be a back region with its tools for shaping the body, and a front region with its fixed props. There will be a team of persons whose activity on stage in conjunction with available props will constitute the scene from which the performed character's self will emerge, and another team, the audience, whose interpretive activity will be necessary for this emergence. The self is a product of all those arrangements, and in all of its parts bears the marks of its genesis.[4]

A radical view—radically *sociological* and not easily reconciled to other radical views such as Minsky's; we have not only ideas about a multiple self, but multiple ideas about a multiple self.

I mention Goffman's work here not only because it was brilliant sociology—a peek into the forbidden backstage of society—but also because it was *popular* sociology that was read by many people and became yet another part of the growing public lore about the social construction of reality. And its insights also became woven into our socially constructed reality. I knew architects in the mid-1960s who had read *The Presentation of Self in Everyday Life* and were enthusiastically designing places of business that would better accommodate the desire of people to perform for others: clothing boutiques with little stages where a woman could strike a pose while trying on a dress; restaurants with dramatic entranceways where an arriving couple could be framed for all to see.

At about the same time that my architect friends were designing theatrical department stores, Eric Berne brought out his famous work of pop psychology, *Games People Play,* which gave us yet another map of the multimodal mind (in his system the three main players in our psyche are called Parent, Child, and Adult) and an intriguing description of how in our interpersonal lives we make up little stories and entrap others into becoming players—usually the heavies and the losers—in our private dramas.[5] He described about three dozen games that people play, and gave them catchy names like "Ain't It Awful," "If It Weren't for You, I Could," "Let's You and Him Fight," and "Now I've Got You, You Son of a Bitch." Berne's ideas were not exactly new—he acknowledged influences such as Freud's tripartie (ego, id, superego) mind-map, Harry Stack Sullivan's interpersonal theory of psychiatry, and Moreno's psychodrama. But Berne was good at showing how interpersonal relations (and problems) are grounded in social constructions of reality—the games between people, the personal stories we make up to explain who we are and how we fit into the larger scheme of things (Berne called these "life scripts"). His work gave rise to a new school of therapy (transactional analysis), and *Games People Play* is one of the very few psychology books that gave its title to a popular song.

Berne's book was, like many cultural events of the 1960s, a preview of postmodern things to come: now there are schools of psychotherapy based on constructivism, which start from the reasonable proposition that if human life is indeed lived within constructions of reality, then we can deal with emotional problems as creative opportunities—challenges to reconstruct, perhaps in collaboration with a therapist or a life partner, our stories about who we are and what is going on.

CONSTRUCTIVIST THERAPY: A GAME OF ETHICS AND POLITICS

A course of constructivist psychotherapy is not at all like one of those Freudian detective stories in which the doctor ferrets out the "facts" of the problem, decodes dreams, and hands down the correct interpretation of the neurosis to his patient in a manner resembling that of Sherlock Holmes as he explains a case to the slow-witted Watson.

Constructivist therapy is not so much a technique as a philosophical context within which therapy is done, and more a product of the *zeitgeist* than the brainchild of any single theorist. One person frequently cited as its ancestor is the American psychiatrist George Kelly, who wrote extensively about the role of "personal constructs" in emotional health and about the potential for dealing with problems by examining (and changing) one's beliefs. "Whatever exists," he insisted, "can be reconstrued."[6] But there are other similar approaches to psychotherapy that do not identify themselves as "constructivist," and are based on European sources such as the French philosopher Paul Ricoeur's *Time and Narrative.* These approaches work with a part of the human psyche that is surprisingly neglected in many schools of therapy—the form-giving, meaning-making part, the narrator who at every waking moment of our lives spins out its account of who we are and what we are doing and why we are doing it.

The constructivist therapist draws the attention of the patient or patients (many constructivists are family therapists) to the story, the "frame": the context of language and meaning *around* whatever it is that has been identified as the "problem." And that context becomes the object of analysis. Patients and therapist together try to get a clear idea of what the various stories are—there are likely to be several of them—and who holds them and where they came from. From there, the work becomes a creative attempt to "reframe" the problem.

Obviously this can be a difficult process, especially when the object of the therapy is a family group, since each participant is going to have a different idea of what the context is. As an article in a professional journal puts it, the family is like "a number of playwrights who have been invited to present little playlets, simultaneously, and on overlapping stages. Furthermore, each playwright, since he or she was going to be present anyway, has been given a part in every other playwright's productions."[7]

The therapist enters this situation as a friendly editor, not necessarily in possession of the facts or even of a better way of discovering them, but as a facilitator who will attempt to help the client or clients draw out the various stories and see what can be done about revising them. And the therapist does this not with a blithe "whatever turns you on" morality but with a conviction that the whole therapeutic effort will be an exercise in ethics, a cooperative attempt to create a set of values for living together. Furthermore, the constructivist therapist acknowledges this to be a *political* exercise, as full of deals and compromises as a budget bill.

Constructivist approaches frequently come up hard against problems that have been defined as "physical" or "genetic" and therefore not likely to be brushed aside with a handful of words.

To give an idea of how a constructivist therapist might deal with such a case—and also to illustrate that constructivism is not a magic pill that immediately cures all ills—let me briefly summarize a case involving a depressive man and his wife. The husband, thirty-nine, had been going through severe episodes of depression ever since his adolescence. He was the sixth of eight children, and both parents, alcoholics, had died when he was in his teens. He had attempted suicide once and had been hospitalized twice. He had been diagnosed as manic-depressive and placed on lithium (the standard manic-depression prescription) and had also been given tricyclic antidepressants. His psychiatrist had pronounced his condition inherited and incurable.

The couple came to a family therapist, who invited them to take a look at the various stories about the man's condition. These fell into two groups representing the two prevailing ideologies about depression: the biological (it is a physical disease of genetic origin) and the psychosocial (it is an emotional expression of low self-esteem or a response to painful interpersonal experiences). The therapist asked the couple to identify the various people—themselves, in-laws, mental-health professionals—who had various opinions as to which applied in the man's case: who held which opinion, and how strongly. It became apparent that the couple was at the center of a battling host of conflicting medical opinions, each of which carried its own freight of *moral* opinions about who was responsible for the problem and what was the right way to deal with it.

The couple of course asked the therapist what *his* opinion was—what the hell, one more couldn't hurt—and he replied that he didn't really know what caused the man's depression. There were good books that said depression was caused by biochemical abnormalities in the brain, and there were good books that said it was caused by emotional distress. There was no definitive study about depression—particularly none that they could apply with certainty to this particular case.

He invited the couple to try an experiment—rather, to try *another* experiment, since they had already tried several that had not worked. They would alternate between days of thinking and acting as if the problem were primarily biological, and days of discussing how they would handle things if it were predominantly psychological. On each day, they would adopt the moral obligations and behaviors appropriate to the "frame." They would do this four days out of the week, and improvise freely on the other three days. The couple thought this sounded like fun, if nothing else, and left the therapist's office.

Thus was outlined a fairly standard episode in the course of constructivist therapy—which, as it happened, was never carried out at all.

On the day after the consultation, the husband went into the deepest depression he had ever experienced. His wife, afraid he might attempt suicide again, sent him off to stay with one of his brothers. His condition improved quickly, and he returned home. The couple never did start the experiment, but they found that they were able to work much more effectively with their regular therapist. The depression did not recur, and after six months the man stopped the tricyclic medication. After two years, he discontinued the lithium also and was by that time actively involved in the local chapter of Adult Children of Alcoholics. He did have one more depressive episode, briefly, after he was transferred by his employers during a reorganization.[8]

I have cited this example of constructivist therapy here not as proof that physical/genetic factors in depression can be ignored—which I don't believe—or that constructivist therapy is the last word in mental health. I have never had an opportunity to observe a course of such therapy at close hand, although I have seen a lot of work in both individual and group therapy that tried a bit of reframing. Most therapists try a bit of everything.

And that, really, is the point I want to make. The struggle with meaning, the weaving of stories around our pains and joys, the conflict between different ways of making sense of the events of daily life—they are present in every form of therapy, and also present constantly in the existence of people who have never sat in a therapist's waiting room. Consider a battle between a married couple as husband and wife both attempt to impose their meanings on the events of their shared life. Consider the story revising that goes on when someone in trouble turns to a therapist, a cult leader, a self-help book, a church, a group such as Alcoholics Anonymous. Ask yourself how many times in your life you have had the uncomfortable feeling that you were being a character in somebody else's melodrama—perhaps a "sting" in which you got to be the entrapped criminal. Consider your own internal monologue, in a time of extreme stress, as you slip and slide around in a morass of words and possible truths in search of some coherent *story* about things that will give you a place to stand and figure out how you need to get on with life. Consider, for that matter, what is going on in your mind now as you decide what story to tell yourself about my story about stories.

The postmodern constructivist and narrative-based approaches to psychotherapy are new and different in many ways, but they are not ventures into New Age solipsism; they do not believe that life's difficulties can be simply reconstrued away. Donald Polkinghorne, a psychologist who has specialized in the education of psychotherapists, writes:

> When organizing past events into meaningful stories, narrative configuration is not simply a personal projection that has no relation to worldly events. When the acknowledged task of a narrative is to organize and make actual past events meaningful, it is required to attend to the accepted reality of those events. Nevertheless, narrative meaning consists of more than the events alone; it consists also of the significance these events have for the narrator in relation to a particular theme. For example, the death of one's mother in a personal narrative cannot be repressed as if it did not happen; however, the interpretation and significance of one's mother's death may also vary, depending on its placement within a narrative scheme.[9]

Polkinghorne also argues that narrative understanding is not just an approach to therapy, but a way of comprehending what it means to be human—what a "self" is. He finds it futile to try to define the self on the basis of a fixed boundary between the individual and society, and prefers to think of the self as a narrative, a plot continually being revised with much creative borrowing from other sources:

> Cultures do provide specific types of plots for adoption by its members in their configuration of self. These plot outlines are carried and transmitted in the culture by mythic stories and fairy tales, by tales of heroes, and by dramatic constructions. In North American culture, they are conveyed by motion pictures, television dramas, comic books, and novels. Although the content of each life is unique to a person, it can share the characteristics of a general plot outline. For example, personal life stories can be emplotted according to the outline of the tragic tale in which a person of good will and innocence is overcome by much pain and suffering, or according to a general heroic tale in which the person understands himself or herself to be engaged in a struggle for principles.[10]

The task of the therapist who is working from this perspective is to identify the plot that governs the patient's life and to see if a more positive one can be constructed—and believed, and lived by. Constructivist therapy is another sign of the times, one way that some people manage to take on the sometimes-frightening idea of reality as fiction and make it an approach to growth and moral responsibility.

TO BE SOMEBODY FEMALE

The world's largest course of constructivist therapy, the women's movement, has been under way for some decades now and shows no signs of nearing termination. If it ever does finish its work, no civilization in the world will be the same.

The women's movement—I think more than any political effort in our time—is an attempt to change not only laws and power structures, but social constructions of reality. And some of its activities, like consciousness-raising groups, were innovative mixtures of politics and psychotherapy, based on understanding the linkage between personal and political change.

It is hardly surprising, then, that women are deeply involved in every aspect of the postmodern dialogue. As psychologist Maureen O'Hara puts it: "When every 'system of truth' we've ever known, from the oldest myth to modern medical science, has concluded that women are biologically, intellectually and morally inferior, that we are at once dangerous and naturally nurturing, that we are unsuitable for public office and should be protected and subjugated—then you bet feminists have a stake in conversations about 'truth' and 'reality.'"[11]

The questions feminists raise go to the very heart of our most commonplace assumptions about human life. Isn't gender itself another one of our dreamed-up categories, built on doubtful assumptions and maintained by a fuzzy and culturally defined boundary that we try to persuade ourselves is a clear and "natural" one? Don't different societies have entirely different ideas of what it means to be male or female? Doesn't the language embody biased statements about the difference between the sexes, beginning with the words "man" and "woman," with woman (from *wifman*) defined only as a sort of annex to the man? "Such is the dilemma of the woman speaker," writes philosopher Andrea Nye: "That the categories of patriarchal language distort what she might like to say. . . ."[12]

So women have produced their own works in the sociology of knowledge, in cognitive science, and in critical studies—and major figures in the postmodern intellectual world such as the French semiotician Julia Kristeva. They have challenged the gender assumptions and inequities built deeply into every social construction of reality, and they have proposed alternate realities.

Alternate realities, of course, because if old beliefs about womanhood and ways of being female are to be dispensed with, then new beliefs and new ways are called for. And some women recognize that the new beliefs and new ways are matters of choice. They see the task as not merely discovering the true femininity that lies beneath the false patriarchal construct, but creating something that has not existed before, not even in the never-never land of prehistory.

The women's movement has its own versions of the objectivist-constructivist polarization—more than one version. One such polarization, the one that has been around the longest and gotten the most publicity, is between female traditionalists, such as Phyllis Schlafly, who defend the old female roles and "women's lib" feminists who think it is time for some new ones. Another polarization is between women who want to discover a new "essential femininity" that is different from the current models but that is *natural,* derived from deep and eternal principles, and those who want to be more frankly creative about it.

O'Hara believes that some of the New Age models of feminist reality—the idea of women as "goddesses" or "priestesses" (women are born spiritual), the mystique of "eco-feminism" (women are born environmentalists)—offer "a comforting antidote to the usual sense of insignificance most women experience in their daily lives," but that all such affirmations of an inborn, biologically based femininity in the end only "perpetuate ways of thinking about human realities that themselves justify attitudes and social practices that have disenfranchised women for millennia."

O'Hara calls the constructivist position "a harder pill to swallow," because it leaves the question of biology's contribution to consciousness veiled in mystery, sees biology as relevant but yet only a starting point from which personal and social symbolic reality must be constructed. And then she makes a very interesting statement, which, if correct, tells us a lot about how people respond to the process I have called the collapse of belief. She says that the despair, the anomie, the fear of emptiness are mainly the property of privileged white European males who see *their* world crumbling about them. She continues:

> What I feel, and read in the work of feminist poststructuralists, is an enormous sense of relief, hope and responsibility. Far from despair, the idea that each of us recreates reality with each encounter fills me with wondrous hope, empowerment and community connection. If there is no absolute truth "out there" to create pristine "expert systems" that can somehow solve our problems mathematically . . . if we accept that when we enter into dialogue we *both* change; if it is true that we *co-create* reality, which in turn creates us—then we are called to a new kind of community. If I can make culture I must act responsibly. If I can only ever be part of the creation I must act humbly. I'd take that over being a goddess. . . .[13]

The feminist constructivists and deconstructivists now constitute an important intellectual movement in their own right. Much of their work is first-rate and much of it is far too difficult to be of much use to ordinary working men and women who might like to find out what is going on in such circles. Kristeva is every bit as murky as Derrida; in that regard, full equality has been achieved. But there is something very simple and immediate about women's stake in the social construction of reality that comes through in statements such as O'Hara's and that may have a great impact on how we go about figuring how to live and be in the postmodern world.

It is very hard for a woman to be somebody without bumping up against social constructions of reality. And the problems that arise for women when they recognize that many of the daily activities of life are structured in rules and definitions that somebody created, that might conceivably be re-created—these problems are not readily solved by modern-era political stances, left or right. I recently heard a woman begin a lecture by saying, "I was married twice, once to a conservative and once to a radical. Neither one of them took out the garbage."

If and when more women see that their daily effort to be somebody is both driven by social constructions of reality and limited by them, and act on that perception, the postmodern era will reach not only every culture, but every household.

CAMP CULTURE: BEING SOMEBODY IN QUOTES

One of the most popular ways of occupying old social forms is the cultural game playing I described earlier as "camp": living between quotation marks. The idea of camping is to do something, but do it with an understanding that it is only semireal. If the game works at all well, you get some of the fun of participating in it that people got when they took it more seriously, and you also have extra added advantages, like the ability to change games from time to time and the opportunity to make fun of people who *did* take it seriously.

If you are attracted to the glamour of war, you can participate in a structured war game during which you wear a uniform and carry a weapon that shoots harmless but noisy charges at your enemies. If you always wanted to be a cowboy, you can go off to a dude ranch where you get not only the standard trail rides and barbecues, but—in "working" dude ranches—the opportunity to ride off with the cowboys and herd real cattle.

Entertainment, fashion, marketing, and the popular arts are full of camp, much of which boils down to young people enjoying things their parents and grandparents enjoyed—Humphrey Bogart movies, swing, tap dancing, drive-ins, Hawaiian shirts—while doing so in a way that makes it clear to one and all that they are just kidding. The nostalgia boom of recent decades is based on that sort of camp, as was the pop art of Andy Warhol and Roy Lichtenstein, with its paintings of soup cans and cartoon characters. In the 1960s, at about the same period of time that Susan Sontag's article was published and the campy *Batman* TV series appeared, Robert Venturi wrote a book celebrating the architecture in Las Vegas, which until then people had thought was just in poor taste. It turned out *that* was camp too, and now we have postmodern architecture that is all camp: building with a giggle. In the 1960s, architects were designing buildings in which people would perform; postmodern architects, taking the logical next step, design buildings that are performers themselves, camp performers, standing between their quotation marks, imitating other kinds of architecture but letting you know they are not being serious about it.

The "Doonesbury" comic strip ran a story that admirably illustrates camp in action: JJ, the upwardly mobile artist whose life and consciousness is that of trendy New York yuppie chic, is commissioned to redecorate the private yacht of Donald Trump, whose life and consciousness appear to be that of plain old American big bucks. Trump points to a ceiling and tells JJ he wants her to decorate it with about fifty Greek gods and a bunch of swans—"In the Michelangelo style, of course."

"Okay," says JJ, "I think I finally get it, Mr. Trump! You're looking for neo-classical kitsch, a kind of grand comment on bad taste! What a hoot! Ha! Ha! Ha!"

Trump gives her a frosty look.

"Or GOOD taste," she decides quickly. "You're commenting on good taste!"

"No," says Trump, "I'm just paying for it, and I want it by Monday!"[14]

Both JJ and Trump are collaborating on creating an environment that plays out Trump's—and America's—fantasies of the tycoon existence. JJ, the postmodern, wants to play the game as if it is a game. Trump wants to play it for real.

Camp Item: The newspaper carries a story about the incomparable Del Rubio sisters, "performing triplets who have emerged from decades of obscurity as a novelty act playing middle-of-the-road music at convalescent hospitals to become the latest darlings of the camp followers in the underground." The middle-aged middle-of-the-road ladies are shown, photographed in a campy pose with their guitars, beehive hairdos, and still-shapely legs revealed between short pants and white boots. The review-article reports that the Del Rubio sisters, working from a repertoire that included "Besame Mucho" and "I Left My Heart in San Francisco"—all sung badly but with innocent enthusiasm, according to the writer—had been madly applauded by "a packed house of hipsters almost half their age."[15]

Camp Item: The fashion editor reports a return of hippie styles: "Like, far out," she begins. "The 60s are back . . . Get ready to see a slew of 60s fashions as spring styles hit the racks. Designers on every level are working to a countercultural beat." She describes several of the hot items, such as designer tie-dyed clothes, peasant dresses, and mirrored vests. A photograph shows a denim-clad model posed in the act of mischievously carrying away a couple of street signs that say "Haight" and "Ashbury." Its caption says: "Student protestors lived in garb like this Legends and Fables jean jacket, complete with granny glasses in the pocket flap ($276) . . ."[16]

Camp Item: With a few friends I drive up to Elko, Nevada, to take in the cowboy poetry convention, an annual gathering that draws cowboy poets, several thousand spectators, and a lot of media attention. The streets of Elko are full of people in fancy cowboy clothes—a curious thing to observe from my own point of view, since Elko is my old home town and when I was a boy there the men mostly walked around in business suits. The cowboy-poets come bringing different talents and different ideas about how seriously they take the contemporary cowboy game. Some are heavily, even solemnly, into the traditional mystique of life on the range; others seem more inclined to kid around about it. One performer says, "A lot of these guys don't know what it feels like to sit in a saddle any more, but I still earn my livin' the old-fashioned way—tourism." He proceeds to tell about his cowboy adventures as a guide on a Montana dude ranch.

We often call the cowboy an American myth; we might as easily call it an American fiction, a curious reality/unreality that becomes curiouser all the time as fewer people eat beef but the market for Stetsons remains healthy. The cowboy life has been heavily saturated with fantasy for a long time (I remember the buckaroos on our ranch sitting around the bunkhouse reading *Ranch Romances*), and as time goes on and the Marlboro men ride steadily through our minds, it becomes more and more a game—one that you can play with your own degree of awareness that it is a game.

Spy magazine reports that camp is on the rise: "This," say the writers, "is the era of the permanent smirk, the knowing chuckle, of jokey ambivalence as a way of life. This is the Irony Epidemic." They identify camp as primarily a pastime of the 1960s generation, noting that their parents were on the whole "disinclined to dress up in outfits amusingly evocative of the Hoover era, or to see the inherent comedy in their new tract houses."

The article mentions a curious gesture that has entered the vocabulary of nonverbal language: air quotes. You have seen air quotes. The hands go up, a pair of fingers marking the invisible quotation marks around—well, around yourself, around whatever you are saying that, you want it understood, you don't exactly *mean*.

> Air quotes abound nowadays. Air quotes eliminate responsibility for one's actions, one's choices. Bob tells co-workers with a grin that he's got to get home to—raise hands, insert air quotes here—"the little woman," or to "the wife and kids," as if his family didn't really exist. . . .
>
> Betty tells friends she's "ultra-Type A" and, with air quotes, "a yuppie madwoman," so they won't imagine she actually enjoys her 12-hour days at the firm.[17]

The authors deride Bob and Betty and all their fellow campers as shallow people who have avoided making a choice—but I think we would do better to recognize that they are complex human beings who have made subtle adjustment to a difficult period in history, the time of collapse of beliefs and beliefs about belief. Neither dropped out nor dropped in, they exist—as we all do in varying degrees—somewhere in the twilight zone of an era, wearing their Hawaiian shirts and bravely waving their air quotes.

THE DRUG ROUTE: HOW TO BE ANYBODY, OR BE NOBODY AND FEEL GOOD ABOUT IT

Every society appears to have a few mind-altering substances in its repertoire: some of these are gentle modifiers of mood or energy, and some are brain-bashing invaders that transform all concepts of personal and cosmic reality. In the 1960s, when drug use came out of the closet and became a part of the public reality of Western civilization, it was commonly believed that the psychedelics (such as LSD) enabled the user to "drop out" of socially constructed reality and to "tune in" to a cosmic reality beyond culture: with the right drugs, you would find the Real World, and the True Self.

But it became apparent rather soon, to everyone who wasn't stoned while in the process of thinking about it, that the matter was a good deal more complicated. LSD users learned quickly that the "trip" could be vastly different according to the concepts and expectations, the "set and setting"—the social construction of reality, in short—that they took with them into the experience. And, despite the exhortations of Timothy Leary, people did not seem to "drop out" of their culures when they ventured into psychedelia—rather, they frequently found themselves deeply engaged with their cultures, albeit in creative and colorful new ways.

Lewis Yablonsky, a sociologist, did a study of the hippie subculture in the 1960s and, in the process, took the obligatory acid trip. Like many trippers he had intense emotional experiences, fantasies of being in various civilizations—and also fantasies about musical comedies and 1930s movies with Ronnie Reagan and Dick Powell, and overriding everything else a sense of himself as "true blue Lew—a sincere American patriot." When he wrote a book about his hippie adventure he entitled the acid chapter, "Red, White and Blue."[18] Whatever the experience was, it was anything but a drop-out—although a lot of his Americana did seem to have quotation marks around it.

People who use drugs are still inside their cultures, and the cultures are still inside them. But, as I have been trying to show in the foregoing pages, people are finding a lot of new ways to occupy the traditional cultural structures, and—to put it another way—a lot of new ways to process the richness of our symbolic existence, all the dramas of self and other, through their multimodal minds. Human life is becoming playfully—and publicly—multidimensional in a way it never was before.

This would be the case even if there were no funny chemicals around. But as it happens, there are a lot of funny chemicals around. Just as we are culturally eclectic, able to draw daily on the symbolic storehouse of thousands of societies past and present, so are we able to draw on a vast storehouse of mind-altering substances discovered over the millennia: everything from marijuana to magic mushrooms to cocaine to opium to vodka martinis. And to further complicate the matter, people are ingeniously creating new substances all the time and finding ways to make the old ones even stronger than they used to be. Sensimilla marijuana grown in many parts of the world today is several times more powerful than the Acapulco Gold and Maui Wowie that blew the minds of hippies young and old a few decades ago. Crack, some say, is instant addiction.

This complicates even further any attempt to generalize about what is real and true for the members of a contemporary society. Although politicians effortlessly make pronouncements about what the American people really believe, the evidence is strong that at any given time a considerable portion of said American people are shooting up, snorting cocaine, swallowing pills, tripping out, smoking dope, getting drunk, or in any of a myriad other ways turning their minds into processors of private dramas that have only the shakiest of links to the official public reality. This is not only a matter of domestic custom, but of international agriculture and trade. Every morning peasants in South American mountains get up and go to work tending coca plants to produce substances that will ultimately disappear up noses in Beverly Hills, while laborers in Scotland tend their vats to produce whiskey that will ultimately wash down the throats of men in South America who make their money in the cocaine business. A lot of people in the world—and a lot of agricultural land—are engaged in the production of substances that help human brains play around with reality. The early postmodern years are easily the dopiest in human history.

The anthropologists tell us that there is nothing unusual about the ingestion of mind-altering substances—indeed, it is probably more the norm of human life than a deviation from it—and report that many societies we call "primitive" managed to have drug use without a drug problem. Perhaps it had once been a problem, but they had successfully ringed it around with prohibitions and rituals; these were unified homogenous societies, which undoubtedly made it easier for them to manage the drug experience. So managed, it became a special part of social life—a sanctified glimpse beyond the society's ordinary construction of reality that deepened the sense of membership in the culture (and undoubtedly the belief that it contained vast wisdom) rather than alienating the individual from it.

We don't have many such rituals in the contemporary pluralistic world; instead, we have rampant experimentation and enormous problems: addiction, crime, diseases such as AIDS spread by needles, young men slaughtering one another in the city streets, countless deaths and injuries from drug- and alcohol-related accidents, immeasurable damage to the health and productivity and sanity of the society and individuals within it. And the U.S. government found it necessary to launch a "war on drugs" to deal with the problem.

Clearly it is a problem, but I am not at all sure that "war" is the best metaphor for it—the best way to construct the reality of how society should approach such a situation. If we do insist on calling it a war, it is very likely to turn out to be another Vietnam.

The clearest publicly expressed alternative to the "war on drugs" approach to the problem is legalization—of some currently outlawed substances or, in the more extreme libertarian scenario, of all. This is a dubious panacea, too, in view of the extreme potency of some of the substances currently available, the utter lack of knowledge about their long-range effects among many of the consumer population, and the demonstrated willingness of many promoters to sell anything to anybody, regardless of the effects.

If we ever find a "solution" to the problem that currently roars through the streets and the headlines and, unfortunately, the brains of a considerable segment of the population, it is going to be through some middle way that manages to combine—as some societies have done in the past—prohibition with permission.

Let me sketch out a scenario of what such a society might look like. Call it a story. I present it with full knowledge that it would be difficult, perhaps impossible, to put into practice—although no more difficult nor impossible than the ones that are currently being discussed.

Imagine a society—a vast pluralistic one like postmodern America—that found itself up to its ears in mind-altering chemicals, many of which were being used in ways highly destructive to the individual users, and many of which were producing socially costly side effects such as crime and disease. The society's response—not just the government's, but the more-or-less coordinated activity of many different people and groups with many different sets of value and belief about such matters—was to search for ways for drugs to be used as productively as possible.

This called for much research, much gathering and dissemination of information, much give-and-take. It was very hard for some groups to accept the possibility that drugs were here to stay, that the society simply lacked the power to prohibit or control them entirely; it was equally hard for the libertarians to accept the idea that some substances had to be proscribed, and the proscriptions had to be strictly enforced.

Starting small, the society managed to get some rough social consensus that some kinds of drug use were, well, at least not *too* bad: peyote for Indian religious rituals, LSD for the terminally ill, a few drinks and maybe even a little grass for people who weren't about to pilot an airliner or perform brain surgery. This wasn't easy, but it provided a base that was then widened by the creative efforts of many different people and groups—ranging from religious organizations to scientific bodies—to find ways to make drug experiences available to people who were ready for them in ways that enhanced their lives.

In time (as long as this is a fantasy I may as well make the most of it), the society became extremely wise in the use of its chemical cornucopia. Many people were helped by the use of drugs in contexts such as religious ceremonies, psychotherapy, artistic events, psychological research, and social occasions. Many others found that they could get along fine without any such assistances. Some kinds of drugs and many kinds of drug-related behaviors—such as driving while intoxicated—were firmly and effectively prohibited. There was much diversity within a very loose social consensus. And the social learning continued, with constant research and continual changes in norms and customs in response to it.

Some moves in this general direction were discussed, as I recall, in the 1950s and 1960s: Aldous Huxley offered a benign and attractive picture of mescaline use in his book *The Doors of Perception*, the National Institutes of Health ran LSD experiments for years, many psychotherapists used it until it was proscribed (I remember meeting a Czech psychiatrist about that time who was amazed that you could buy LSD on the streets in America but doctors couldn't use it in clinics), and various leaders of the counterculture were talking with varying degrees of plausibility about the need to create "new sacraments" involving marijuana instead of Manischiewitz.

One can hardly blame Middle America for failing to be carried away by some of the prodrug rhetoric of the 1960s. Much of it was unbearably arrogant in its conviction that drugs were the One True Path. Theodore Roszak, who was no admirer of the druggier aspects of the counterculture he otherwise sympathetically chronicled, quoted this piece of agonized philosophizing from *The East Village Other*, in an article entitled, "CAN the World Do Without LSD?" The writer said: "Here's where those who have and those who have not had LSD part company—at least as far as knowing what the subject under discussion is . . . Can a person be human without LSD? Or, let us say, without THE PSYCHEDELIC experience? The answer, as far as the writer of this article can see, is a highly qualified, cautiously rendered, but emphatic, definitely NOT."[19] So much for most of the human race.

Although Timothy Leary and his followers were a little extreme in their claims about the wonders of the psychedelic drugs, and demonstrably hasty to persuade everybody (including themselves) that enough good dope turned the user into a superior human being, they were, I believe, onto something in their angry conviction that the attempt to stamp out all use of psychedelics (which began to seem to many Americans a pretty good idea) was a form of thought control beyond the capability of any government to undertake or carry out.

We will have to come to terms, as we stagger into the postmodern era, with the hard-to-avoid evidence that there are many different realities, and different ways of experiencing them, and that people seem to want to keep exploring them, and that there is only a limited amount any society can do to insure that its official reality is installed in the minds of most of its citizens most of the time.

THE SEARCH FOR GOODNESS

Being a multimodal person and a moral one is never easy, even in a society that has one official version of what constitutes goodness. You may have noticed this already. Parts of us want to be good—or at least seen as good—and parts of us want to wave a finger at goodness and do something-or-another else whether it gets a merit badge or not. And the more pluralistic the social context becomes—the more value systems available to us, and the more complex our ideas about goodness—the harder it gets. You don't get to be good for everybody. You can be a model Christian, and a lot of people are going to think you're an uptight jerk. You can be a model Muslim, ready to die for the faith, and a lot of people are going to think you're a murderous terrorist.

As more people become capable of distancing themselves from official systems of value and belief, curious new ideas about goodness emerge. The struggle of blacks for dignity and self-respect in a white-dominated society brought forth a remarkable reversal of the language, in which "bad" came to mean "good." To be a "good nigger" was to be an uncomplaining and servile loser; to be a "bad nigger" was to be rebellious, proud, contemptuous of the white man's value system—and hence good. And so "bad" became young people's jargon for anything hip and fashionable, and English became even harder to figure out than it had been anyway. Other groups play their own complex game with official reality structures as they seek to redefine themselves: many feminists have come to similar conclusions about the old model of the "good woman." You know the "good woman": she is either virginal or drowning in children, and in either case is lost in admiration for the qualities of the male sex and deeply grateful to God and society for having placed her in her present position. Many women seem to have found this a sort of goodness they didn't much need.

Rebellions of certain groups against certain localized social goodnesses are not really too hard to understand, even by those who don't approve of them. But what are we to make of Satanism and other rebellions against goodness itself? What other than a generalized feeling that the social versions of goodness are not absolutes—perhaps even, as some seem to be saying, the very contrary force of the deeper reason of nature? Some people reject the old absolutes; other people try to establish new ones.

As we move into the postmodern era, we move into a new stage of the human struggle to evolve as a moral being. We do not, as so many fear, cease to be moral animals and slide into hedonistic or savage normlessness. But neither are we completely subservient to the various holy tablets containing eternal prescriptions about what we should and should not do. It ceases to be a secret that morality is socially defined, and with the revelation of that secret, a conviction is born in the minds of many people—see, for example, the works of Karl Marx and Michel Foucault—that social definitions of morality (which are of course another name for social constructions of reality) are power grabs and conspiracies.

And in this climate of moral uncertainty we have, as of course we must and should, entirely new ways of looking at the ancient question of what constitutes the good person. In place of philosophies that measure the morality of people in terms of how well they conform to the official codes, we have psychological schemes of "moral development," which suggest that the most virtuous people are not necessarily high performers by these older standards.

The main sources of contemporary work on moral development—at least the main psychological sources—are Jean Piaget and Lawrence Kohlberg. Piaget, who is frequently included among the patron saints of the sociology of knowledge, worked out a theory of cognitive development identifying various stages of growth at which the mind becomes capable of handling successively more complex concepts. Kohlberg, whose major works were first published in the late 1960s, took this one step further—the cognitive stages become stages of moral development—and in the process sketched out the first clearly postmodern theory of virtue.

Kohlberg's work, anticipating constructivist therapy, focused on the frame rather than the picture, on story rather than action. To understand the level of a person's moral development, you had to find out not what a person did but why he or she did it, what the action *meant*.

He based his research on stories about situations that involved conflict and moral choice. The favorite one went as follows: A man's wife is dying from cancer, and a drug is available. But the druggist wants a high price for it and refuses to let the man pay later. The man breaks into the store to steal the drug. Should he have done that?

Most people said yes, but gave reasons that revealed different styles of moral reasoning. One might say the man needed his wife's services and shouldn't let anything get in his way; another might justify the act in terms of conventional morality; a third might have even higher moral aspirations than those of conventional society and say, for example, that the man ought not only to steal the drug but then make the act known in order to inform others about the problem.

Out of this research emerged Kohlberg's famous moral-development scale, showing six different "levels" of growth. At the lowest level, people understand little more than their own needs and the chances of being rewarded or punished. At Stage 2, they begin, in a primitive way, to recognize that other people have needs and a few trade-offs may be in order. At Stage 3, they move into a "good boy" orientation based on getting approval for pleasing and helping others; people at this stage tend to see that society is "really" a system of roles, and to think of personal success as a matter of performance in role. At Stage 4, they see society as really a system of rules; this is the orientation of the "law and order" conservative. At Stage 5, people recognize that all rules are in a sense arbitrary, and develop an orientation toward negotiation and "social contract" rule making. The person who has evolved to Stage 6 becomes more inclined to rely on his or her personal conscience and welcomes moral challenges as opportunities to discover what is "right" logically and universally.[20]

Many later researchers have criticized some aspects of Kohlberg's work—some have challenged its applicability to other cultures, others have accused it of being sexist. Carol Gilligan of Harvard argued that Kohlberg's justice dilemmas were irrelevant to women, and that women have a "different moral voice" based on their orientation to relatedness and caring.[21] Many feminists accepted this enthusiastically, while others have criticized it as sexist in its own way, popular mainly because, as psychologist Martha Mednick puts it, "it meshed so easily with the pro-family women's nature ideology that has become the dominant public rhetoric."[22] In any case, Kohlberg's system is far more complex than the simple outline I have presented here; nobody thinks that we all go around being perfect twos or sixes. The essential vision is what is important in Piaget's and Kohlberg's work—and that is a view of human beings as social animals who develop systems of morality as naturally as they eat and breathe.

For those who think of moral development this way, a social environment of conflicting realities and conflicting moralities is, at least potentially, an excellent matrix in which to grow people of highly developed moral character. Conflict—certain kinds of conflict, conflict in which moral issues are made explicit—can create the situation in which people become capable of moving from one developmental stage to the next. Morality, then, is the product of hard-won wisdom, a way of being that expresses wherever a person happens to be along the (hopefully) never-ending path of understanding and reunderstanding life, constructing and reconstructing the rules of relationship between self and others.

This perspective, if you follow it to its logical conclusion, adds a few more tons to the burden of trying to be somebody. It requires us not only to make moral choices, but also to add to our life-making responsibilities the task of creating and re-creating our ideas of what morality is. It also tells us that different people, depending on where they happen to be along the personal path of moral development, will have entirely different ways of dealing with the transition into the postmodern world—and entirely different kinds of resistance to it.

The contemporary early-postmodern world in which we take on these tasks is a rich field in some ways, a barren one in others: clearly there is plenty of moral pluralism around, but the moral dialogue is anything but brilliant. We need for moral development not only conflicts, but public role models who show what a mature and morally responsible person is like, and myths and stories that deal creatively with the moral issues of our time. And in the latter areas, contemporary mass democracy is seriously deficient.

CHAPTER 7

Democracy's Dilemma

The postmodern era could become the true age of liberation, something like what was dreamed of by the great spirits of democracy. Thomas Jefferson, who declared himself the enemy of all forms of tyranny over the human mind, might be pleased to see a society so busily unshackling itself from belief systems. But would he welcome postmodernism in its totality? I doubt it. Jefferson was a good Enlightenment rationalist who dwelled amid the certainties of philosophy and science, and would probably not appreciate having some wise-guy deconstructionist from the big city coming along and telling him no truths can be held to be self-evident (or that if you do hold a truth to be self-evident, you're probably sneaking some contradictory truth into your statement about it).

Democratic institutions as we know them in the West, and as they are now being adopted by other societies around the world, were created to accommodate different opinions and different interest groups—even different religions if they didn't get too far off the page—but not different realities and certainly not different ideas about what (if anything) reality is. Alexander Hamilton, the true architect of the American system of governance, was primarily concerned with the need for institutions that could moderate the conflict among factions. And factions to Hamilton were nice neat categories, identifiable things like, say, fish or zebras. You knew one when you saw it. Individuals were single agents; the Constitution meant what it said; history was a record to be read and learned from, not an indeterminate babble. Hamilton was himself a complex man who may well have been bent on self-destruction when he entered into the fatal duel with Aaron Burr. But the public discourse of his time, the world in which he and his colleagues created the Republic, was one which believed in the attainability and permanence of objective truth.

And when Hamilton felt the need to influence public opinion in favor of the Constitution, he put his arguments into a series of brilliantly rational essays, the *Federalist* papers, which are still read by students of politics and literature. Today, anyone who wanted to engage in such an opinion-shaping campaign would go at it entirely differently. First, you would hire a PR man. Then you would mount up a media campaign if you could afford it, and loft a few more banalities out over the airwaves: get that Constitution a new image.

We have seen in our lifetimes, and are seeing now, an evolution of democracy into something quite unlike what it was a couple of centuries ago. First, plain demagoguery evolved into propaganda, and propaganda has been evolving over the past few decades into the art and science of story making and image-management that saturates every aspect of governance. This might be fine if the products of it were wise and challenging narratives that accommodated the complexities of our time and helped us create better personal and social realities. But unfortunately the stories and images created by the various political dream merchants and accepted by most of the American people are more in the league with Rambo movies and Harlequin romances.

The general drift of political PR in mass democracies is to give the public simple get-happy stories of the Grenada variety and to avoid bad news. Every good political pro knows that optimism sells, and that, given the choice between two candidates in an election, the public will generally vote for the more optimistic one. Jimmy Carter's presidency is best remembered for two unforgivable sins against optimism: one was that he spoke of an American "malaise"; the other was that he presided over the Iranian hostage crisis, a global spectacle in which the United States appeared impotent—which is totally incompatible with the American self-image. The lesson to be learned from this, if you are one of the enormous corps of well-paid and talented men and women who practice the profession of political image-management, is to keep the public happy. Maintain the good-guy American story at all costs. No gloom and doom stuff. And fire that guy who wrote the "malaise" speech.

The collapse of old beliefs, and of old beliefs about belief, create an unprecedented opportunity for the political story-makers: In the absence of deeply held and socially enforceable constructions of reality, new ones can be created more freely—and naturally these should be *palatable* realities: just give people what they want. But the story-making, meaning-manufacturing machinery of postmodern society is enormous and multidimensional and not entirely under anybody's control. Competing stories emerge; *information* emerges in gargantuan quantities, so much that we scarcely know how to assimilate it or evaluate it, and in some cases—the greenhouse effect, for example—are strongly tempted to deny it entirely. Who *knows*? One scientist says one thing, another one says something else. Science isn't what it used to be; it's no longer the final fountainhead of hard facts.

The dilemma of democratic governance in the postmodern world could easily be summed up as a tension between fantasy and reality: between the beguiling stories spun out by the political mythmakers and the hard truths of a host of threats beyond our boundaries and, yes, a malaise or two at home. And at one level the situation is precisely that.

But we no longer live solely on the first floor. Postmodern voices remind us that people and societies are always engaged in the story-making, even mythmaking embroidery of life as we live it, and that although information—such as scientific data—cannot easily be denied, neither can it be mindlessly embraced as cold and objective authority. Information, even the inert numbers that we crunch through our computers, is socially constructed reality; it has its own politics. And so we move into a much more complex stage of democracy's evolution, one that Jefferson and Hamilton could scarcely imagine, in which we seek better stories and better information and better understanding of both. We struggle toward a higher level of public dialogue, even while we are surrounded by story-making activity that is at the same time amazingly sophisticated and remarkably stupid.

EARLY CALIFORNIA DREAMING

In the early 1930s, at about the same time that Adolf Hitler was raising the curtain on his brilliant work of political dramaturgy in Europe, a new profession was being born in the United States.

The profession was political campaign-management for hire—media-based campaigning—and it was what Victor Hugo would have called an idea whose time had come. America had already become a country dazzled by the mass media—the movies, the network radio programs, the glossy new magazines—but the political pros had not quite caught on. The urban political machines were smug in their power and set in their ways. Candidates were selected in the proverbial "smoke-filled rooms," and campaigns were usually based on the tried-and-true strategies of building coalitions, taking good care of the party faithful, and getting out the vote at election time. Campaign organizations might reluctantly spend a little money on billboards, but most of the old pros regarded advertising as a way to sell toothpaste, not a tool of politics.

Clem Whitaker, a public-relations man in California, saw different possibilities, and teamed up with his wife, Leone Baxter, to start a new business. Whitaker and Baxter offered a complete package of campaign-management services to groups or candidates, for a straight fee of $25,000 to $50,000.[1] The firm had two subsidiaries: the Clem Whitaker Advertising Agency, which handled the purchase of space and time in the media; and the California Feature Service, which supplied a weekly clipsheet of editorials and news features free of charge to small-town newspapers. Whitaker and Baxter managed their first campaign in 1933, a referendum involving the development of water resources in the Central Valley, and won handily. The next year, they were hired by their first live candidate, a Republican nominee for lieutenant governor who was running against a Democratic ticket headed by novelist Upton Sinclair. Sinclair, muckraking journalist and novelist, had previously run for office several times as a Socialist candidate, but had never come close to being elected. When he changed his party membership and entered the primary, establishment Democrats could not agree on a candidate to oppose him, and to everyone's surprise including his own, Sinclair became the nominee.

Whitaker and Baxter put on a campaign of a sort that California—indeed, democracy—had never seen before. The core of it was an unprecedented utilization of the media, all organized around a central story of what the campaign was about: it was a holy crusade to save the state from "Sinclairism," which was represented as more or less the same thing as communism. The message went out to the public in radio commercials, newspaper ads, brochures, leaflets. Whitaker and Baxter hired an artist to draw editorial cartoons that they distributed to accommodating newspapers. The Hollywood film industry mobilized in the service of a political cause for the first time: the studios raised a half-million-dollar campaign fund (part of which came from an assessment of one day's wages against employees). A series of films were produced and exhibited as newsreels in the theaters. One showed mobs of vagrants (actually actors) supposedly on their way to California to get in on Sinclair's welfare schemes. Another—also filmed in a studio with actors—showed an elderly lady telling an inquiring reporter that she intended to vote against Sinclair "because I want to save my little home. It's all I have left in this world." A suspicious-looking bearded man with a Russian accent told the same reporter he intended to vote *for* Sinclair: "His system vorked vell in Russia, vy can't it vork here?"[2]

Sinclair was vulnerable to this sort of thing: he had written books—which gave the opposition a vast amount of material to use against him—and he based his own campaign on a long list of untried economic reform ideas that, he was breezily confident, would end poverty in one or two years. He called this the EPIC plan—standing for End Poverty in California. Sinclair had never held a public office, and the largest political unit in which he had ended poverty up to that time was the Upton Sinclair family. But if Sinclair's campaign had its own elements of soap opera, it was a far less sophisticated drama than the one his opponents were staging, and it had the disadvantage of being cluttered up with a lot of ideology and detailed proposals; Sinclair had no clue of the first rule of the new politics, which is that you keep it simple and keep it vague. He lost, of course, and Whitaker and Baxter went on to long and prosperous careers.

You can see, in hindsight, various reasons why this kind of politics flowered early in California. For one, the state's more traditional political machinery had been dismantled a couple of decades earlier by a reform movement. And California was already slouching toward postmodernism in the 1930s. It had a highly mobile population of people who had recently moved there from somewhere else and who tended to keep moving after they arrived. This made old-style political organizing difficult if not impossible. As Carey McWilliams put it in his classic study *California: The Great Exception*, "There are neighborhoods in Los Angeles in which it would be safe to say that not more than two or three families in an entire block are known to one another. Try to boss such a neighborhood."[3] It was not only the neighborhood that was ceasing to function as a solid framework for political organization, but (according to the students of "mass society") a whole congeries of factors such as class status and ethnicity that once had helped people define their personal identities and their political interests.[4] Semidetached from traditional social settings and from the constructions of reality that went with them, the floating masses of suburbanites and apartment-dwellers were ready to connect, via the media, to the image of the larger entity, California, of which they were somehow a part, and which was getting itself ready to—pick your drama—either end poverty or stamp out the menace of Sinclairism. Sinclairism looked a lot like an ideology, and ideology was aging as badly as machine politics. Any ideology's monopoly on absolute truth was doubtful, and besides, ideology was no fun; ideologues always wanted you to read some dull book.

Whitaker understood the great potential for reaching this mass public in a new way—touching it not with ideology or even with promises, but with drama. Summing up his political wisdom in a speech to the Los Angeles chapter of the Public Relations Society of America years later, he said:

> There are thousands of experts bidding for every man's attention—and every man has a limited amount of leisure. Then we must recognize, too, that in almost every human being there is a great craving just to be lazy, at least part of the time, and a wall goes up when you try to make Mr. and Mrs. Average Citizen *work or think* when all they want to do is relax. . . .
>
> The average American, when you catch him after hours, as we must, doesn't want to be educated; he doesn't want to improve his mind; he doesn't even want to work, consciously, at being a good citizen.
>
> But there are two ways you can interest him in a campaign, and only two that we have ever found successful.
>
> Most every American loves *contest*. He likes a good hot battle, with no punches pulled. He likes the clash of arms! So *you can interest him if you put on a fight*!
>
> No matter what you fight for, *fight for something*, in our business, and very soon the voters will be turning out to hear you, providing you make the fight interesting.
>
> Then, too, most every American likes to be entertained. He likes

> the movies; he likes mysteries; he likes fireworks and parades. He likes Jack Benny and Bob Hope and Joe E. Brown!
>
> So if you can't fight, PUT ON A SHOW! And if you put on a good show, Mr. and Mrs. America will turn out to see it.[5]

Clem Whitaker and Leone Baxter became powerful figures in California politics—powerful in no conventional sense; they never held public office, or even formal positions in the Republican party, which provided most of their clients. Their success produced a host of imitators—professional campaign-management firms are now involved in campaigns everywhere—and, much more important, was part of a revolution in the *style* and *techniques* of political campaigning. The utilization of media, the management of image, the avoidance of an excess of ideology and detailed programs (the disastrous presidential campaigns of Barry Goldwater in 1964 and of George McGovern in 1972 have convinced contemporary political pros that the last thing you want to do is throw a lot of tiresome proposals at the voters) all support the thesis that Daniel Bell advanced in 1960 in *The End of Ideology:* that we had seen "an exhaustion of the nineteenth-century ideologies . . . as intellectual systems that could claim *truth* for their views of the world."[6] With the old ideologies losing their authority, space was opened for new ways of defining political truth—for entirely new conceptions of what politics might be.

Whitaker and Baxter helped to change the face of American politics. They did not make politics any more dishonest than it had ever been. What they did was more subtle, and more revolutionary: they recognized, and acted explicitly on the recognition that politics could be not only a struggle for power, but a medium of *entertainment.* They thus accelerated the progress of public affairs toward the systematic orchestration of pseudoevents, and their success laid the foundation for that protracted pseudoevent known as the political career of Ronald Reagan.

A STAR IS BORN

On a memorable November evening in 1966, I was at the Biltmore Hotel in Los Angeles, watching the televised election returns with Stuart Spencer of the Spencer-Roberts campaign-management firm, when the word came through that Spencer's client Ronald Reagan had been elected governor of California. I was there as a journalist, working on an article about the latter-day Whitakers and Baxters—and Spencer-Roberts had just come to the top of the heap.

I had no idea, of course, when we went upstairs for cocktails and speeches, that I was going to the victory celebration of a man who would eventually become president of the United States; this seemed most unlikely to me, although Spencer predicted it that evening. What the Reagan victory signified to me and to most people at the time—the story then current in California—was that the voters were reacting to recent upheavals such as the Free Speech Movement in Berkeley and the Watts riots in Los Angeles. These represented to many people unpermissable breakdowns of law and order. And those disturbances were also, of course, the focal points of a spreading concern that the whole country—and California in particular—was going through some kind of cultural breakdown and/or revolution, something along the lines of what Timothy Leary and other notables of the time advocated: nothing less than a massive rejection of the values and beliefs of Western civilization.

Reagan's gubernatorial campaign had been tailored to respond to these concerns. In one speech, he had told the scandalized members of a southern California women's club about an anti-Vietnam War protest dance in Berkeley that turned into an "orgy," and said that the university had "finally reached a point where the morality gap is so great that we can no longer ignore it." In another, a major TV address, he asked whether the public should meet the students' "neurotic vulgarities with vacillation and weakness," and called the streets of California's cities "jungle paths after dark, with more crimes of violence than New York, Pennsylvania and Massachusetts combined."[7] Stu Spencer told me that his firm had chosen to make morality the main theme of the campaign.[8]

Spencer-Roberts ran a slick campaign, a state-of-the-art job of management that of course made maximum use of their candidate's formidable media skills. It is profoundly ironic, a piece of history to make a deconstructionist's mouth water, that Ronald Reagan, who came to political power as a representative of a popular urge toward the restoration of old and understandable American values, did so by campaigning with the most sophisticated media techniques, so skillfully used as to make his opponent's campaign look like a creaking Model-T by comparison. As Reagan went on to the presidency, many political observers noted other paradoxes, commented on how strange it was that a twice-married movie star, a longtime resident of the closest thing around to a modern Babylon, could somehow emerge as the incarnation of the clean-cut simple values of small-town America.

Ronald Reagan was the first postmodern politician. Presented to the public as the antidote to a counterculture that was leading the march away from modern culture, he took the society even further from its connection to the certainties of the modern era.

He did not embody the constructivist urge toward the creation of higher moral principles, nor did he ever announce the death of a belief system. But he understood the power of free-floating symbolism, rooted in nothing at all. Nobody could ever call the man logocentric. He would, of course, use a statistic or two if it came in handy, but neither his promises nor his performances were rooted in any dreary objectivist search for quantified reality: the students at Berkeley did not become measurably less neurotic and vulgar after he took office in Sacramento, nor did the streets become measurably safer. Neither did he deliver on the larger and more amorphous dream that was always suggested by his personal manner and by so much of his campaign material: the dream of bringing us back to the small-town, straw-hatted, wisecracking but hardworking, white, Protestant, and middle-class America of the Norman Rockwell paintings and the old Ronald Reagan movies. That America had never existed anyway, and the only way we could return to it was by means of a sort of high-camp politics that spread a veneer of folksiness across the face of a turbulent and pluralistic society.

Reagan was unusually well qualified to make the most of the public-relations industry that had emerged in recent decades as a new and increasingly organized manufacturer of social reality. Much has been made of his acting background, and of his extensive reliance on PR men. It would be as accurate—and give us a better understanding of his skills—to note that for a long while Reagan had been a PR man himself. In the mid-1950s, over ten years before he ran for governor, he had gone to work for General Electric in a corporate-image position that involved acting as host on the weekly *G. E. Theater* TV program; visiting factories to boost employee morale; and representing the corporation in public appearances around the country at which he delivered, time and time again, a vague and peppy speech about Americanism.

Reagan's unique qualification lay not merely in his speaking skills or his camera savvy—those are not too hard to come by—but in a certain kind of *intellectual* training that had equipped him admirably to take a leading role in the politics of the nonevent: he had managed to go through a long and rather successful professional career that did not require him to develop any concept of truth; the truth was simply whatever entertained the audience. Most contemporary professions took form during the modern era, and do have and teach a concept of absolute truth. The law, for example, is a proud collection of techniques for arriving at objective certainty: the deposition, the oath to tell "the truth, the whole truth and nothing but the truth," the findings of fact, the agonizing efforts to establish the "intent" of the authors of the Constitution. Yes, realists and postmodernists have been blowing up those courthouse statues; yes, there are plenty of crooked lawyers. But the concept of nonsubjective truth is there, and deeply instilled in many lawyers. Other professions have comparable foundations; myths of absolute reality. Training in those professions has tended to produce objectivists. Ronald Reagan's professional experience, from the early radio days when he worked for station WHO in Des Moines, simulating play-by-play descriptions of baseball games while actually broadcasting from a studio and making up the action on the basis of information supplied by telegraph, was constructivist. He lived in a happy Kantian interaction with the noumena, improvising realities out of them as he went along, and always managing to find a public that liked what he created. Many men, having reached the high public levels at which he found himself, would have been ashamed of a past so full of light fiction. But Reagan never was, and engagingly told stories about his sports-announcing days, about fun times on the sets at Warner Bros., about "The Speech" that he delivered again and again and again to admiring crowds of G. E. executives. He enjoyed the game.

As president of the United States, he tended to be bored with the dreary details of office, excessively preoccupied with the more glamorous adventures such as battling the bad-guy Sandinistas in Central America; he was well served by some of the subordinates to whom he delegated power and nortoriously ill served by others. But delegate he did, of course, because governance did not really interest him; being president was what interested him. And the public, on the whole, was quite happy with the performance. Nobody ever looked better relaxing at the ranch in western clothing, nobody waved more presidentially to the press while striding across the White House lawn to the helicopter. The government—well, it went its indeterminate way, as governments do. There are a lot of people in a government, after all. They had a few disasters, a few successes. Things seemed to be in pretty fair shape, and the president looked great.

Ronald Reagan was not an evil man, unless you extend your definition of evil to include intellectual carelessness on a heroic scale. Some of his recent predecessors in the office, notably Johnson and Nixon, showed stronger flashes of good old-fashioned Iago-style evil. He was merely an innocent constructivist, a postmodern primitive. People who agree with my assessment of him will no doubt feel that if this is what postmodernism looks like in politics, we are in big trouble. I think that concern is well founded. Once we are detached from the old sense of reality, there may be new dangers—definitely including the danger of, as Neil Postman put it, amusing ourselves to death.

The Reagan administration was not a one-man show, of course. It was effective not merely because it had a good leading man but because it was made up of an extraordinarily skilled corps of professionals who mobilized all the resources of the White House—and those are a lot of resources—in the service of public relations. The Reagan PR strategists included, at various times, James Baker, Mike Deaver, David Gergen, Larry Speakes, and pollster Richard Wirthlin. They made the presidency a media-oriented machine, and in effect made the media an unwitting part of the presidential team. As Mark Hertsgaard puts it in his history of the press and the Reagan presidency:

> Both Deaver and Gergen recognized that to engineer mass consent in the modern media age, the government had to be able to present its version of reality to the public over and over again. Neutralizing the press, by limiting journalists' ability to report politically damaging stories, was necessary but not sufficient. The press had to be turned

> into a positive instrument of governance, a reliable and essentially non-intrusive transmitter of what the White House wanted the public to know.[9]

What the government did in the Reagan years was not always easy to discover, but what it *said* it did was put forth to the media—and through it to the public—with relentless clarity. Early in the morning of every White House working day came the "line of the day" meeting in which top strategists would decide what news would be fed to the press that day, how the story should be angled, and who would be primarily responsible for it. The word would go out via conference call to senior officials, who were expected to tailor their own comments to the press accordingly. This kind of coordination made it possible for the White House to put through the messages it most wanted the public to get, and to exercise "spin control"—which is really story control, shaping the context of meaning surrounding an event and giving it positive or negative connotations.

Great care was also given to the visual images, the still photographs and TV footage in which the public saw its president in the very act of presiding. Well-staged visuals could vividly communicate the image of the rather passive Reagan as an active, take-charge sort of guy—out there talking to workers in the factories, meeting with world leaders, standing at the border between North and South Korea with a pair of field glasses.

Presidents before and after Reagan have employed the techniques of public relations effectively, put spin control ahead of leadership, but no administration in American history has been quite so dominated by what was once thought of as secondary to the substance of governance. A disgruntled White House aide who quit the Reagan administration after it excluded the press from the Grenada invasion said:

> The whole thing was PR. This was a PR outfit that became President and took over the country. And to the degree then to which the Constitution forced them to do things like make a budget, run foreign policy and all that, they sort of did. But their first, last and overarching activity was public relations.[10]

The most serious shortcomings of the Reagan administration lay not in what it did, however, but in what it didn't do. One thing it didn't do was pay any serious attention to the accumulating evidence of threats to the global environment. The evidence was available. The federal government has agencies that were created specifically to gather such information. One such, the Council on Environmental Quality, is located organizationally within the executive office of the president and geographically close to the White House. During the Carter administration, CEQ was highly visible and influential: it produced the *Global 2000 Report*, which was the most complete survey of the state of the biosphere that had been put together by any government anywhere. In the Reagan years, CEQ shrank to insignificance and the *Global 2000 Report* became about as popular a piece of literature around the White House as the collected works of Ted Kennedy. A White House official told an acquaintance of mine that global environment worries were generally regarded as "laughers" in the higher circles of government. Any staff person with a good feel for how to win approval and get ahead had sense enough to avoid bringing up such stuff; you didn't want people to think you were some sort of wierdo environmentalist.

By such subtle taboos are social constructions of reality maintained by those in power. A government generates enormous amounts of information and creates many stories, but only a few are chosen to become the main themes that define the national purpose. And the story of taking responsibility for the well-being of the global environment definitely did not become the plot line of the Reagan administration. The media-management style of politics naturally favors certain kinds of stories as likely to work well with the presidential image, and it's hardly surprising that a president who used "Morning in America" TV commercials in his campaign for reelection played down the story of an endangered biosphere.

Ronald Reagan was a leader. He led us into the postmodern era, and his historical importance is not that he was unique, an actor who got lucky, but that he was extraordinarily good at a kind of politics that everybody now practices.

RADICAL THEATER

Ronald Reagan and the high-priced progeny of Clem Whitaker are not by any means the only people who have figured out how to manipulate the media and dramatize issues. Indeed, politics and theater have become inseparable; anyone with a cause today thinks about how to dramatize it, and there is as much stagecraft on the left as on the right.

The civil rights demonstrations of the 1960s were among the great political dramas of all time. Out of the chaos in the South, a strong story came through: American citizens were being systematically deprived of the rights that, according to what we had all been told countless times, American citizens are supposed to have. The drama as it played out in scenes of demonstration and confrontation was powerful and moving, full of vivid images: blacks and civil rights workers on the road to Selma, fat cops and billy clubs against them.

The whites in the Deep South who resisted the civil rights demonstrations, and who resented the roles that the drama assigned to them, spoke often of "outside agitators." They felt invaded by hordes of radicals and do-gooders and reporters and photographers, people who did not understand them and their way of dealing with things. But what was happening was not so much that outsiders were coming into the South as that the South was being taken to the world, ripped out of its old context and thrust by the news media onto the center of a global stage in which the drama was there for all to see. When demonstrators chanted "the whole world is watching," they were announcing the arrival of the postmodern era, in which time and space can be magically modified by media of communications, in which boundaries are not what they used to be, and in which ancient social constructions of reality can wither in an instant under the bright lights of global scrutiny.

The Deep South's SCR—the one that said, "We know how to handle things here and the darkies are happy"—had not been in the best of shape anyway. The darkies knew it wasn't true for them, and a lot of the whites had trouble with it also, particularly when they had to defend it to outsiders. There seem to be few limits to the realities a society can create and keep alive as long as it is left alone, but the Deep South had never been exactly walled off from the world. Then in the 1960s, whatever walls there were came tumbling down, and the Deep South was in our living rooms.

Passion, drama, conflict. Put on a show, and Mr. and Mrs. America will turn out to watch.

It does not demean the civil rights movement to call it a piece of political theater, in some ways akin to the kind of huckstering that was in the early stages of turning the amiably air-headed Ronald Reagan into a president of the United States. Drama and the staging of dramas and the competition between dramas have become a central part of mass democracy. What made the civil rights movement such a compelling drama was the quality of the moral conflict; the Gandhian tactics showed people not merely fighting for what they had coming, but risking their lives in the service of a higher principle. If the demonstrators had marched down the road to Selma with submachine guns, we would have had a drama down around Kohlberg's Stage 1. But they marched peacefully, and put on a show that moved a nation.

Another thing in favor of the demonstrators' cause was that they were on the side of the Constitution. They were mounting an assault on the reality structure of the Old South—and, although this was less clear at that time, on our images of black people—but they were not challenging basic American values and beliefs. They were only demanding things that are enshrined in the Bill of Rights and the Fourteenth Amendment and in all our rhetoric about freedom and equality. They were asking the country to live up to its own ethos.

I am sure there were plenty of self-serving agendas among the demonstrators and do-gooders, societies of mind on all sides, all kinds of personal fantasies being acted out. But out of it emerged some constructive moral discourse, some closing of the gap between our public ideals and our actions, some tangible gains embodied in civil rights legislation. We made a little progress, and we would not have made it when we did if some people had not put on a fight and put on a show, and got Mr. and Mrs. America to watch.

But political theater does not automatically help us become wiser and more compassionate people. Such outcomes require certain situations, and certain commitments. Many people know how to dramatize issues and manipulate the media—or be manipulated by the media into producing the kind of political action that excites the public—but not many people know how to dramatize issues to any *purpose*, such as expansion of our moral or intellectual understanding. Nor do I see many political activists willing to consider the possibility that some issues are simply not going to be better understood through being dramatized for the media and the masses.

Certainly there was not much evidence of such thinking in the later years of the 1960s when the country was getting drunk on political drama and melodrama, tragedy and comedy—more assassinations, more protests and counterprotests, a war, and—what fun!—a presidential election.

By 1968, America was well into a kind of political/media frenzy that no society in the past had ever experienced. Basic American values and beliefs were being openly challenged; this produced a new kind of radical, a different approach to revolution. Gone, at least gone from the public eye, were the dour and dedicated types who fought obscurely for their cause. In their place were whimsical media characters who seemed to be based more on Tristan Tzara and the *surréalistes*. Consider the difference between a 1930s archetype of a politically committed person, Robert Jordan in Hemingway's *For Whom the Bell Tolls*, and Jerry Rubin of the 1968 Chicago demonstrations and the subsequent Chicago Seven trial. Jordan's story is played out among a band of simple peasant revolutionaries who are trying to blow up a bridge—one small part in a complex military story that they barely comprehend; he does his part, and dies. In the movie version of the book, he is played by the tight-lipped Gary Cooper. Jerry Rubin's story is played out in front of the cameras, in a huge media event that the whole world is watching. He does not bother to blow up any bridges. He is a postmodern revolutionary, engaged in the blowing of minds; he and his colleagues are out to upset our social constructions of reality. He is of course played by himself, and instead of dying in obscurity, he decides to change his image and goes to work on Wall Street.

The big times in Chicago in 1968, during the Democratic national convention, were a different kind of drama from the civil rights marches of a few years earlier. They were much more pseudoevent, ambiguous and capable of being interpreted in many ways. All kinds of exciting things were going on in Chicago; what did they mean, and what did they accomplish? Were the riots and battles with police outside the Democratic convention hall swaying the opinions of the delegates, or of the public who watched the events on television? If so, were they being moved toward an anti-

Vietnam War position, as many people a few years earlier had been moved toward a pro-civil rights position? Who knew? Undoubtedly many of the protesters believed they were pushing history in the right direction. But Abbie Hoffman, sometime before his death in 1989, wryly remarked to a reporter: "1968 was a great, wonderful year. They don't make years like that anymore. And if it weren't for our efforts, we'd have a president today sending troops off to exotic countries like Lebanon and Grenada and bombing cities like Tripoli."[11]

When political action gets to be as much fun and games as it got to be for Abbie Hoffman and some of his friends in the late 1960s, a huge bawdy confused drama in which you have a rousing revolutionary-hero role and the whole world is watching, you don't really have to have tangible political victory to feel "empowered." You are already getting a kind of gratification that is the envy of millions of others who would love to get themselves so solidly into the act. The drama becomes an end unto itself.

I am not accusing Hoffman and Co. of being hypocrites. The old-fashioned idea of hypocrisy really doesn't tell us much about the motivations of political activists, especially what happens to political activists when they get into the political theater. I am sure they believed in what they were doing, wanted an end to the war, and probably would have undergone some personal suffering to bring it about. But they were not suffering; that message came through clearly amid the confusing and contradictory events of the times; they were having a great time on that big stage. And to make it even more fun they told themselves, and us, a story that the fun and games were a new and painless form of political progress. Rubin wrote that "Yippie is the gestalt theater of the streets, compelling people by example to change their awareness. Entering a Congressional hearing room in a Paul Revere costume or wearing judicial robes to a court proceeding is a way of acting out fantasies and ending repressions."[12] Christopher Lasch, in *The Culture of Narcissism*, countered:

> Acting out fantasies does not end repressions, however; it merely dramatizes the permissable limits of antisocial behavior. In the sixties and early seventies, radicals who transgressed these limits, under the illusion that they were fomenting insurrection or "doing gestalt ther-

> apy on the nation," in Rubin's words . . . had so few practical results to show for their sacrifices that we are driven to conclude that they embraced radical politics in the first place not because it promised practical results but because it served as a new mode of self-dramatization.[13]

The radicalism of the 1960s has become another cultural artifact—a sort of historical media event, endlessly replayed and reinterpreted, written about and documented in films and television. Most of the nostalgia casts the young radicals of the time in a heroic role, but once in a while dissenters like Peter Collier and David Horowitz come along with a contrary message. In their 1989 book, *Destructive Generation*, Collier and Horowitz (who were both editors of the radical magazine *Ramparts* in the sixties and later became Reagan Republicans) blasted their former allies on the New Left as a bunch of preening juveniles, stoned on slogans and fantasies of power.[14] The book received politically correct reviews—writers on the left called the authors turncoats, the conservative *National Review* called them "eloquent converts"—but David Burner, reviewing it in the *New York Times*, pointed out that Collier and Horowitz had moved from left to right without any real change in their melodramatic style of perceiving political reality: "The large denunciations, the obsession with enemies, the delirium of half-sleep remain." He went on to say:

> For Mr. Collier and Mr. Horowitz the matter is quite simple. Their radical politics of the 60s were wrong; their conservative politics of today are correct. This assumes that a correct position could have been found amid the realities of a repressive and brutal Vietnamese Communism, a weak and brutal anti-Communist Saigon and an American war that could only pile up bodies. What the authors might have found—what numbers of Americans on both sides of the Vietnam question had found or had possessed from the first—were skepticism, ironic perception and judgment. The concept of discovery offered by the authors of "Destructive Generation" is that of switching sides.[15]

But deep engagement with the ironies and tragic complexities of the human condition may get kind of dull. If such a position can be dramatized, fine; if it can't, it may remain the property of small minorities of people, ignored by the millions who watch the TV shows and elect the presidents. This is the issue that mass democracies are going to have to come to terms with: whether we can construct our large-scale public realities in forms that enable us to grow and change and engage the difficulties of life in adult ways, or whether we will inevitably gravitate toward simple fables of good guys and bad guys.

David Burner noted that many people formed a deeper and wiser view of the Vietnam experience—and, I suspect, many people formed a deeper and wiser view of war itself during those difficult, dramatic years. The protest movement, including the Yippie contingent, no doubt contributed something to that. But the signal-to-noise ratio was not good. There was a kind of moral emptiness in much of the anti-establishment posturing, something that appeared to many people to be not youthful idealism, but plain immaturity. The old propaganda-fed American fantasy that we are always the good guys in a war took a serious beating; the protestors relentlessly ridiculed that fantasy, but in the process many of them became caught up in a good-guy/bad-guy fantasy of their own.

Now we are far into the age of biopolitics, with governments being forced to deal with new issues—deforestation, global climate change, biotechnology, protection of genetic resources—for which their institutions were not created nor their leaders trained. These are enormously complex and troubling issues, and in a way you can hardly blame the image-makers of the Reagan years for wanting to leave all the environmental stuff out of their fantasies of a new era of American power, prosperity, and popularity—it kind of tended to deconstruct the story.

But environmental problems can be dramatized too, it turns out; simple stories with simple plots can be forced down on top of them, creating opportunities for some people to be the heroes in stirring dramas that provide great personal satisfaction for the participants. As environmental concerns have moved to the forefront of public consciousness, new organizations get into the act—organizations like Earth First!, who are scornful of dull political techniques such as lobbying, and instead practice various forms of Yippie environmentalism. This ranges from demonstrations (with the demonstrators dressed in animal costumes to dramatize the plight of endangered species), to acts of vandalism (such as tearing up the strawberry plants that were to be sprayed with "ice minus" bacteria in a California biotechnology test), to "spiking" trees (driving a spike deep into a tree so as to cause damage to a power saw and injury to a person who tries to cut the tree down).

The antics of Jeremy Rifkin, his personal drama of saving the world from biotechnology, provide an excellent example of the ongoing degradation of protest politics. Rifkin came on the scene in 1977, at a National Academy of Sciences forum on recombinant DNA research, when he and a group of his followers disrupted the meeting by singing "We shall not be cloned" to the tune of "We Shall Overcome."[17] Anybody who noted that event should have had a good idea of what was coming. It was, first of all, an attempt to insert into a difficult issue of science policy—safety regulations—an image that was dramatic, sexy, easy to understand, and totally irrelevant to what was going on. Nobody was cloning human beings or had any interest in doing so; that was not the reality of the scientists or the administrators—but it was the reality that Rifkin sought with some success to impose upon the event. He also managed to borrow some of the moral intensity of the civil rights movement, the feelings wrapped up in the tune of "We Shall Overcome," and graft it by a sort of semiotic gene transplant onto an entirely different set of issues.

Rifkin's approach to his biotechnology crusade mixes drama—conflicts, charges, Frankenstein scenarios such as his warning that use of the "ice minus" bacteria to prevent frost damage to crops might have major effects on the climate—with attempts to back up his positions with absolute truths. He circulated a "theological letter on biotechnology" to convey the impression that God is opposed to it, and in various writings (including a book entitled *Who Should Play God?*) has repeatedly passed down the word from nature that we do not have her permission to splice genes or do tissue culture. Those acts embody the two main techniques of political persuasion available in a society where (a) ideologies are defunct, and (b) nobody really knows anything about the issues being debated: dramatize all issues down to TV-news simplicity, and pull Absolute Truths out of your sleeve to back up what might otherwise have to be presented as mere personal opinions.

On both the political right and the political left, we see a general recognition that reality is not what it used to be and a general willingness to create for the public any reality that serves one's political purposes. Conservatives wrap themselves in the flag—George Bush's crusade for an amendment against flag burning is a classic example of an attempt to get personal political mileage out of a symbol—but also manufacture realities with a skill that often leaves liberal opponents in the also-ran column. Radicals sometimes embrace traditional political values or official American norms—such as the Bill of Rights—and at other times celebrate the blow-it-all-away nihilism of Yippies or punk rockers, and at yet other times flirt with the new fundamentalism of ecotheology.

Although everybody with a political agenda routinely professes great respect for the wisdom of the American people, the actual behaviors reveal not respect but thinly veiled contempt.

THE APPROXIMATE NATION

And while we struggle to make sense of the various fictions offered us daily from left and right, we must also struggle to make sense out of the fiction of America itself.

We noted in a previous chapter that one of the most central fictions of politics is the fiction of a "people"—an aggregation of human beings distinguishable from other aggregations of human beings and therefore capable of being organized into a political unit; an "us" that can be identified as separate from "them."

The United States of America has always had a particularly hard time with the "people" fiction. Its people obviously didn't spring out of the soil. They came to it from many different places, and had to take it away from the people who were already at home on it. And when Americans did begin to form patriotic identities, it was usually a loyalty to a state—a kind of loyalty that nearly scuttled the nation-building enterprise at the beginning and again in the Civil War and that still gives Washington trouble from time to time.

Then there were the massive waves of immigration, much of it from parts of the world far different from those that had sent earlier colonials over to become Vermonters or Virginians. This caused a great deal of anguish about the future of American cultural traditions, and led to the creation of a new American culture. There is a difference between merely having a culture and not giving the matter much thought, versus having an *idea* of culture itself, so that you think of your culture as a thing to be admired and preserved. What you really do when you seek to preserve a culture is create it. Americans created an odd mix of ideology and state religion called "Americanism." You don't hear much about Americanism any more, but there was a time when newspapers regularly editorialized in favor of it and outside observers commented on how odd it was that a nation should be so self-conscious about its value and belief system.

How could you not have some kind of an "ism" when you were trying to get several million human beings of all sizes, shapes, colors, classes, religions, and cultures whipped together into a "people" that could function as a nation in a world of nations? Something had to be created, and then passed on to the newcomers. And so, in the early years of the twentieth century, "Americanization" was a keystone of federal policy. The government had a post of director of Americanization under the Department of Interior, and a variety of educational programs designed to help immigrants (in the words of a Bureau of Americanization publication) "renounce allegiance to their old and prepare to live or die for the glory of the new—America."[18] I have a photograph of an Americanization class of this period. It shows a classroom full of immigrant women watching four American ladies in costumes of the revolutionary era sewing an American flag—the Betsy Ross tableau. On the front wall of the classroom is a poster that says, in enormous block letters, BE LOYAL. All this was some decades before brainwashing as such, but the Americanizers had an idea of some of the fundamentals—particularly the importance of getting people to redefine their personal identities.

Creating and maintaining the identity of a "people" always mobilizes the arts, and in America the mass media played an enormous part. American culture, for better or for worse, is pop culture, and the American consciousness of the twentieth century rode on waves of media: the slick magazines, the coast-to-coast radio shows, the movies, television, records, and discs and cassettes. Maybe there are some purists off in their ivory fortresses who can imagine an American culture apart from the mass media, but for most of us it is quite impossible. We swim in that sea of symbols day and night, and in one way or another we must deal with it. Our intellectuals write learned discourses about Hollywood movies, and our nihilistic punk rebels parody pop culture with an emotional intensity that seems to mix equal parts of love and hate for the objects of their obsessive concern.

War is another great people-molder, and World Wars I and II were enormously useful to the Americanizers. World War II was a marvelous media event for those of us who had the good fortune to be a long way from the shooting. As a boy of hero worshipping years I felt totally immersed in it, thousands of miles from any battlefield. The radio filled my room with an endless chant of battle songs, patriotic songs, songs of servicemen separated from their girls and girls separated from their servicemen but vowing not to sit under the apple tree with anybody else. In the streets my eyes were dazzled by posters, flags, men in uniform. And, unsatiated by the daily dose, I went with my contemporaries to the movies every weekend for the adventures of the Army Air Corps, the Marines, the Fighting Seabees, John Wayne going over the top, Dana Andrews handsome and brave—but in an offhand, wry, American way—in his gallantly crushed pilot's cap.

There are undoubtedly many reasons why some slightly amended version of the same story couldn't be successfully packaged and sold again in the 1960s: GI Joe returns. Good-guy Americans overcome evil aggressors and are welcomed joyously by the people they have come to liberate. Many people tried to fashion such a story; the sad and confused history of the Vietnam years includes its share of media symbolism: the "Ballad of the Green Berets," the indefatigible Bob Hope entertaining the troops. But mythmaking is an imprecise art, and somehow that particular reality did not prevail. In the long run, it is just another story worn down by too much information, too many rival realities. And instead of a new myth of America united, we had the defiant taunt of the counterculture musical *Hair,* in which the Vietnam War was described as white people sending black people over to kill yellow people to defend the land they took from the red people.

In the confusion and cultural conflict of the Vietnam years, America ceased to be a nation.

I mean that it ceased to be a nation in the traditional modern meaning of the word; obviously, the United States of America continues to be a fully accredited nation-state, with a federal government that functions rather well, a strong economy, a role of leadership in the world, and more or less distinct boundaries around it.

But the nation-states of the modern era had to be capable of great creations of fiction—the kind of fiction that the Americanizers tried to create, the kind that mobilizes people to go to war with other people—and I see very little evidence that the United States of America is capable of going to war. Serious moves in that direction—such as the Reagan adventures in Central America—are immediately compared to Vietnam, not to the happily hyped crusade against Hitler and Tojo and Mussolini. Even the Grenada invasion, an artfully managed nonevent that never threatened to interrupt anybody's college education, produced its protest movement. No doubt a Pearl Harbor would mobilize us against the attacker, but the United States is not likely to be presented with another drama like that one—and without some such provocation, not able to get the public solidly behind any really costly entry into a situation as ambiguous as Vietnam was, or as Nicaragua has been in more recent times. We are no longer capable of war. The United States of America has evolved into something very like the nation-states of the modern era, the sovereign war-makers—but something else, something we do not yet know how to define.

This idea, thus baldly stated, will no doubt strike many readers as far-out. However, I have heard the same thing said, a bit more cautiously and usually with a note of regret, by men with stars on their shoulders. And always said off the record, because there are stage and backstage areas in the postmodern mass democracy. For the audience, you pretend that the old reality structure is still in place; among your colleagues, you admit that it isn't.

And that is one of the reasons that we invest so much energy in professions of loyalty to that structure, in keeping the myths of America pumped up and visible to the crowds—because we doubt very much that there is anything underneath it.

The issues that will face us in the years ahead will not have so much to do with whether we are capable of war, as whether we are capable of peace—of maintaining a pluralistic society that does not have to hold itself together by kitsch symbolism, does not have to manufacture pseudowars to make itself feel good, and can change. Change will be the tough one. As more and more people recognize that the institutions we have are human and fallible in nature, pressure for new and much different ones will inevitably rise; all things may not be possible, but many people may be hard to persuade that anything at all—such as great changes in the distribution of material wealth—is impossible. We may well face major global environmental disasters that call for huge, dramatic, and rapid shifts in a whole range of public policies. These are issues that we may not be able to reduce to simple dramas, and will have to face in a new political world, without the old myths, without many people having bought the new ones—without, in fact, a great deal of unity except an accident of history and geography that puts all 250 million of us in the same country.

I suspect (and hope) that we will find our principles, norms, and values to have a great deal of mileage in them, even though we come to realize that they are merely human creations. Many people knew that already and wonder what it is the crits and their enemies are getting so excited about. Most of the framework of American governance can be serviceable to a people (who aren't quite a people) finding their way into a world that nobody has seen before—not perfect, not the final word, but useful until something better comes along.

DEMOCRACY'S DILEMMA

Democracy is based on the noble and clear idea that people are capable of governing themselves—which means that they are capable of understanding what is happening and making rational decisions about it.

But it is becoming extremely difficult to understand what is happening. Although the main ingredients of understanding—stories and information—are present in abundance, they do not come together in ways that lead the masses to wise engagement with their world.

It is frequently said that we are living in the "information age"—meaning that our time has, among its other delights, an unprecedented amount of information. We also have, of course, an unprecedented range of activity concerned with gathering information, sorting it, filing it, recording it, buying and selling it, transmitting it, and otherwise pushing it about. I write these words at a table with two computers on it, next to a filing cabinet, in a room full of books.

Information overwhelms us, and it overwhelms our beliefs. Most of the belief systems that people found satisfactory in older and simpler times came into existence as stories that adequately arranged the information that was available at a certain point into coherent explanations of life, but the accumulation of further information becomes a constant source of irritation: the information has to fit the story, or the story has to change to fit the new information, or the information has to be denied or repressed. The Christian church has been in retreat before science for centuries, countless clerics agreeing wholeheartedly with Martin Luther's characterization of knowledge as mistress of the Devil. That battle is still on, as the creationists lamely try to beat back the deluge of scientific research that fails to confirm the Genesis version of how we got here.

Political ideologies are not in much better shape. Daniel Bell's declaration of the end of ideology appears to have been a correct assessment of what was happening to the master systems of thought about governance and power. They, too, tend to deconstruct as accumulations of contradictory data come in. Marxism, perhaps the most impressive intellectual edifice of them all, might have outlasted other ideologies if there hadn't been so many Marxist governments around—each providing mountains of evidence that The Revolution wasn't turning out quite the way it was supposed to.

Yet if the more rigid ideological systems, the old explanations of where we came from and where we are going, seem to be in some trouble, the human mind continues to think in terms of stories—naturally seeks to order experience, looks for explanations of sequences of events, is attracted to dramas.

The dilemma of democracy is that, while governance issues grow ever more complex and information more copious, the systems of mass communication make it ever more possible for political operators (left, right, and center) to distort this complexity—to reduce it down to simple stories most people can understand without too much trouble, and can believe as long as they don't take in too much information.

We move every day into a world that makes greater demands on the intelligence of citizens, while the energies of our communicators are focused directly on the creation and dissemination of idiotic stories about what is going on. Any political aspirant who does not play the Clem Whitaker game is in serious danger. It is a long time since Adlai Stevenson launched a political campaign by saying, "Let us talk sense to the American people. Let us tell them there are no gains without pains." Stevenson lost that election to a man who had a much nicer smile.

I don't know if this problem is soluble. One way people attempt to solve it in practice is to separate image from substance, stage from backstage; campaign symbolism and White House glitz create their own reality, one with only occasional points of contact with the substance of government. Where they do contact, image comes first. And as we become more given to mass-media politicking, we may be driving a deeper wedge between politics and governance than there has ever been. While governance becomes more complex, politics becomes more simple-minded. The public is beguiled with media images, noble lies, theatrical poses, and half-truths disguised as absolute verities. Never have there been such easy answers to such hard questions.

One thing we might reasonably do in attempting to think our way into the postmodern era is to recognize that, once we let go of absolutes, nobody gets to have a position that is anything more than a position. Nobody gets to speak for God, nobody gets to speak for American values, nobody gets to speak for nature.

Arthur Schlesinger, Jr., one of the last of the great liberal intellectuals of the modern era, showed a surprising hospitality to the possibilities of the postmodern era when he wrote:

> It is this belief in absolutes, I would hazard, that is the great enemy today of the life of the mind. This may seem a rash proposition. The fashion of the time is to denounce relativism as the root of all evil. But history suggests that the damage done to humanity by the relativist is far less than the damage done by the absolutist—by the fellow who, as Mr. Dooley once put it, "does what he thinks th' Lord wud do if He only knew th' facts in th' case."[19]

Lacking absolutes, we will have to encounter one another as people with different information, different stories, different visions—and trust the outcome. Because once we enter fully into a world in which reality is socially created, democracy is all we have left, and it is a much bigger game than the one Thomas Jefferson and Alexander Hamilton played a couple of hundred years ago.

PART FOUR

FAITH AND FREEDOM

CHAPTER 8

The Magic Bazaar

Some people really believed that the modern era was going to bring an end to religion, the final triumph of reason over superstition: God is dead, remember? Instead, we seem to be in a world with more religion than there has ever been before. However, the situation is not really one to warm the heart of a true believer; the growth seems to have been quantitative rather than qualitative—more things to believe in, but not necessarily more of what we used to call belief. G. K. Chesterton once said that the trouble when people stop believing in God is not that they thereafter believe in nothing; it is that they thereafter believe in anything.

Nowhere is the reality-diversity of postmodern life more evident than in the area of religion. Opinion surveyors occasionally explore the belief systems of contemporary people, their views of the cosmos, their religious convictions and superstitions. And the findings are an amazing revelation to anyone who really believes we are living in a secular-humanist society. It turns out that beneath the rational surface of the more-or-less secular "realism" that is supposed to be our official worldview—and not too far beneath it, either—lurks a seething cauldron of cults and faiths of all description. Surprisingly large numbers of people profess a surprisingly wide range of belief, from fundamentalism through all manner of spiritualism and superstitions to black magic and Satanism.

In some ways, we have not come so far from the medieval days when there was one Christianity for the intellectuals and another for the common people. We have today an official worldview professed by the majority of people who hold positions of power in government and business: essentially a secularism with a dash of religion thrown in for respectability. If you sampled the beliefs publicly held by representatives of this elite group—presidential candidates, for example—you would find little diversity.

But out there in the Republic is religious diversity of a sort never seen anywhere. We are the inheritors of beliefs and practices from centuries past, and from civilizations all over the world. And the climate of toleration is, on the whole, excellent. It is not too good an idea to be a card-carrying Sufi if you want to be appointed to the Supreme Court, but on the other hand you can probably make a good living at it. In the Middle Ages you could be burned at the stake for practicing witchcraft. Today you can write books about it and appear on television.

Never before has any civilization openly made available to its populace such a smorgasbord of realities. Never before has a communications system like the contemporary mass media made information about religion—all religions—available to so many people. Never before has a society allowed its people to become consumers of belief, and allowed belief—all beliefs—to become merchandise.

THE BELIEF BASKET OF THE WORLD

For the creators and consumers of religious reality, the United States is a marvelous marketplace. You can look around and find an endless variety of belief systems with stories about everything, explanations of everything, myths and morals for every taste.

We have, to begin with, the Bible: Old Testament stories of the six-day creation, the flood, the parting of the Red Sea, the visions and burning bushes and pillars of salt; and New Testament stories of miracles and resurrection from the dead. We have the Roman Catholic version of the story of Christ, which adds that his mother was not only a virgin but was conceived free of Original Sin so she would be worthy to give birth to him. We have the Seventh-day Adventists, followers of a Baptist minister who predicted that Christ would come to earth in 1844. We have the Church of Jesus Christ of Latter-day Saints, whose founder, Joseph Smith, was (its members believe) visited by angels, one of whom gave him plates of gold inscribed with what is now known as the Book of Mormon and that told of tribes who came to America several centuries before Christ.

Then we have imports from the Orient, some that have been around for a long time and some just off the boat: Buddhism;

Islam; Yoga; Vedanta, based on Hinduism; and Theosophy, based on Buddhism and other Eastern teachings. We have the Rosicrucian order, a modern re-creation of an ancient esoteric tradition; and Eckankar, which teaches about the spiritual travel of the Soul Body.

We have uniquely American religions such as the Church of Scientology, founded by science fiction writer L. Ron Hubbard.

We have Satanism and witchcraft, beliefs that so many societies have tried so hard to stamp out, now flourishing in the marketplace. Satanism, to be sure, is in some trouble these days owing to reports of satanic rites involving child molestation, but for some years its most visible promoter, Anton S. LaVey, founder of the Church of Satan, was sort of a celebrity. He published three books (one of which, *The Satanic Bible,* sold widely) and was a special adviser on the occult to the movie industry; he also played the part of the devil in *Rosemary's Baby.* The basic principles of LaVey's version of Satanism sound more like a manifesto of yuppie go-for-it than anything diabolically evil. They are, exclamation points and all, as follows:

1. Satan represents indulgence, instead of abstinence!
2. Satan represents vital existence, instead of spiritual pipe dreams!
3. Satan represents undefiled wisdom, instead of hypocritical self-deceit!
4. Satan represents kindness to those who deserve it, instead of love wasted on ingrates!
5. Satan represents vengeance, instead of turning the other cheek!
6. Satan represents responsibility to the responsible, instead of concern for psychic vampires!
7. Satan represents man as just another animal, sometimes better, more often worse than those that walk on all fours, who because of his divine spiritual and intellectual development has become the most vicious animal of all!
8. Satan represents all of the so-called sins, as they lead to physical or mental gratification!
9. Satan has been the best friend the church has ever had, as he has kept it in business all these years![1]

In a sense, the opposite of the last declaration may be true: one of the things that is keeping Satanism alive is the obsessive interest that some conservative Christians have in it. Although LaVey did manage to publish a few books, most of the literature about Satanism comes from nervous Christians who have recorded in vivid detail all the stories about satanic rites and practices—profanity, desecration of sacred objects, ritual slaughter of animals, murder and rape and mutilation of human victims—found in rumor and folklore. Yet another form of social construction of reality: the opponents give life and longevity to that which they oppose. Gordon Melton says in his *Encyclopedia Handbook of Cults in America* that "the Satanic tradition has been created by generation after generation of anti-Satan writers. Sporadically, groups and individuals have tried to create groups which more or less conform to the Satanism portrayed in Christian literature."[2]

Witchcraft—yet another part of the contemporary American religious scene, and not in a way that a Salem Puritan could ever believe—has some similarities to Satanism, both in its back-to-nature urges and its deliberate roguishness. But it is much more out in the open, less dependent for its existence on the imagination of its enemies, and in some circles downright trendy.

It comes in many packages: national witchcraft organizations include the Church of Circle Wicca, Saxon Witchcraft, the Covenant of the Goddess, and the Temple of the Goddess Within. According to my main reference source, over thirty thousand people in North America consider themselves witches and neo-pagans, and slightly over half of those are women. Witchcraft has a strong feminist appeal, all the more so because of the patriarchal structure and sexual biases of so many mainstream religions. All Wiccan groups worship goddesses and have female priests and honor the memory of the many women persecuted as witches. There are also lesbian separatists such as Zsusanna Budapest of the Susan B. Anthony Coven in Venice, California, who advocate all-female covens. (The only witch I have ever gotten to know personally is PBS radio reporter Margot Adler, a likeable person who is among other things a granddaughter of the great psychiatrist Alfred Adler and author of *Drawing Down the Moon,* one of the better-known books on the subject. Her husband, a psychologist, tells me he thinks of witchcraft more as a form of therapy than as a religion.)

And in addition to the various beliefs I have enumerated here, all of them with organizations and books and newsletters and rituals and groups of followers, there are many others that defy categorization: *The Encyclopedia of American Religions* mentions in its "other groups" section the Nudist Christian Church of the Blessed Virgin Jesus, which was founded by an Iowa man named Zeus Cosmos and seeks to establish clothes-optional public places across the United States; and the Kennedy worshippers who, soon after the assassination of President John F. Kennedy, began to report various contacts with the dead president's spirit, healings, and other miracles. A John F. Kennedy Memorial Temple was established in Los Angeles as the latter movement's headquarters.[3]

Other religions come and go, of course: I expect somebody to found a First Church of Joseph Campbell any day now.

And then there are the ever-present folk beliefs, such as astrology. I sometimes think astrology is America's true national religion. I certainly meet more people who want to explain events to me on the basis of the movement of the planets than people who are visibly involved in the cosmic struggle between God and Lucifer.

Astrology is a nice, user-friendly belief system. It doesn't ask much of you, and it explains any number of things: it tells you why you are the way you are, why your friends are the way they are (isn't that just like a Scorpio?), and why the things that are happening today are happening today. Although it is a body of beliefs that are quite capable of being tested and falsified, the charges of skeptics bounce off it like bullets off of Superman's chest. A recent book by one group of skeptics tells of a French investigator who placed an ad in a Paris newspaper offering: "Completely free! Your ultra-personal horoscope: a ten-page document. Take advantage of this unique opportunity. Send name, address, date and birthplace. . . ." He got about 150 replies, and sent them all the same horoscope, that of a man who had murdered several dozen people and dissolved their bodies in quicklime. He enclosed with each horoscope a self-addressed envelope and a questionnaire, asking about the accuracy of the reading. Ninety-four percent said the horoscopes were right-on descriptions of themselves, and 90 percent said their positive assessment of it was shared by their families and friends.[4] Most people with whom I have discussed astrology—people who believe in it—are usually eager to grant that there is a lot of foolishness connected with it, and many charlatans in the field, but the fools and the charlatans always seem to be somebody other than the person I am talking to and the person who did his or her horoscope.

Although the mass media tend to be rather contemptuous of unconventional beliefs, the media on the whole play an extremely important part in helping beliefs find their followers and potential consumers find things to believe in. You can pick up a publication such as the *Psychic Reader*, which circulates free of charge in the San Francisco Bay area, and find listed therein more clairvoyants, crystal dealers, and sorcery supply shops than anyone could ever hope for. You can also find the number of the Deja Vu Hotline, which provides "professional psychic readers for Clairvoyant, Business, Past Lives, Career, Body Weight, Future, Relationship and other types of readings."[5]

PRIMITIVE CHIC

Religion has its fads and styles, like everything in the symbolic universe—waves of belief washing this way and that—and the current wave of spiritual style in the Western world is washing in the direction of the past. The most stylish forms of religion in the United States at the moment are the primitive ones; shamanism, in particular, is very much in vogue.

My mailbox is a highly sensitive instrument for detecting these trends. I am on any number of human-potential and New Age mailing lists, and can hardly help noticing the changes that take place over the years in the kinds of announcements and promotions the daily post brings. I note very little on group therapy these days, nothing at all on encounter, still a fair number of advertisements for ways to open myself up to becoming wealthy and/or improve my sex life—and lots of shamanism.

The contemporary shamanic scene would certainly not be what it is, and quite possibly would not exist at all, were it not for Carlos Castaneda and his series of best-selling books. Castaneda's adventures with the old Indian sorcerer Don Juan may or may not be accounts of the real truth in the objectivist sense, but they are without question the reality of late-twentieth-century shamanism.

Castaneda has created it, much as Christian writers have created contemporary Satanism. The person who picks up an advertising brochure knows exactly where he or she is, immediately recognizes the archetypal characters such as the old wise man/woman and the young American apprentice. And there are plenty of advertising brochures. Castaneda himself was reclusive and most uninterested in making it possible for his readers to take up shamanic careers, but others are much more helpful.

I frequently receive mailings from the Dance of the Deer Foundation, inviting me to participate for a few hundred dollars in various programs led by a young man named Brent Secunda, who describes himself as a student of Don Jose Matsuwa, a 109-year-old Huichol Indian. "The purpose of all the activities," a recent brochure says, "is to guide participants to the direct experience of Huichol Shamanism, its ceremonies and pilgrimages to places of power and to help them integrate the elements of shamanism into their lives."

The Window to the West Foundation, located down at Carmel, not far from the Esalen institute, sent me a brochure offering a number of programs such as the following:

> *A Spiritual Warriors Journey*
> With Tom Little Bear $150.00
> Join other men and women on a spiritual warriors Journey to reconnect with our primal instincts. Spend 3 days living the way our Ancestors did for thousands of years, with the spirit of your power animal and the sacred mystical powers of the universe. You will learn how to make fire, arrows and lodges, all in the old way. Learn how to stalk, hunt and gather your own food. We'll paint our faces and dance, sing and drum together under the full moon. By building a sweatlodge near a creek, we'll go through a series of purification ceremonies to cleanse our bodies, minds and spirits of negativities and toxins and to come into a better relationship with the Great Spirit, our Mother Earth and all things that surround us. This journey will forever change your life. Call for dates.

Most of the shamanic events offered in this way feature Indian practices and teachers, but once in a while I get something a bit different. A leaflet that came recently from an organization called Aloha International offered courses in Hawaiian Shaman Training; one of them, an evening program, was entitled "Manifesting

Money"—something that I had never thought of as part of primitive religion, but which is very much a part of the New Age spiritual scene.

Castaneda's work has generated many literary imitators, the most successful being Lynn Andrews, who produced a female mirror image of the Don Juan stories. In her various books, she flies off to distant locales in search of secret teachings and has spectacularly good luck at it—far better than that of the countless frustrated hippies who tried to follow the path of Carlos Castaneda. Wherever she goes—and she has written books about travels to many different parts of the world—some native teacher, appropriately female, turns up almost immediately and initiates her into ancient and secret knowledge. Andrews is another one of the nonreclusive shamans: she lives in Beverly Hills, travels the lecture circuit, and gives private sessions in "spiritual counseling" for—according to the *Los Angeles Times*—$150 an hour.

There are also a number of neo-pagan organizations in the United States. Paganism is, philosophically, closely related to shamanism and to witchcraft, and pagan organizations are usually identifiable by their connection to a certain ethnic tradition: Norse, Druidic, and Egyptian are the most popular.[6] The people who belong to these groups are not necessarily of Scandinavian, English, or Egyptian origin, of course, nor are the rituals and practices of the organizations closely based on those of the ancient traditions they perpetuate: very little is known of those traditions. Neo-paganism, like shamanism, is a postmodern religion, not a premodern one.

Much of the reaction to postmodernism is not a reassertion of modernism, but a hankering for premodernism. Some people, of course, want to get back to the scientific rationalism and confident progress of the modern world, but there is a stronger and simpler appeal in getting back further yet—back into premodern religions and attempts to re-create premodern life-styles.

Obviously some of this is linked with despair over environmental problems—the belief that we can only solve them by retreating to the times before they existed, to the pre-industrial ways of living and producing that, whatever their drawbacks, didn't produce any Chernobyls. But myths of a lost Golden Age, cults of the Noble Savage, have been around a long time, since before the Industrial

Revolution, and what we are seeing now is a revival of those dark romantic urges.

The old romanticism comes back and blends in with the present, takes on environmentalist fervor and New Age millenarianism. At the time of the Harmonic Convergence a few years ago, the word went out along the New Age circuit that, according to the Mayan calendar, August 16, 1987, would bring a major cosmic event, a powerful configuration of the planets that would possibly be the End of the World or, as some believed, the End of Civilization. A young woman in Berkeley said, "If civilization collapses, we'll all become hunters and gatherers again." She seemed to think this would be a good thing; I had a hard time envisioning almost 250 million Americans hunting and gathering.

The idea of hunting and gathering as the best way of life has become quite popular recently, much more popular in some circles than the idea of simple farming as the best way of life. Many of the new primitives regard the beginnings of agriculture as one of humanity's major steps in the wrong direction. Most of the people who are drawn to such ideas do their actual hunting and gathering in grocery stores, but the *feeling* is there; it takes the form of a religion, is expressed by participating in American Indian rituals—or primitive-style rituals that are created anew. Primitivism and shamanism now form a subculture, with its own organizations, its own publications—handsomely produced slick-paper magazines like *Shaman's Drum*—and of course its own belief system.

The new primitivism is now a well-established part of Western society, and I do not expect it to fade away. I expect it to grow, in fact, as many people find it an attractive way to distance themselves from the stresses and uncertainties of the contemporary world. As we move into the twenty-first century, look for large numbers of people to be doing everything possible to turn back, as far back as the imagination will carry them.

CULT AND COUNTERCULT

A few years ago, over two thousand followers of the Reverend Sun Yung Moon got married, all in the same ceremony. They wore formal dress, and their march to the altar looked like a parade. The brides and grooms had not chosen each other, in the normal hit-

and-miss fashion that most of us are familiar with; rather, the mates had been assigned by church authorities. Some of the people who got married that day had not even been previously introduced to the mates they pledged to spend their lives with.

In South America, nine hundred followers of the Reverend James Jones stood in line at a vat of poisoned Kool-Aid, and yielded up their lives and the lives of their children in obedience to their leader.

In Poona, India, and later in Oregon, followers of Baghwan Shree Rajneesh stood in line to be admitted to the status of *sannyasin*, in which they would be given new names—take on a new identity and wear a necklace with a portrait of Rajneesh. They also contributed their money, and watched in admiration as their spiritual teacher amassed a fleet of over ninety Rolls-Royces.

The scene varies, the specific acts vary in content—simple, hedonistic, sincere, silly, reverent, suicidal—but the basics are usually there and immediately recognizable: first of all comes the leader, with his or her message—a body of beliefs, a prophecy, a way of dealing with personal problems. Then come the followers, and then come acts of submission to the leader.

Nothing about cults is inherently postmodern; they are a familiar pattern of human organization, a recurrent fact of life in the symbolic universe. Beliefs proliferate like weeds wherever people are found. But there are differences in the way cults function now. The postmodern era has created a uniquely hospitable environment in which the cult can thrive. The mass communications media not only provide a means by which the leader's reputation and message spread, but also provide, for some, a significant source of income from the sale of books, cassettes, and other merchandise. Cult leaders do get roughed up considerably in the media, but I suspect that few of them, for all that, would willingly go back to the old days of their predecessors who trudged along dusty roads and spoke to small gatherings in marketplaces.

And the legal climate has improved: not much remains of the whole repertoire of crucifixions, inquisitions, and other strategies whereby societies used to patrol the boundaries of reality, enforcing established beliefs and stamping out deviant ones. Cult leaders do manage to get themselves into a lot of trouble, but they don't get burned at the stake much these days. Cult leaders often claim that they are unfairly discriminated against—that their organizations deserve the same treatment as conventional religions, which are merely cults that got lucky. And they are quite right: Jesus was a cult leader, the Buddha and Mohammed were wandering gurus in their times. The Puritans were a cult, and so were the Quakers. It's another fuzzy boundary situation.

But the word "cult" has a meaning, and one that most of us understand. It signifies, among other things, reality in the making, new belief systems (usually variations on old ones) trying to become established. It signifies people trying desperately to reduce the range of choice in their lives by making one controlling choice to accept a certain body of teachings as the final word about what is real and what isn't. And it usually signifies a leader, a heavy dose of personal charisma. A remarkable transaction takes place as a cult forms—the followers agreeing to let some single human being become their primary definer of cosmic reality, the leader willingly taking on that role. Powerful psychological needs are involved, and I sometimes think that the leader is the greedier of the two parties to the transaction, a person who desperately needs a horde of uncritical followers to get a fix on his or her own reality.

And uncritical they are. When people decide to put some person in the role of The Teacher, they show a fascinating willingness to construct everything he or she does—every stupid, pointless, flaky, or fascistic action—as a part of his or her Teaching. After events in the Oregon Rajneesh commune deteriorated into what would look to most people like complete and dangerous looniness—wiretappings, drug use, poisonings, importation of thousands of street people to vote in local elections, buildup of an arsenal of rifles and semiautomatic weapons, finally criminal charges against the leaders and virtual collapse of the whole setup—many followers remained convinced that Rajneesh had designed the whole thing as a part of his teaching. "I wouldn't have missed the experience for anything," one said. "Bhagwan showed us at firsthand how power corrupts. He showed us how Fascism comes into being. Where else could you learn something like that?"[7]

Another common feature of the contemporary cult is the tendency to make increasing demands for loyalty and time on its members. This is psychologically sound, a way to deal with the problem of wavering, lukewarm followers. If you escalate the demands on individual members, require them to participate more and more intensely, they are going to be either pushed out or pushed in—in to total commitment. I had an opportunity to observe this dynamic firsthand in the 1960s when my wife and I were members of the Synanon organization in Los Angeles.

Synanon, then riding high, had expanded beyond merely being a rehabilitation center (and a good one) for drug addicts, and had developed a program called "Synanon for Squares," which mainly consisted of allowing nonaddicts to become dues-paying nonresident members of the organization and participate in weekly sessions of the rousing encounter-group process they call "the game." But if you signed on for that kind of membership and thought that was all it consisted of, you were wrong.

Every week, people invited us—rather forcefully—to come around and participate in some other activity: come join the group that's going to stay up all night and paint the kitchen. We got equally forceful invitations to donate things or money to Synanon. The invitations came with the message that if you didn't do more you were sort of a dilettante, a hypocrite, not really into the program. It became clear that you either made Synanon a major part of your life—all of your life, if you wanted—or got out. We got out, and watched from a distance as Synanon went down into its own whirlpool of cult madness.

Recently the newspapers reported on a fairly typical kind of conflict that had arisen within an organization called the Aggressive Christianity Missions Training Corps, a small authoritarian religious sect whose members wear military uniforms and whose leaders, a married couple, have the rank of brigadier generals. One of the cult's ex-members, a woman, had sued the group. She claimed they had brainwashed her. The group's leaders said they had merely disciplined her for having committed "spiritual adultery" by being excessively involved with her own family.[8]

Some cults develop beliefs involving prophecies of coming world events—the millennium, Armageddon—and a special role for the cult's members. So they have not only certainty about what is real, but important roles in a cosmic drama. The Arica organization, a religious movement that was going strong in the 1970s, sent out the word from its leader, Oscar Ichazo, a South American student of Gurdjieff and other teachings, that a "wave" was coming in the next few months, a massive upheaval of civilization, and that Arica members should hold themselves in readiness to assume positions of leadership when this took place. (Sociologists have written some interesting studies of what happens when cults dedicate themselves to a specific prophecy and then it doesn't occur.)[9]

Cult and countercult activities have become a familiar part of postmodern life, as different groups with different realities struggle for hearts and minds. All too frequently the hearts and minds in question are those of young people—children who have not only left the family home but relocated themselves into a new belief system, one totally alien to their parents and their Sunday school teachers.

Since the 1960s, countercult movements have grown in dedication and numbers—there are at least as many organizations fighting cults as there are cults, and quite possibly more. And they come in many packages: some are merely conservative Christian groups concerned primarily about *other* Christian groups that deviate too far from orthodoxy. These have been around for a long time, trying to straighten out Christian Scientists, Seventh-day Adventists, Mormons, Jehovah's Witnesses, and other such deviates. More recent crusaders, of course, tend to be more concerned about non-Christian beliefs. One anticult authority, Ronald Enroth of the Spiritual Counterfeits Project, uses the term "cult" exclusively for Eastern and occult groups, and calls the unorthodox Christian groups "aberrants." However, an equally prestigious authority in the field, Professor Gordon R. Lewis of the Denver Conservative Baptist Seminary, says the term "cult" should apply only to deviant Christian movements. These are tough times not only for absolutes, but also for definitions. But despite these relatively minor quibbles, conservative Christian leaders tend to agree that they are doing battle against Satan himself. "Satan," says anticult writer Dave Hunt, "is the author of every cult and false religion, and his imprint is clearly seen on them all."[10] The Christian anticultists, then, have got themselves cast into one of the more gripping dramas around.

The conservative Christian groups have done a lot of writing, preaching, and organizing against cults, but haven't accomplished all that much. The most aggressive and effective anticult movements have been secular ones backed by parents—people concerned less with saving souls and protecting Christian orthodoxy than getting their children away from the guru and back into the American mainstream.

In the 1960s, a man from southern California, whose daughter had abandoned her fiancé and her nursing career to join a Texas cult called the Children of God, joined with another man who had had a similar experience with a family member. The two formed a secular anticult organization, at first known as the "Parents' Committee to Free Our Children from the Children of God," later condensed to "Free the Children of God," FREECOG for short, and later yet reorganized as the "Volunteer Parents of America." In the early 1970s, Ted Patrick, one of the group's founders, developed the most effective and notorious weapon in the anticult wars, deprogramming.

Deprogramming was brainwashing. In order to "free" a cult member, the deprogrammers first had to kidnap him or her. Then came a period of forced detention combined with the familiar techniques for remodeling personal reality: interrogations, deprivation of privacy, assaults on belief and identity, and all the rest.

This was pretty rough stuff for a society that is supposed to believe in freedom of religion and freedom of choice, and the deprogrammers ran into heavy opposition—not only from groups like the American Civil Liberties Union, as might be expected, but also from the National Council of Churches and even from anticult organizations. Walter Martin, one of the leading Christian anticult writers, said in 1980: "I cannot stand behind such practices. It is true that cultists have been blinded . . . but it is also true that they have the right to make up their own minds, and we should not stoop to unChristian tactics to accomplish God's ends."[11]

The debate about deprogramming goes on, and often comes close to being a debate about social constructions of reality in general. Some sociologists have claimed—often with evidence to back up the charge—that cults practice their own forms of brainwashing to get and keep their members firmly in the fold. These include such techniques as constantly repeating doctrines, applying intense peer pressure, manipulating diet and depriving the member of sleep and privacy, forcing the member to cut all ties with the outside world, using rituals as affirmations of belief, and inventing new vocabularies that construct a new reality for cult members.[12]

But you can find sociologists such as Dick Anthony who argue, and also present good evidence, that membership in a cult (he prefers the term "new religion") usually has a positive effect on the mental health of the individual. Lowell Streiker, a northern California counselor, is also a defender of the new religions—and believes that the anticult movement has become a cult in itself, a "cult of persecution" essentially no different from witch-hunts and McCarthyism. Streiker says that what the new religions do to their members is no more a form of brainwashing than what society does to everybody: "Somebody being converted to a demanding religious movement is no more or less brainwashed than children being exposed to commercials during kiddie programs which encourage them to eat empty calories or buy expensive toys."[13]

KEEPING THE FAITH

We commonly think of religions as things that "last" for measurable periods of time, rather like the statues and cathedrals that represent them. And there is some continuity of certain central doctrines. Contemporary Christian anti-cult groups commonly use the Apostolic and Nicene creeds as standards by which to judge deviant movements, and Buddhists still learn the "four noble truths" that were uttered, it is said, by Gautama himself.

But religions are living entities, and they live in human minds. And they change as the times change and as human consciousness changes. There is little similarity between the worldview of the fourth-century Nicene Fathers and that of the twentieth-century conservatives who try to keep their faith intact by using the Nicene Creed—no more than there is between the California Indians of a thousand years ago and the people who play the Carlos Castaneda game in the Big Sur mountains.

Some kinds of religious change are visible and easily documented, others relatively invisible. We know that Christianity has gone through tumultuous events in recent centuries—the Reformation, the increased power of secular constructors of social reality, the institutionalization of freedom to choose other religions or none at all—and such changes inevitably bring modifications in the actual beliefs of those who still keep the faith. The ancient faith that is advancing into the postmodern world is not quite the faith of our fathers.

Take the matter of Heaven and Hell.

The hope of being rewarded in Heaven for a virtuous life on earth, the fear of being punished amid fire and brimstone for an evil one, have been central to the reality of believing Christians for centuries—and an endless source of material for Sunday sermonizing. But *Newsweek* reported, in a recent Easter issue, that Christian clergy are not much given to talking about the afterlife anymore; some avoid the subject because they think their listeners don't want to hear about it, and some because they don't believe it themselves. "The problem," a theologian told the magazine, "is that the (mainstream Protestant) clergy simply don't believe in the afterlife themselves, either the Biblical view or any other view."

Newsweek commissioned a poll, with curious results. First, it appeared that, however much doubt there may have been behind the pulpits, the pews were filled with believers: 94 percent of Americans said they believed in God, 77 percent said they believed in Heaven. Of those who believed in Heaven, three out of four thought they stood a good chance of getting there. However, they had all kinds of ideas about what the afterlife might be like—ideas that expressed personal preferences rather than religious dogma.

What really surprised the *Newsweek* writers was the discovery that Hell was nowhere to be found. Nobody other than a small minority of fundamentalists believed in its existence, and nobody even appeared to be much interested in the subject. "Hell disappeared," a church historian said. "And no one noticed." It had been quietly fading away for a long time, apparently—along with Calvinism and other visions of a stern and punitive God—and research revealed no mention of it at all in the indices of several scholarly journals of theology. Even the Roman Catholic church, although still officially committed to a belief in the possibility of eternal damnation, had virtually nothing to say about Hell in documents such as the publications of Vatican Council II.[14]

The Catholic church, as the Western world's largest structure of absolutist belief, is an especially interesting place to look for clues as to how traditional religions may adjust to the postmodern world. The church, a premodern institution, has already scored a remarkable achievement in surviving through the modern era; can it survive in a time when both beliefs and beliefs about belief are changing with unprecedented speed?

THE POPE'S PREDICAMENT

If I had to identify the one person in the whole world most discomfited by the coming of the postmodern era, I think I would nominate His Holiness the pope.

If you look at it one way, his job is an enviable one: high prestige, plenty of perks, tenure. But it requires him to be infallible, and these are tough times in which to have to be infallible.

Infallible he is: the doctrine of papal infallibility, as adopted by the First Vatican Council in 1869, declared that when the pope speaks *ex cathedra* on matters of doctrine, his definitions are "irreformable of themselves and not because of the consent of the Church." Armed with this tradition, he is, as one church historian put it, "the last of the absolute monarchs."[15]

Yet although the Roman Catholic church still clings to its image as keeper of absolute religious truth, absolutism has been fighting a losing battle for decades. As early as 1962, when Pope John XXIII convened the Second Vatican Council, it was obvious that there was a strong split between absolutists and those who favored a much more constructive attitude toward religious teachings. The church was suffocating under its load of doctrines, and so were its members. Bishops at Vatican II spoke openly what many priests and churchgoers must have secretly felt: that it was ludicrous to teach that eating meat on Fridays or missing mass on Sundays was a mortal sin. "Is this reasonable, and how many Catholics believe this?" demanded the outspoken patriarch of Antioch. "As for unbelievers, they merely have pity on us."[16]

Many official truths were revised by Vatican II, yet the final documents of the conference revealed the terrible crisis in which the Roman Catholic church finds itself: the council clung to the myth of the church's teachings as eternal truths, denied that it was changing even at the very moment when it showed itself to be changing and changing for the better. Unable to take a decisive step into the postmodern world, the church is deeply divided, with many of its members clinging resolutely to the past while others make up entirely new versions of Christianity.

Although the Roman Catholic church is the world's largest organized religion, with some 900 million members, it is eroding alarmingly and in several different ways. In 1971, the Vatican commissioned a secret study that leaked to the press and revealed that from 1963 to 1969, over 8,000 priests had asked for permission to leave the priesthood, and nearly 3,000 others had left without waiting for permission. The study estimated that over the next five years, 20,000 more would leave—and the estimate proved to be far too low. In Ireland, one of the great strongholds of Catholicism, there were, at the end of 1987, 6,000 priests and over 1,000 ex-priests. In the United States, there are now over 17,000 ex-priests.[17]

In some parts of the world—notably Latin America, another great stronghold, a place where, it is often said, you are Catholic just by breathing the air—another kind of erosion is taking place. Latin Americans are flocking to Protestant churches—not just Protestant, but Evangelical. In the Evangelical churches they sing hymns, hold hands, call one another by their first names. Richard Rodriguez reports that there are now more than 50 million Protestants in Latin America, that conversions are taking place at the rate of four hundred an hour, and that demographers are estimating that Latin America will be Evangelical by the end of the twenty-first century. What are the reasons? In part, it seems to be that people identify the Roman Catholic church with Latin America's failures, and its pain. "Generals are not the point of Latin America," Rodriguez writes. "Drugs are not the point of Latin America. Catholicism is the point of Latin America. . . . Latin America suffers because it is Catholic. Babies. Guilt. Fatalism."[18] Turning away from the failures and the fatalism, young men are attracted by the gringo preachers with their fancy suits; older men and women respond to its praise-the-Lord hopefulness. And the church fathers tell one another that the wanderers will come back, even though what they see is more and more of their own flocks wandering.

Even among those still within the church, belief is highly selective, which is not at all the way faith is supposed to be in a religion with a body of explicit doctrine and an infallible leader. Pope John Paul II, striving desperately to keep his flock from straying into distant postmodern pastures, insists that the church should be a "teacher of the truth. . . . Not a human and rational truth, but the truth that comes from God. . . ."[19] And on many occasions he has stated that the faithful do not have the privilege of window-shopping among the church's doctrines for those they find acceptable; they must accept the authority of the whole package. But his followers, many of them without even seeming to give the matter much thought, simply reject church teachings that do not strike them as human and rational.

A *New York Times*/CBS news poll found that 68 percent of American Roman Catholics favored the use of artificial birth control methods, 73 percent favored divorce and remarriage, and 55 percent favored legal abortion to save the mother's life or in cases of rape or incest. Asked whether is was possible to disagree with the pope and remain a good Catholic, 80 percent said it was.[20] In another poll, 93 percent of respondents told *Time* magazine they believed "it is possible to disagree with the pope and still be a good Catholic."[21] Clearly, infallibility is not what it used to be; great numbers of people see religious doctrine as something to be thought about, accepted selectively, changed with the times—not as something handed down from God. And once one link is broken in the chain that connects personal morality to absolute reality, the damage is done; even though the person may continue to enjoy the security of church membership, it is no longer the old-time religion.

"Curb your dogma" was the slogan on placards waved before Pope John Paul II when he visited San Francisco in 1987. Gays, their subculture deeply shaken by the endless waves of deaths from AIDS, would like to turn to religion—but gay Catholics, according to reporter Bill Kenkelen, "are particularly angry at the Catholic Church because, unlike other religious denominations, they believe it has denied them both respect and compassion by its emphasis on homosexuality as a sin."[22] Homosexuals are one group—a considerably larger one than church officials care to admit—that will be a continual source of dissent as long as the church clings to its present doctrines.

Women are another. Long the true rock of the church, faithful and obedient to its teachings, women have become increasingly restive. Many Roman Catholic women—including nuns—openly campaigned for changes in the official teachings regarding abortion and birth control. Organizations such as Catholics for a Free Choice publish surveys showing that a majority of Catholic women agree with the statement "The Church is too far behind the times," and that a great majority (77 percent) disagree with the statement "The Pope is never wrong when he speaks on matters of faith and morals."[23] The insistence on clinging to (and attempting to enforce) positions that most female members disagree with, the overall second-class status of women within the church, and the issue of ordaining women as priests are not only sources of internal trouble, but major factors in the decisions of many nuns to resign, and of other women to choose other paths in life.

Eugene Kennedy, a professor at Loyola University in Chicago, believes that the church is splitting apart into what he calls "two cultures," each with its own reality. "First Culture" Catholicism is the institutionalized church; "Second Culture" Catholics are almost invisible to the First Culture, and in turn refuse to pay a whole lot of attention to its power struggles and doctrinal disputes:

> They are definitely not the unobservant Catholics in name only who have, like the poor, always been with the church; neither are they actively rebellious, nor do they stand in the front ranks of those described as dissidents. They are psychologically independent of the canonically erected, clerically layered, heroically envisaged church that appears, according to the papers and television, to be the only one that exists.
>
> Second Culture Catholics . . . do not listen to supercilious discussions about whether purple should be replaced by blue as a liturgical color, and they cannot imagine that anybody, except the profoundly unreconstructed, would consider the latter as possessing religious significance. Culture Two Catholics do not follow the strictly ecclesiastical "news" whose buzz can be heard constantly in the pillared halls of the First Culture.[24]

Unable to understand such Catholics—unable, perhaps, even to perceive their existence—the official church keeps itself busy stamping out what it does understand, which is dissent: twenty-four nuns who signed a full-page *New York Times* ad affirming the principle of freedom of conscience on abortion were ordered to recant. Leonardo Boff, a Brazilian spokesman for liberation theology, was sentenced to a year of silence. John McNeil, a Jesuit priest who praised homosexual love, was silenced and then excommunicated. Charles Curran, who advocated liberal positions on birth control, divorce, and sexual behavior in his courses on moral theology at the Catholic University of America, was dismissed under orders from Rome. Matthew Fox, a California priest who mixed Catholicism with ecology, feminism, and New Age spirituality, was sentenced to a year of silence.

The leading figure in most of these disciplinary actions was not Pope John Paul II, but his lieutenant, Cardinal Joseph Ratzinger, prefect of the Vatican agency called the Congregation of the Doctrine of the Faith—and once known as the Holy Office of the Inquisition. Cardinal Ratzinger has carried out the duties of his office energetically, and along the way also upgraded the claim to absolute truth of the doctrines he was charged to protect. The faithful, he declared, must give "submission of intellect and will" not only to those teachings covered by the doctrine of infallibility, but also to other "ordinary" teachings. What that meant, in effect, was pulling fairly recent pronouncements such as prohibition on birth control up by their bootstraps into the realm of unquestionable truth.

Of all the deviations from doctrine, none has been more troublesome than liberation theology. Ironically, this explosion of religious/political activism got its impetus from the official church, from Vatican II. The conference inspired priests with a view of the church as protector of the poor, with the revolutionary idea that religious leaders should teach them to seek a better life on earth instead of waiting for their reward in the hereafter. It opened the door to a postmodern understanding that oppressive social structures of value and belief were mere human creations—human and sinful. Gustavo Gutierrez in Peru reinterpreted the doctrine of sin to include such actions as U. S. behavior toward Latin America and the Peruvian oligarchy's treatment of the country's peasants.[25]

In 1968, at a bishops' conference in Colombia, delegates from all over the Western hemisphere adopted a list of radical, politically oriented declarations based on Gutierrez's ideas. And at this point, a good portion of the Latin American clergy came into open opposition to the military-political establishment and to the church's traditional stance of placing itself in alliance with political authority while declaring itself nonpolitical. Whether the good bishops knew it or not, they were declaring war. As I read various accounts of the conference, I get a strong impression that many of them didn't know, were riding on a wave of 1960s euphoria, and thought the world would give way easily to their new ideals. But within the next ten years, 850 priest and nuns had been killed. And Cardinal Ratzinger had made it his chief priority to stamp out liberation theology, which he and Pope John Paul II regarded as an ungodly mixture of Christianity and Marxism.

There are definite elements of Marxist thought in liberation theology, particularly in its emphasis on class conflict, but liberation theology is not pure Marxist doctrine. It is not, in fact—and I speak of it in the present tense because it clearly has not been stamped out—pure anything doctrine. It is a new system of value and belief, created, as new systems usually are, out of bits and pieces of old systems of value and belief, with no apparent feeling of obligation to swallow any of them whole. It is pushing toward a new vision of the church, as more a Third World institution than a European one, and as far more pluralistic in doctrine and practice than it has ever been.

A spirit of innovation is definitely in the air, and it is incompatible with absolutism. Christ becomes a revolutionist in Brazil, an environmentalist in America. God himself gets a sex-change operation. A black priest in Washington, D.C., establishes an independent church called the Imani Temple, African American Catholic Congregation, and says a mass with African drums, bells, rattles, and folk songs.[26] A witch named Starhawk teaches at Holy Names College in Oakland. The center does not hold.

Yet, even while the infallible pope strives to keep his church from straying too far into dissent and disarray, he must deal with renegade reactionaries who think it has strayed too far already—and who produce their own kind of dissent and disarray. Followers of the ultraconservative French archbishop Marcel Lefebvre (who was excommunicated in 1988) reject the reforms of Vatican II and defiantly hold traditional mass—in Latin, and without that peace handshake. "We won't give in to relativism and modernism," declares an American bishop of Lefebvre's Society of St. Pius X. "Our Lord never said, 'I'm OK, you're OK.' Our Lord said, 'If you refuse me, you're going to hell.'"[27] A member of a St. Pius congregation in New York says, "With fundamentalism, we've found structure; things are clear now, black and white."[28]

So goes the church—in all directions.

ALMOST-POSTMODERN THEOLOGIES

The postmodern world sports as many theologies as cults, sects, movements, practices, and opinions. There is more theology than there has ever been—and there is no theology at all.

There is no theology because there really never was any theology. The word "theology," meaning knowledge of God, is its own contradiction in terms. God is the name we give to that which is beyond our knowing, and theology, as a profession for experts about that which is beyond our knowing, was in trouble from the outset. Yet the human mind yearns for understanding of the beyond, for what Paul Tillich called "ultimate concern," and in the twentieth century, the century of space and science, it has stretched toward images of the beyond quite different from the large bearded gentleman painted on the Sistine ceiling. And the theologies keep coming.

Several different twentieth-century theologians have tried, and to some extent succeed in, producing religious ideas that have something to offer to the postmodern world—not so much because of what they say about God, but because of what they say about the human condition. Like Pico della Mirandola's Renaissance vision of Adam as empowered to cocreate himself, they offer religious visions of a creative, dynamic human role in the world's reality—both in taking responsibility for what is, and in shaping what it becomes. Wolfhart Pannenberg's thought is known as "the theology of the future"—for its idea that we experience the freedom and sovereignty of God by facing the power of the impinging future, with its vast possibilities and unseen realities.[29] Another German theologian, Jurgen Moltmann, offers the "theology of hope," in which God is seen as having created the conditions that make it possible for us to innovate in the world, and sometimes succeed in our efforts, and thus have reason to hope.[30]

Of all contemporary theologies, process theology, which is based on the work of the English philosopher-mathematician Alfred North Whitehead, has had the greatest impact on postmodern thought. Whitehead came to America after a distinguished career as a mathematician at Cambridge and the University of London, and in 1924 became a professor of philosophy at Harvard, where he developed his "process metaphysics." (I sometimes wonder if Harvard knows how much it has contributed to postmodernism, or if it wants to know.)

Whitehead had a radically different idea of God, and a radically different view of the way we tend to think about reality. His God is changing along with everything else. He didn't like the idea of a permanent God, and he thought our notions about such a God were inseparable from our strange habit of thinking that reality had to have some existence outside of consciousness. He located the God most of us have heard about as a product of the Greek quest for the ultimate cause and the ultimate truth:

> The notion of God as the "unmoved mover" is derived from Aristotle, at least so far as Western thought is concerned. The notion of God as "eminently real" is a favourite doctrine of Christian theology. The combination of the two into the doctrine of an aboriginal, eminently real, transcendent creator, at whose fiat the world came into being, and whose imposed will it obeys, is the fallacy which has infused tragedy into the histories of Christianity and into Mahometanism.[31]

This "vicious separation of the flux from the permanence," he said, is at the root of our sense of ourselves as separated from God, and also at the root of our faulty thinking about the nature of truth itself. It leads to "the concept of an entirely static God, with eminent reality, in relation to an entirely fluent world, with deficient reality."[32]

In the process view, there is no ultimate reality to which things happen, and consequently we don't need—in fact should be on guard against—the absolutes we make up to describe ultimate reality. Whitehead, agreeing with the American pragmatist philosophers such as William James, with whom he had made common cause, thought that the "intolerant use of abstractions is the major vice of the intellect."[33] Writing about the same time that Karl Mannheim was doing his pioneering work in the sociology of knowledge, he also understood that we tend to give our abstractions independent lives. His term for reification was "the fallacy of misplaced concreteness."

Whitehead's thinking is currently much in vogue among young theologians, who find it a provocative and useful way of asking the big questions about the cosmos, and highly unpopular among more conservative thinkers, who don't regard it as theology at all. I sort of agree with both. It is provocative and useful, and it isn't theology. It is intellectually iconoclastic, and—by posing huge questions about the nature of the cosmos—also reveals that any final answers are not to be trusted.

I once heard an old man, Bernard Loomer, one of the leading scholars of process theology, give a guest sermon in a church.

Loomer had spent his life at the highest levels of religious philosophy—he was for many years dean of the divinity school at the University of Chicago—and what he had to say, after all those years of thinking about God, was this: "We are born in mystery, we live in mystery, and we die in mystery." He died not long after that, and left me thinking that I had been privileged to hear an honest and heartfelt statement from an unusually wise theologian.

CHAPTER 9

The Two Faces of God

Although the religious/spiritual scene is, to say the least, highly diversified, certain patterns run through it like figures in an oriental carpet. One such pattern, likely to jump into the foreground of our consciousness as ancient and not-so-ancient faiths struggle to find their places and their followers in the postmodern world, is the tension between two ways of being religious: the exoteric way and the esoteric way.

These are not exactly melodious terms, and I feel a little apologetic about asking readers to grapple with them—but they are precise terms, and to know the difference between the two is to open up a new perspective into the issues we have explored in the previous chapter. Most religious controversy has to do with belief; the exoteric-esoteric dialogue has to do with beliefs about belief.

The exoteric and the esoteric are the objectivist-constructivist polarization that we have seen in other fields—and are by far the oldest manifestation of it, foreshadowing by thousands of years the argument that has broken out in so many different guises in the postmodern world. They represent religious paths that move in opposite directions. They take different approaches toward the social construction of reality, and they produce different kinds of political power.

It will take us a while to get the feel of this distinction, but to begin with I will define exoteric religions as doctrinal, esoteric religions as mystical. Exoteric religions, such as institutionalized Christianity and Islam, are reified and deified belief systems that explain all reality and are capable of serving as a complete system of values and beliefs for a society. They are concrete, publicly available in scriptures and other official teachings; there is nothing secretive about them.

Mystical religions, such as Sufism and Zen Buddhism, are primarily traditions of individual instruction, somewhat coy in their way of going about their business, with strikingly different ways of transmitting knowledge—ways so different, in fact, that people sometimes wonder if they have any knowledge at all, or any real interest in transmitting it.

In a doctrinal religion the initiate or convert is presented with a clearly visible body of information to learn. Study your catechisms, kid. In a mystical tradition the student is given to understand that the truth is not to be learned in that fashion; the truth is something one must discover for oneself.

The history of religion is a history of the two tendencies pushing and pulling at one another. Sometimes the tension between the two becomes unbearably strong and culminates in crucifixions and inquisitions; at other times the two seem to be complementary, like the yin and yang of oriental symbolism or the two faces of a coin, each a kind of truth and useful in its own way.

IF YOU SEE THE BUDDHA ON THE ROAD, KILL HIM

Centuries before existentialism, modern art, or the sociology of knowledge, teachers such as the Buddha were describing the illusory nature of socially conditioned consciousness and urging people to "awaken" to a different sense of reality. Although Buddhism has become encrusted with exoteric formalisms and beliefs, at its heart it is not really a religion in the Western sense (it has nothing whatever to say about God) but rather a system for the development of consciousness. And that system is based not so much on learning in the Western sense as on unlearning: perceiving the illusory nature of social constructions of reality, particularly the illusion called ego.

Zen is perhaps the most radical of many iconoclastic reform movements that have periodically arisen over the long history of Buddhism—movements aiming to scrape off some of the encrustation and return to the pure essence of the teaching (or unteaching). "Iconoclast" means image-breaker. Iconoclasm expresses the ancient reluctance to be taken over by religious signs and symbols, to let the map become the territory. It is the same concern that prompted the biblical commandment against creating graven images, the Judaistic prohibition against using the name of God.

Zen emerged first in China around the seventh century A.D. as a

Buddhist school based on meditation: the word for meditation is *dyana* in Sanskrit, *ch'an* in Chinese, *zen* in Japanese. Meditation is a practice of sitting in silence and either obstructing the flow of internal verbalization by counting breaths or repeating a mantra, or learning to observe the mind's internal chatter as if from a distance. All of the techniques have the same goal, which is to open a gap between experience and the reification of it in words and symbols. Zen folklore is full of iconoclasms: I have read of monasteries where Buddhist scriptures were used as toilet paper. Zen sayings like "If you meet the Buddha on the road, kill him" would warm the heart of an old-time Parisian *surréalist* or a contemporary punk rocker.

The most famous of all the Zen proverbs is a question: "What is the sound of one hand clapping?" That in itself is enough to scramble anyone's mind—but look at a few more:

> A monk asked Nansen (an early Zen sage): "Is there a truth that has not been preached to men?"
>
> "There is," said Nansen.
>
> "What is this truth?" asked the monk.
>
> Nansen answered: "This is not mind, this is not Buddha, this is not a thing."[1]

> Here is a man on a tree holding one of the branches in his mouth, but neither clinging to any of them with his hands nor touching the trunk with his feet. Someone at the foot of the tree asks him, "What is Zen?" If he does not answer the question, he cannot satisfy the man, but if he speaks, even a word, he will at once fall down to death. At such a moment, what answer would you make if you were he?

> A monk says to his teacher: "My mind is troubled, will you pacify it for me?"
>
> "Certainly," the teacher replies. "Bring me your mind and I will pacify it."
>
> "Sir, I cannot."
>
> "There. I have pacified your mind."

> A monk asks his teacher: "Does a dog have enlightenment?"
>
> The teacher answers: "*Mu*." (No!)

Each of these is in the form of a dialogue between a monk and a sage, and essentially consists of the sage saying something that doesn't make a whole lot of obvious sense—sometimes *some* sense, other times absolutely contradictory messages. In either case the metamessage, as in a piece of deconstructionist text analysis, is that the text itself is fallacious, a prison of words from which one must somehow seek to escape. Deconstructionists are not, on the whole, terribly encouraging about the prospect of escaping ever; but Zen teaches that there is a possibility of escape, into enlightenment or liberation, a state of being in which one sees the world differently.

If Zen is remarkably similar to deconstruction, other Buddhist teachings are remarkably similar to constructivist cognitive science—particularly in their attack against the idea of the individual that Minsky calls the "single agent fallacy." Buddhism departed from the mainstream of ancient Indian religion with an explicit rejection of the *atman*, the central core or essence of the individual—an idea roughly comparable to the Christian doctrine of the soul. The Buddhist teaching is that such an idea is reification, a blind alley: *anatman*, said the Buddha. No atman.

In the Buddhist view, the experience of an individual is a lot of things happening—so many that it is wiser and less dangerous to think of oneself as a lot of things happening than as one thing happening. A parable in the Tibetan Buddhist tradition likens the individual to a sort of crowded town meeting. Once in a while somebody in this assembly gets up and makes a speech and carries the majority along with him on a certain course of action. Sometimes everybody has different ideas of what to do, and there are violent disputes. Sometimes members of the group leave or are forced out, die, or lose their voices. New ones come along, become bolder, and gain influence—even to the point of setting themselves up as dictators over the rest. Each of these members represents a component of the mind—an instinct, belief, tendency, or desire that is the product of ancient social and biological processes (*karma*) whose original beginnings are not known. Put together, in whatever order they may happen to be in at any given moment, they make up the "person."[2] This is from writings that predate by several centuries the publication of Minsky's *Society of Mind*.

I am not trying to prove here that Buddhism in any particular guise is "the same as" postmodern cognitive science or critical theory. Although Buddhism is in a sense an institutionalized attempt to break free of social constructions of reality—of culture—it is also, wherever it arises, a part of the very culture it is dealing with.

It is expressed in language even where it seeks to transcend language, and Buddhism frequently becomes equated in people's minds with certain specific beliefs—such as reincarnation—which really only get in the way of understanding the radical beliefs-about-beliefs that are at the heart of Zen and some schools of Chinese and Tibetan Buddhism. Western students often become confused about this, load on all sorts of cultural artifacts along with the transcultural message, and conclude that they have to go to some monastery in Japan to locate their true minds.

Although esoteric religions are not the same as postmodernism, they afford us a rich set of tools from which to get some perspective on our own cultural artifacts (even though we should not expect to escape totally from our cultures) and gain a deeper understanding of what is happening in our time. And Zen is only one of them, one that happens to be well organized and well known. There are others, such as Sufism.

THE DERVISH DECONSTRUCTIONISTS

The philosophy that has become known in the West as Sufism is a convenient description for a vast variety of schools and traditions that have existed in the Near East for immemorial centuries. No clear borderlines separate Sufism from other streams of oriental religion such as Hinduism and Buddhism—or, for that matter, from Judaism and Christianity, each of which has its own esoteric schools. Sufism, sometimes called "the heart of Islam," has ancient historical roots in the Arab world, in Persia, in Afghanistan, and in India—and today can be found thriving not only in those places, but also in South America, Europe, and the United States.

The Sufis have their own meditative practices—including the whirling dance of the dervishes—and their own stories that use words to try to guide the student *through* words into some form of "higher knowledge." Some of these are extremely difficult to make any sense out of in an ordinary way; others we would recognize as jokes; still others are more like what we would call parables, and are fairly easily translated invitations to take a critical look at ordinary reality. Consider, as an example of the third group, the story of the changed waters:

According to this tale, mankind was warned by Khidr (a mysterious teacher who often appears in Sufi stories) that all the water in the world, except that which was saved in a special way, would disappear and be replaced by different water—and that the new water would drive men mad. Everybody ignored the warning except one man, who collected good water and stored it in a safe place. When the forewarned day came, all the streams and wells went dry, and the man began to drink from his cache. And when he came out among other people, he found that they had all gone quite insane: they thought and talked differently, and they did not remember that they had been warned. And worst of all, when he tried to talk to them, they thought *he* was crazy. For some time, he continued to drink his own pure water, but he could not bear the loneliness; after a while he gave it up and drank the new water, and became like the rest, and forgot all about what had happened or where the water of sanity was, and was regarded as a madman who had become sane again.[3]

Nothing in this would strike a contemporary reader as particularly unusual—it could come straight from the pen of Timothy Leary or R. D. Laing—but we are looking at a story that has been circulated, used as a sort of teaching tool, for centuries.

In some of the Sufi stories you find what seem to be morals about reification. Tea is a recurrent theme, and seems to stand for wisdom or insight into the illusory nature of reality. It is something that comes from the East, that some people know how to appreciate for what results from using it and others begin to deify and turn into some*thing* that is revered in and for itself. In other stories a wise man comes along and says something worth hearing: some people listen to what he has to say, take it in, and forget about the man; others want to build a temple on the place where he stood when he said it.

EXOTERIC RELIGION: YOU BETTER BELIEVE IT

Esoteric religion focuses inward, on the transformation of personal consciousness; exoteric religion focuses outward on bodies of doctrine, symbols, rules, the organization and its visible structure. The most purely, radically esoteric schools view the outward teaching as a convenience, a vehicle sometimes useful and sometimes an obstruction—and never to be taken too seriously. D. T. Suzuki, who introduced Zen to the West, warned: "Whatever art or knowledge a man gets by any external means is not his own, does not intrinsically belong to him; it is only those things evolved out of his inner being that he can claim as truly his own."[4] A Zen saying describes all of Buddhist doctrine as nothing more than a finger pointing the way. Conversely, in the most extremely and purely exoteric religions, the outward structure takes precedence and becomes a thing revered, something to be protected against desecration—and the religious person is warned to be ever on guard against inner thoughts or feelings that threaten to conflict with the tradition. For the esoteric, the outward teachings have no existence apart from subjective consciousness. For the exoteric, the faith is real, rooted in the cosmos, above and beyond humanity.

Exoteric, doctrinal religions lend themselves nicely to becoming established religions, supported by the authority of a state and in turn supporting the authority of the state by teaching that it flows directly from God. The doctrine of the divine right of kings is but one example of many doctrines that have given shaky structures of human power the majesty that comes with being the earthly manifestation of cosmic order. Thus monarch, government, laws, offices are detached from their origins in more-or-less ordinary human minds and transformed into separate entities—reifications—with extrahuman reality.

It is easy to be critical of these political deals that have so persistently been cut between priests and monarchs, but it is hard to deny that exoteric religion *works* as a shaper of coherent social orders. The religion embodies the society's construction of reality; its doctrines make that reality available and more or less understandable to everybody. (If there are some parts of it you don't understand, you just figure, well, you're not that smart; the truth is there even if you don't quite get it.)

A doctrinal religion is a giver of order. It places the society and its institutions within the order of the cosmos, confers upon arrangements such as social classes and land ownership a rationale without which they might not make a whole lot of sense, and even creates psychological order within the individual citizen by determining which energies are to be encouraged and which repressed. It explains everything, and its explanations give it great power, because they are a shelter against the empty blue sky of meaninglessness.

Sometimes established doctrinal religions tolerate and even encourage esoteric schools; the esoteric schools in turn keep a low profile, go quietly about their business, and teach their students to obey the laws and respect the social traditions even while they are developing an ability to see the social construction of reality as arbitrary and illusory. The simple people who (presumably) have no capacity to learn about such things accept the SCR as the Scriptures describe it, say their prayers, obey the commandments, and look forward to getting a better deal in Heaven or in their next incarnation.

But there are certain inherent tensions between the two approaches, constant sources of trouble. Esoteric teachers tend to view religious doctrines with some skepticism and occasionally with outright scorn. Authorities in established religions sometimes revere the holy men and women, the meditators and seekers of visions—and sometimes have them killed. Esoteric experience and thought may well be close to the source of all religions, but it also can get in the way of the real business of established religion, which is maintaining social order.

The classic parable of a doctrinal religion's urge to cut itself off from its esoteric source is Dostoyevski's tale of the Grand Inquisitor: Christ returns to earth—specifically to Seville in the time of the Inquisition, where every day fires are lighted to the glory of God and heretics burned in public for sins of deviation from the official truths of the church. He is welcomed by the people, who recognize him and weep and follow him through the streets. But he is not welcomed by the Grand Inquisitor, who regards him as a nuisance. The two have a long conversation in which the Inquisitor lectures Christ about the realities of human nature—which are that people want to be told what to believe, and furthermore want to have everybody believing the same thing:

> This craving for *community* of worship (says the Inquisitor) is the chief torment of every man individually and of all humanity from the beginning of time. For the sake of common worship they've slain each other with the sword. They have set up gods and challenged one

another, "Put away your gods and come and worship ours, or we will kill you and your gods!" And so it will be to the end of the world, even when gods disappear from the earth; they will fall down before idols just the same.

The Inquisitor tells Christ that he missed a really good opportunity to do something worthwhile for humanity during his time on earth. He could have deprived people of their freedom, guaranteed them stability and plenty to eat, and established a good solid social order in which everybody would have been happy. But he blew it:

> Instead of taking men's freedom from them, Thou didst make it greater than ever! Didst Thou forget that man prefers peace, and even death, to freedom of choice in the knowledge of good and evil? Nothing is more seductive for man than his freedom of conscience, but nothing is more painful. And behold, instead of furnishing a firm foundation for setting the conscience of man at rest for ever, Thou didst choose all that is extraordinary, vague, and conjectural; Thou didst choose what was utterly beyond the strength of man. . . .[5]

Having railed at Christ extensively, the Grand Inquisitor first condemns him to be burned, then changes his mind and orders him to go and come no more. Christ departs, and the Grand Inquisitor goes about his business of establishing the Christian kingdom on earth.

YIN AND YANG

The ancient Chinese yin-yang symbol—a circle divided into two nestled segments, each reflecting the other and each containing within itself the seed of the other—is an elegant representation of many things that are opposed yet not entirely opposite: of male and female, of course, and also of the two religious tendencies we have been discussing here.

No religion is ever static and unchanging; religions, like ecosystems, are forever in transition. Esoteric religions frequently turn doctrinal, and exoteric religions give rise to spirituality.

Esoteric teachings are in constant danger of freezing into doctrines. Every spiritual teacher lives with the temptation to go beyond being merely a guide on an individual's path of self-discovery (a "dangerous friend," as the Tibetans sometimes put it) and turn into a messiah. Empire-building agendas regularly emerge among the followers. Frances Fitzgerald, in her account of events in the Rajneesh commune, catches the organization at the very cusp: ". . . developing all the institutions of a church." The guru's chief lieutenants were given new and pretentious titles, and a booklet entitled *Rajneeshism* was published, giving instructions on rituals, sacraments, and religious holidays. On the organization of the church, the booklet stated:

> The ecclesiastical organization of the religion is overseen by the Academy of Rajneeshism.
>
> There are three categories of ministers: *acharyas, arihantas,* and *siddhas.* The category into which a candidate is placed depends on the particular type of energy he or she possesses: introverted, extroverted or a synthesis of the two.
>
> To be eligible for the ministry, a person must have the following experience and training: a minimum of
>
> —two years as a neo-sannyasin
> —two years of participation and practice in meditation
> —two years of participation in religious discourses and teaching with guidance
> —one year of worship-meditation or apprenticeship in Rajneeshism
> —specific orientation for the ministerial duties

This is not unusual for an organized religion, but it is rather odd for a movement whose founder was on record as having stated: "It will not be possible to make a dogma out of my words. . . . Every institution is bound to be dead. . . . I am destroying your ideologies, creeds, cults, dogmas and I am not replacing them with anything else." Followers had expressed similar ideas about the movement's role: "Bhagwan is like Gurdjieff," one said. "His function is blowing preconceptions."[6]

So even iconoclasm, even postmodern blow-their-minds quasi-punk iconoclasm, can magically turn to the production of new icons.

And although esoteric schools are dedicated to the pursuit of freedom, they manage to create tyranny with surprising frequency. The reasons for this are complex and probably vary from case to case, but one part of the process is fairly constant and not too hard to understand: this is the power relationship that comes into play between teacher and student. The former is the keeper of the truth—which becomes all the more valuable for being unstated and mysterious, not to be gained merely by reading the scriptures or performing some spiritual exercises—and the student is the seeker of it. Something like a psychoanalytic transference often occurs in this situation, the teacher becoming an object of love and a figure of great authority over the student's life. In this situation, the personality defects of the teacher are overlooked or transformed into paradoxical evidences of his great wisdom, while the personality defects of the student are magnified. The student is given to understand that his or her opinions, characteristics, and attempts to understand are manifestations of ego—especially when they involve negative feelings about the teacher. The Carlos Castaneda books regularly present such situations: Carlos frequently bickers with Don Juan, but the reader always knows that he is merely resisting the Truth; never, never are we allowed to consider the possibility that Don Juan may be, in any region of discourse, simply full of shit.

Let us say—in a spirit of generosity to the countless people who have entered into such relationships over the millennia and will probably continue to do so—that this way of going after some of the more difficult kinds of wisdom is effective in some conditions and produces exactly the kind of results that it should. Whether it does or doesn't, it is clearly a dangerous game.

The dangers are many. The teacher may exploit the student sexually, psychologically, or economically. The student may be taught a lot of seriously flawed wisdom if the teacher doesn't know as much as he thinks he does. Or the school may become a vehicle for the ego promotion of the teacher and his teachings. The teacher may metamorphose from friend/mentor into guru-going-on-messiah. His writings may become scriptures, his sayings pearls of wisdom to be recorded and distributed to the world. The approach to teaching may become reified, turn into a thing with an institutionalized existence of its own.

The adventures of the twentieth-century Indian teacher Jiddu Krishnamurti and the Theosophists are a remarkable personal drama involving these issues. The Theosophical Society was (and is) an international religious organization with an eclectic collection of beliefs and a sizable membership, including several members of the English nobility who contributed generously to its progress. Its president in the early 1900s was an Englishwoman, Annie Besant. Theosophy was based on esoteric traditions of the East, but the society of which thousands of people became members had all the trappings of an organized religion: a doctrine of an invisible hierarchy of Occult Masters, and a quite visible hierarchical organization involving levels of initiation.

Krishnamurti, the son of a man who worked on the Theosophical Society's estate near Madras, was chosen when he was only thirteen to be educated and prepared for a major role—nothing less than that of World Teacher, Messiah of the twentieth century. Mrs. Besant took him to be educated in England and on the Continent, and created a special international suborganization—called first the Order of the Rising Sun and later the Order of the Star—to support his progress and prepare the world for his Coming.

Mrs. Besant and the man who had first noticed the young Krishnamurti—her confidant, Charles Webster Leadbeater, a former clergyman and longtime student of the occult—believed that the young man had great spiritual potential. It turned out they were right, but things did not work out at all according to their plan. As the time drew nearer for Krishnamurti to assume his role as World Teacher, his public statements began to become alarmingly iconoclastic. He took to telling people to search for the truth within themselves and not in external authorities. Finally, in 1929, he dissolved the Order of the Star—deconstructed it, so to speak, in the presence of Mrs. Besant, three thousand of its members, and a sizable radio audience. To his shocked mentor and followers, he said:

> I maintain that Truth is a pathless land, and you cannot approach it by any path whatsoever, by any religion, by any sect. . . . If you first understand that, then you will see how impossible it is to organize a belief. . . . If you do it becomes dead, crystallized; it becomes a creed, a sect, a religion, to be imposed on others.[7]

The Krishnamurti affair illustrates both tendencies: a collection of esoteric teachings trying hard to turn into a church, and an esoteric teacher destroying a religious structure to go his quixotic way.

THE USES AND MISUSES OF ESOTERICA

Many people in the Orient have used esoteric teachings such as Buddhism as a source of guidance in life, without feeling that they needed to make the teaching their "religion" or—more to the point—to regard themselves as particularly religious. I expect that many people in the West will do more or less the same thing; indeed, many have already. We have seen books on Zen-and-the-art-of just about everything.

Esoteric teachings have many things to offer, including guidelines for motorcycle maintenance. Three aspects of such teachings are useful to people looking for practical guidelines for survival in the postmodern world.

First, they offer an idea of a religious life without a concept of God—in fact, a religious life that is dedicated to sweeping away concepts of God as soon as they begin to appear in the mind. Religion without theology, a refreshing thought: there is a lot to be said for the proposition that, as in the famous mot about war and generals, religion is too important to be left to the theologians.

Second, they are systems for learning about the illusory nature of our own thought processes. We have a lot of good theoretical work on that subject from the cognitive scientists and the literary critics, but very little recognition that mastering it, really integrating it into one's worldview, may be a difficult process of personal change and not merely an intellectual exercise.

Third, they directly challenge the assumption that if you lose your conviction in the absolute truth of any concept or doctrine you are automatically headed down the slippery slope to meaninglessness and/or immorality. They are, on the contrary, distinctly enthusiastic about the benefits of abandoning any such doctrines—including their own—and then abandoning whatever is left when you think you have abandoned all doctrines. In one Zen parable, a master tells a student to drop what he has in his right hand. The student drops it. Then he is ordered to drop what he has in his left hand, and does. Asked what he has left, he says, "Nothing." "Drop it," says the master. I am not in favor of asking everybody to drop their convictions, and in any case I don't think everybody is going to. But if we are to make it into the postmodern world at all, we are going to have to develop greater confidence in our ability to survive without the certainty that we have any cosmic prop for our values and beliefs. And for some people, an exposure to esoteric teachings may help develop such confidence.

Eastern esoteric traditions have much to offer, and many limitations. If you approach them at all, approach with skepticism. An early expert on the subject has been quoted as saying: "Do not believe on the strength of traditions even if they have been held in honor for many generations and in many places; do not believe anything because many people speak of it; do not believe on the strength of sages of old times. . . . After investigation, believe that which you have yourself tested and found reasonable. . . ."[8] That statement itself should be approached skeptically, especially since it comes from a sage of old times (the Buddha), but it has a ring of good sense about it and also expresses the idea that you can approach this (or any other) body of teaching without feeling that you need either reject it entirely or swallow it whole.

The batting average of esoteric schools is, on the whole, not high. I mean the whole esoteric enterprise, from the Buddha to whoever has come along this week. Such schools have tried valiantly to come to grips with the human condition, to learn and teach about the possibility of living with both freedom and responsibility in the symbolic universe. But they succeed only when they produce people with a high order of insight into the subjects they try to communicate—and they do not succeed all that frequently. The insights of wise men and women become reified as something called Enlightenment, and millions become worshippers of the Buddha. Huge exoteric structures with hierarchies, rules, doctrines, and codes of behavior grow up. Visiting the Orient, gazing at the monumental statues of a man who tried to tell us to let go of our graven images, I stand in awe of the monumental capacity of human beings to miss the point.

We also miss the point if we think that study of esoteric teachings or practices such as meditation will either (a) lead us into a "natural" way of being that is beyond all symbolization, culture, and social constructions of reality, or (b) transform us into morally superior beings.

The search for transcendent experience in religion is quite similar to the search for transcendent experience through publicly defying society (the punk path), battling its political institutions (the revolutionary path), imaginatively lampooning its cultural expressions (the avant-garde art path), searching for the True Self (the therapy path), or submerging the brain in chemicals (the drug path). In these and other experiences, any number of interesting things may happen, you may change as a person and may learn and unlearn many things—but you remain human and still, therefore, a resident of the symbolic universe. You may take on new worldviews, new values and beliefs, but you do not become free of all worldviews, all values and beliefs. The True Self that you imagine you will find is a social construction of reality and so is the New Self that you do find. It may be a great improvement over the self you started with, but it is still inseparable from history, culture, others, words. It may also be inseparable from your guru and his or her philosophy.

Ernest Becker argued in *The Denial of Death* that the various concepts that come into play as people try to strip away all of culture and pursue the "natural being within" subtly become new absolutes, new metaphysics of "power and justification from beyond." The new absolute principle—he said "it can be called, variously, 'the great void,' the 'inner room' of Taoism, the 'realm of essence,' the source of things, the 'It,' the 'Creative Unconscious,' or whatever"—becomes the new Rock of Ages to which the seeker attaches his or her identity, and of which the teacher and the school are the privileged interpreters.[9]

You do not have to become thus enthralled, although the potential for thralldom is ever-present in the needs of seekers, in the dynamics of student-master relations, and unfortunately in the agendas of many spiritual schools that are not altogether sure they want you to become free of attachment to all doctrines.

You can assemble with some selective shopping in the oriental bazaar a worldview that includes insight into the nature of worldviews, and into the workings of your own mind in its daily business of world viewing.

Will you become a better person? You might. You might absorb some of the precepts that are commonly found in spiritual circles—nonviolence, for example—and live by them. You might go through some of the mysterious internal processes that cause us to mature and become more morally alive. And you might not. I know people who are convinced that esoteric teachings and meditation automatically produce better people, and that if we could just get everybody to meditating, the world's troubles would be over. I have never been able to agree. I have seen altogether too much evidence that it is possible to be, simultanously, a holy man (or woman) of high repute and an irresponsible twit.

The esoteric traditions are unfinished business—a long and on the whole honorable and valuable part of our evolution. We have much to learn from them, and they have much to learn. I expect that future comings-together of Eastern and Western thought will carry this evolutionary effort forward and help us find the parts of each that are useful to people in the postmodern world. And I expect that there will be a lot of foolishness along the way. There always is.

PART FIVE

WORLDVIEW

CHAPTER 10

All the World's a Stage

The collapse of belief we have been witnessing throughout the twentieth century comes with globalism. The postmodern condition is not an artistic movement or a cultural fad or an intellectual theory—although it produces all of those and is in some ways defined by them. It is what inevitably happens as people everywhere begin to see that there are many beliefs, many kinds of belief, many ways of believing. Postmodernism *is* globalism; it is the half-discovered shape of the one unity that transcends all our differences.

In a global—and globalizing—era, all of the old structures of political reality, all the old ways of saying who we are and what we are for and what we are against, seem to be melting away into air.

How to have an identity in such a world? Nationalism becomes semiobsolete before it even completes its conquest; national governments everywhere are challenged from front and rear, past and future. They are forced to do battle against premodern tribal and ethnic identities even as they resist the threats to their fragile (and all too obviously fictional) sovereignties that are posed by international organizations and movements and economic forces. The weaker national sovereignty is as an absolute principle, the less secure we are in defining ourselves according to national citizenship.

How about ideology? Throughout the era of the Cold War, global ideologies seemed to be replacing national loyalties as the supreme definers of political reality. For a time, the world appeared to be divided into two opposed belief systems rather than into many nations. But the international ideologies never quite managed to separate themselves from nationalism (Marxism had a particularly hard time with that, was widely suspected of being merely a tool of Russian ambitions), and today hardly anybody other than a few intransigent communists and die-hard anti-communists believes that the world is politically bipolar.

Religion is still a potent definer of political reality and still an explosive one—we may still be having holy wars when we have stopped having any other kind—but it is also the most vulnerable of all to being unveiled as a creation of the human mind.

Each of these sets of categories, each of these ways that people construct who they are and what they believe, is increasingly chimerical, capable of evaporating in a moment when people look at the world with different eyes.

Class and race may prove to be more durable definers of reality, more stable markers of who is "us" and who is "them." But each of these, too, becomes anything but predictable in a postmodern world. The wretched of the earth may be a force for rebellious change because they believe some form of Marxist doctrine about class conflict, or merely because they *cease* to believe in the various social constructions of reality that held their condition to be part of God's own arrangement. Oppressed races grow skeptical (as the world gains understanding of the games oppressors play) about the social constructions of reality that define *their* place and strive to keep them in it.

Everywhere we see not merely one-dimensional political conflict of the kind we once understood or thought we understood—nation against nation, class against class, and so forth, within a clear set of rules—but shifting multidimensional struggles that are sometimes attempts to change the rules. And amid those struggles many individuals manage to change their own rules by changing their political identities. We see the old polarizations, and if we look closely we see new ones: fundamentalism against relativistic and liberalizing trends within religions and cultures and ideologies; localisms against globalism; yearnings for the past against dreams of progress.

It is a world coming together—a global civilization, the first that has ever existed, emerging into being before our very eyes—but one that seems to be, at the same time, in the process of falling apart. It is doing neither, and both; it is becoming a system that is not organized according to belief as we once knew it.

We may not yet have a global civilization that we can recognize as such, but we clearly have a global theater: for the first time ever, all people are more or less capable of knowing they inhabit the same world, and more or less aware of what is going on in it.

More or less. We don't have all living human beings watching the same program on their TV screens, and probably never will—I kind of hope we won't. But yet the number of people who can be aware of the same event has increased enormously. According to the trivia-keepers, more people watched the wedding of England's Prince Charles and Princess Diana than had ever before in human history observed such an event at the same time. According to an apocryphal story related by Neil Postman, one year the Lapps postponed their annual migration, at the height of popularity of the *Dallas* TV series, because they wanted to stay around and find out who shot J. R. Ewing.[1]

I was traveling in Europe in June of 1989, at the time of the heart-sickening events that followed the Chinese students' demonstration for democracy, and it was painfully obvious to me—even more obvious, somehow, than if I had been at home in California watching the news—that Tiananmen Square had become for a time the center of the world. My fellow passengers talked about the events there while I rode a train going from Stockholm to Copenhagen; in newsstands that retailed foreign papers, the same bloody pictures appeared on front pages with captions from half a dozen languages; and in Bonn thousands of students, most of them Asian, marched through the streets shouting slogans; the whole world was watching.

Yet I could not help observing that the whole world was not doing a whole lot more than watch. Some people demonstrated. Most of us read the news and talked about it and felt the deep sadness that comes when you see humanity at its ugliest. Political leaders made impotent noises about sanctions.

I am not arguing that we should have sent in the United States Marines or an international military body; I am only seeking to get at the difficult place that we—and by "we" I mean the human species—have got to, a place in which events sometimes become the objects of global compassion and moral judgment, but in which there is no institutionalized way to prevent such events from being resolved with pure savagery: a global theater, not yet a global civilization—a stage on which are enacted dramas of a scale no Shakespeare ever imagined.

THE GREATEST SHOW ON EARTH

World War II was a war unlike any previous war—a global conflict in which propaganda played an unprecedented role in support of armed combat. When it ended, we moved almost immediately into another global conflict, unlike even World War II—so different we had to invent a new name for what was happening, and called it the Cold War—in which arms played an unprecedented role in support of propaganda. World War II brought forth a new weapon, the atomic bomb, which make it appear to the major powers that there was not much to be gained and literally everything to be lost by entering into another global war. Diverted from that path, they discovered the global theater, and created new weapons of another kind, such as brainwashing and disinformation—weapons aimed at social constructions of reality.

Equipped with the hindsight of history, we can look back to the early decades of the twentieth century and see the new game being played long before World War II began.

In 1921, a year when European artists were taking liberty with old ideas about reality in many ways, a Soviet government official named Aleksandr Yakushev, on a trip outside the USSR, sought out an anti-Soviet exile and told of a vast conspiracy he belonged to, a network of high-level officials in various sectors of government and the military who stood ready to take over as soon as the Communist regime collapsed—which, as he described it, it was about to do. The exile contacted British and French intelligence operatives to inform them that the Soviet economy and political system was foundering, and that Yakushev wished to be of service.

Subsequently, other Soviet officials made contact with anti-Soviets in Europe; they confirmed Yakushev's story that the regime was in a state of near-chaos and that a large secret organization, known officially as the Monarchist Union of Central Russia and more informally by the code name of "the Trust," was working to hasten its demise. Some of the exiles and intelligence agents were suspicious at first, until they saw that the Trust could deliver: it delivered by smuggling families of dissidents out of Russia, getting arms and supplies to counterrevolutionary groups inside Russia, getting fake passports and visas for exiles to enter Russia surreptitiously, blowing up police stations, arranging prison escapes, and getting secret economic and military documents for intelligence services. Within a few years, the intelligence services of eleven of the major Western powers were, according to Edward Jay Epstein in his fascinating account of this invisible war, "almost completely dependent on the Trust for information about Russia."[2] The Trust had successfully created the West's official reality, a story of a crumbling and internally divided Soviet Union.

Toward the end of the decade, problems began to develop. Some exile leaders vanished on their secret missions into Russia. Some of the documents proved to be false. And, most serious of all, the Soviet Union failed to collapse on schedule.

In 1929, a top official of the Trust defected and revealed that the whole operation had been created and managed by Soviet intelligence. This news was of course tremendously demoralizing to Western intelligence services and Russian exiles. The episode left them confused and distrusting themselves and one another—especially when they learned that the official who blew the Trust's cover returned to Moscow and went back to work for Soviet intelligence. "Since the deception had worn thin by 1929," Epstein concludes, "and . . . no longer had a strategic objective, the Soviets decided to liquidate it in the most advantageous way"—leaving the anti-Soviet forces even more mystified than they had been already.[3]

And so began the great show of the twentieth century. The West took up the challenge, of course, and intelligence operations went far beyond the simple game of spying—even beyond the somewhat more elaborate game of counterspying, planting double agents and providing the enemy with false documents. It became a labyrinthine business of creating large and complex realities, stories with as many levels and turns as any Escher drawing. The new word that came into general use to describe such operations was *disinformation.* "When disinformation becomes the art of the state, as in the case of the Trust," says a former CIA agent, "nations use their intelligence services to paint, brush stroke by brush stroke, a picture that will provoke its adversaries to make the wrong judgments."[4]

The art of the state: a phrase to ponder. It is a remarkable development, that creating realities for one's adversaries comes to be regarded as a major function of governance. Perhaps disinformation was a natural evolutionary development in the world of military intelligence. If you have information-gathering systems, it is hardly surprising that false-information-supplying systems should develop. If you have systems such as intelligence agencies and briefing officers that need stories, why should somebody not get into the business of providing the stories they want you to believe?

As the Cold War escalated, became a major global conflict and a major concern of the great powers, disinformation merged with propaganda and new works of art appeared. And the United States honed its own skills in the game—fielded its own double agents, created its own stings abroad and at home. It is said that FBI boss J. Edgar Hoover opposed the idea of outlawing the U.S. Communist party during the height of the Cold War because he had his own agents in most of its key positions and he preferred keeping the party intact so he could identify its members and control what they did; it was our government's domestic Trust.[5] Military men, once they caught on, came up with imaginative proposals for bigger and better pseudoevents: General Edward Lansdale, a CIA planning officer, had the inspiration after Fidel Castro came to power in Cuba of trying to persuade the gullible Catholic Cubans that the Second Coming of Christ was imminent but would pass their island by as long as the godless communist was in power; General Lansdale thought it would be a good idea to have a U.S. submarine fire star shells into the night sky to make it appear that Christ was on the way. Some of his colleagues thought that particular plan was a little bit too daring, and it was never put into play.[6]

The U.S. intelligence establishment also became more sophisticated about dealing with "dangles" (defectors or informers who might be double agents) and the information they provided. In the 1950s, the CIA seriously considered maintaining parallel branches with different "mind-sets": one would operate according to the reality that the spy was for real, the other according to the reality that he was a disinformant.[7]

The games of disinformation and propaganda merged also with governmental policies for informing and misinforming their own citizens. The citizens became more sophisticated too, and did not always accept the stories handed out by their own leaders with the same patriotic gullibility that had been so evident during World War II. Part of the national trauma of the Vietnam years was the widening "credibility gap" between the government and the public, as the government kept putting out the news that all was going well while other news—such as reports on the massacre of civilians by American troops at My Lai and the unauthorized release of the Pentagon Papers with their documentation of how little truth the government had told in its public statements—indicated that everything was not going well at all.

Governments favor the story that all is going well. One of the more bizarre examples of an effort to keep this construction of reality afloat at all costs is recounted by David Wise in his book *The Politics of Lying:* in 1971, an employee of the National Emergency Warning Center sent out, by mistake, a signal that was—as the system was organized for it to do—immediately sent out by the wire services to radio and TV stations all over the country. It said that the president had declared a state of emergency action notification, and all broadcasting was to halt immediately. This was the notification to be used in the event of a nuclear attack, and it was sent out *with* the code word to announce that it was real and not a test. The error was discovered and a cancel notice sent out, but when the fiasco was investigated later it leaked out that one of the tapes which civil defense officials had prepared to be broadcast in the event of a nuclear attack said the enemy had "struck the first blow," and added this reassuring report: "Our Strategic Air Command and naval units have devastated many of his major cities and industrial centers. Our defense forces have retaliated with tremendous effectiveness and probability of victory is good."[8] One can imagine the whole country gone, all major cities blasted away, death and destruction everywhere, and some little radio station still sending out that message that all is well, like the smile on Lewis Carroll's Cheshire cat that remained even after the cat had disappeared.

Nuclear conflict itself, that astounding buildup of weapons and the way the weapons were actually used, is itself the most amazing part of the Cold War. The weapons themselves are so hideously devastating that nobody in his right mind would use them, and yet it did become the most urgent part of defense policy—indeed, the very heart of the whole Cold War—for each major power to pretend that it stood ready to do just that. Steven Kull, a clinical psychologist, interviewed major defense policymakers and found that in extended, probing discussions they sooner or later would set aside the "hardware" aspects of military planning—the need for weapons in order to win shooting wars—and focus on the need to manipulate the perceptions of possible adversaries in peacetime. More important than any of the multitude of theories that shaped the thinking of decision-makers was "perception theory," which said in essence that what counted was not what a weapon could do or what you intended to do with it, but what you could get somebody to believe you intended to do with it. As one prominent strategic analyst explained:

> Strategic weapons are political artifacts first. And when they cease to be political artifacts, then they're entirely irrelevant, entirely without a purpose. . . . The only existence that these weapons have that has any meaning is in political terms. And perceptions is the only relevant category. The only question is to debate how people, in fact, see them—what these perceptions really are.[9]

The nuclear arms race—the biggest military construction project in all of human history, the effort that squats like a fat monster on top of the economies of the world's most powerful nations, that has cast a shadow over the world for decades—is a pseudoevent. And what it reveals to us, as many pseudoevents do, is that we do not quite have control of our reality-making machinery. Indeed, it is more out of control than our bomb-making machinery is. Even after decades of intrigue and intrigue novels, agents and counteragents and doubleagents, we tend to get caught up in our own fantasies. Speaking of what he calls the "greater-fool" thesis (that the nation which will prevail in a time of a nuclear standoff is the one most capable of convincing the world it is ready to blow up everything), Kull says:

> The most critical feature of the greater-fool argument for maintaining the balance is not the idea that there is this widespread illusion about the military significance of the balance. The most critical feature is the prescription to play along with the illusion as if it were real. Logically, this is not a necessary conclusion. It is possible for policymakers to actively work to neutralize the illusion. Furthermore,

> playing along with the illusion is more than a passive response. Behaving consistently with the illusion implicitly confirms and thereby effectively promotes it.[10]

The moral, I suppose, is that you should be careful about what drama you concoct for the global theater (or possibly even for the local one) because you may well end up believing in it—and even get killed in the final act.

SATANIC VERSUS

In the declining years of the Cold War, Iran, a nation striving desperately to keep its distance from globalizing civilization, emerged as a persistent scene-stealer on the stage of the global theater.

In the early 1980s, American public opinion went through something that was not quite a paradigm shift, but still a dramatic change in social reality: it was more a villain shift. Where once all good Americans had understood that the United States and the Soviet Union were natural enemies—which gave the incumbent Soviet leader *ex officio* status as the heavy in our global drama—the role of The Man You Love to Hate was taken over soon after the Iranian revolution by the Ayatollah Khomeini. And for the remaining years of his life, Khomeini held on to his position of arch-unpopularity.

Now, by all the standards of realistic modern-era politics, there is no particular reason why the United States and Iran should have become bitter enemies in a new polarization that seemed at times to supplant the old Cold War conflict, or why Americans should have become so obsessed with the beetle-browed image of the Ayatollah. After all, the difference in size and power between the United States and Iran was enormous, and Iran posed no genuine threat to any concrete American interests. And the Ayatollah was merely a grumpy old religious reactionary. There are plenty of grumpy old religious reactionaries around—I can think of a number of cardinals and rabbis answering to that description—who do not take on such diabolic stature in the American popular mind.

But the America-Iran conflict was not merely played out in the arena of realpolitik; it was played out in the global theater. In 1980, spunky little Iran stood up to Uncle Sam, violated the rules of the diplomatic game by raiding the American embassy, took a bunch of Americans prisoner, and defied us to do something about it. America looked rather foolish, and the whole world was watching.

America and Iran come out of that affair as enemies, a situation that expressed a postmodern polarization and a postmodern logic: America the nation furthest into a constructivist reality, with its incredible jumble of beliefs and beliefs about beliefs, and Iran the world's leading example of a totalitarian absolutist state, its leaders desperately devoted to browbeating the entire population into living within a single social construction of reality. America became Iran's "great Satan" and the Ayatollah became a satanic figure in the editorial cartoons.

Throughout the 1980s Iran continued to annoy Americans, and to occupy, for its size, a disparate amount of attention in the global theater.

And in the latter part of the decade Iran again showed its remarkable ability to occupy the world's attention, as it became involved in the extraordinary global flap about the publication of Salman Rushdie's book *Satanic Verses*.

As blasphemy goes, *Satanic Verses* is not one of the heavyweights. A lot worse things have been said about all religions than what Rushdie said about Islam. His book was not so much anti-Islamic as postmodern: he played games with Islamic truth, and with reality in general. The part of the book that got him in trouble—a passage that took up only seventy of the book's five-hundred-plus pages—was a takeoff on the life of the Prophet Mohammed, in which Rushdie suggested that the Prophet was a very human being and a sharp operator. Any number of Western writers had said the same thing before, and much more bluntly, but Rushdie was only about half-Western: he was an India-born resident of England, and had been raised a Muslim. Indeed, one of the themes of his book was the difficulty of holding on to a traditional identity—or any single identity at all:

> O, the dissociations of which the human mind is capable. . . . O, the conflicting selves jostling within these bags of skin. No wonder we are unable to remain focused on anything for very long; no wonder we invent remote-control channel-hopping devices. If we turned these

> instruments upon ourselves we'd discover more channels than a cable or satellite mogul ever dreamed of....[11]

Not only irreverent toward the Prophet, then, but irreverent toward a fundamental prop of modern reality, the single self. Clearly not to be tolerated.

The publicity about the book began when Muslims in the north England city of Bradford (where one person in seven is of Indian or Pakistani descent) organized a public burning of the book. The real trouble began when the controversy about the book became global—when the Ayatollah Khomeini heard about it and offered a million-dollar reward to anybody who would do right to the memory of the Prophet by murdering Rushdie.

It could only happen in the global theater. Within a *civilization* with norms and laws, such expressions would be dealt with according to whatever formalized procedures happened to be in place: the author would be protected according to the laws of freedom of speech, or the author would be punished according to the laws that put limits on such freedom. And of course in an earlier stage of global development—back when there was little or no contact between the country in which the book was published and the countries in which lived the people who were insulted by it—such a book would not have become a global issue. But the postmodern world has mobility and displacement (a huge Muslim population in England), and rapid communication, and global news media that found it a highly dramatic event.

The Rushdie affair showed how dangerous is the present stage of global development—a stage of communication without community. It also gave a hint of a new kind of problem that now presents itself to national governments, such as that of Great Britain, as they are thrust into the uncertain new conditions of the postmodern world.

Massive global population movements are transforming many nations. Some of the nations—notably the United States—have traditions of taking in and assimilating peoples from divergent racial/cultural/religious origins. Others—notably the European nations—are less accustomed to that role, and have no statue-of-liberty, melting-pot mystique to go with it. They deal with their new populations in different ways: France, which has taken in more immigrants than any other European nation, handles the assimilation problem with Gallic *hauteur*: the state education system teaches the values and beliefs of French civilization, and does not agonize about preserving the language and cultural heritage of immigrant populations. England, like some other countries, has tried to become "multicultural."

Multiculturalism is fine as long as all concerned are in a postmodern frame of mind about their traditions—and especially about their religious beliefs. This means that no particular group, no particular minority community, has any basis for *enforcing* fidelity to its cultural heritage. As columnist William Pfaff put it, in a discussion of the Rushdie case:

> Without a community of values and cultural assumption there is no community at all. Do you believe that Salman Rushdie, or anyone else, has the right to say and publish whatever is on his mind? Do you think the freedom to do so essential to the political community in which you wish to live? Or do you believe that God's truth, as you understand it, should be enforced against false ideas—or even that offenders against that truth deserve to die?
>
> You can believe the one or the other. You can't believe both. A coherent political community cannot exist without a consensus of agreement on one or the other. That is the problem Rushdie and his book are forcing people to confront.[12]

Actually there are several problems. The problem for fundamentalist Muslims in England is how to enforce conformity to an absolutist belief system when you are living in a pluralizing postmodern nation. The problem for Salman Rushdie and other artists (especially bicultural artists who draw their material from one civilization but produce for another) is how to feel truly free to say and publish whatever you want—and to depend on your legal "rights" to protect you against the vengeance of people who believe you have violated a higher law.

And the problem for those who hope for a true global civilization is figuring out how fundamentalist and postmodern worldviews can coexist within it.

Fundamentalism and postmodernism are a new polarization, but not (at least not yet) an overriding one like capitalism-communism became during the Cold War years. They represent one more kind of fragmentation, one more source of conflict. We have many such sources, everything from local parochial loyalties to global-scale agendas.

GLOBAL NOBLE LIES

Although the postmodern world cannot be described by a single story, that does not prevent anybody from trying. The human mind is a prodigious maker and consumer of stories; give it an image of a world and an evolving species, and it will soon produce accounts of what is happening and what is going to happen. Global stories are simultaneously attempts to explain the world—to create a new global reality—and attempts to further the aspirations, hopes, political agendas, and ego needs of different groups of people.

In an article that I coauthored some years ago with Donald Michael, we identified six stories that are competing for attention and credibility in the postmodern world; our subtitle, with no apologies to Pirandello, was *Six Stories in Search of an Author.*[13] We used the term "story" as a commonsense description of ways that people explain how the world got to be the way it is and what is happening and is likely to happen. A story in this sense may or may not be about the same thing as an ideology. Some stories (notably Marxism) are ideologically sophisticated, with elaborate explanatory structures; others are not too steady on their intellectual feet. Our enumeration of six stories was not meant to be a complete inventory, but rather an exploratory description of some ways that people are trying to make sense of the postmodern world.

The six stories are (1) the Western myth of progress, with its enthusiasm for technological change and economic development and its overriding image of a world in which the conditions of life keep getting better for everybody; (2) the Marxist story of revolution and international socialism; (3) the Christian fundamentalist story about a return to a society governed on the basis of Christian values and biblical belief; (4) the Islamic fundamentalist story about a return to a society governed on the basis of Islamic values and koranic belief; (5) the Green story about rejecting the myth of progress and governing societies according to ecological values;

and (6) the "new paradigm" story about a sudden leap forward to a new way of being and a new way of understanding the world.

These aren't neat categories, of course; the human mind being what it is, you find an enormous range of variations and overlaps: fundamentalist Christian boosters of economic progress, for example, and fundamentalist Islamic Marxists. But there are genuine, and in some cases profound and bitter, differences between one story and another—explosive differences, because each story has its true believers and (here is the real powder keg) each story has expansion-minded believers who are convinced it is the one true faith that must prevail and become *the* belief system of global society. Some think the world's future is inseparable from continued Western-style development (the works of the late Herman Kahn proclaimed this); some still believe in the inevitable triumph of global Marxism. You can easily find fundamentalist Christians who expect the whole world to become one big Bible Belt, and fundamentalist Muslims who foresee a global Islamic society.

The six stories are rooted in different historical periods: fundamentalist Christianity and Islam have premodern origins, and aspire to impose upon the world premodern certainties. To anyone who sees the world from outside these belief systems, this appears utterly ludicrous—trying to find instructions in the Bible for what to do about RU 486, or looking in the Koran for what to do about religious movements that came into being after it was written—but clearly many people find it the only way to cope with the complexities of our time.

The capitalist/progress/development story and the Marxist story are both rooted in the modern era and, beneath their differences, share a modern construction of reality: a confidence in materialism and scientific truth; a modern sense of time not as circular but rather linear and progressive, of history not as a decline from a golden era but rather an upward struggle out of ignorance and tyranny. Both borrow heavily from the Darwinian theory of evolution and strive mightily to convert Darwin's ideas about the survival of species into ideological beliefs about the survival of civilizations. Both are *ideologies* as we came to understand that word in the modern era: systems of *political* truth that rest on no divine authority, yet claim to offer basic understandings of politics and governance that are not merely matters of personal opinion.

The Green and "new paradigm" stories are early-postmodern creations that express ways of seeing the world that have become popular since the 1960s. Although neither comes anywhere close to having the millions of true believers boasted by the other four, they both deserve attention. The Greens are a serious political movement in some countries, and their story has the status of an emerging ideology in places where they have little political organization. The "new paradigm" vision is enormously appealing to many people, and has a tendency to surface wherever people gather to talk about globalism and peace. It, too, begins to look like an ideology.

The two overlap in many places, and in many people's minds, but there are important distinctions: the "new paradigm" idea, when applied to the realm of human affairs, predicts a sudden great leap forward in evolution; Green ideology is profoundly reactionary, easily equal to the religious fundamentalisms in its enthusiasm for figuring out how to shift history into reverse.

The "new paradigm" ideology borrows heavily from twentieth-century science, much as capitalism and Marxism borrowed from nineteenth-century science—with equally dubious logic. Pick up any New Age book that talks about global politics, and you will probably find prophecies of an imminent Golden Age combined with citations of Thomas Kuhn and Ilya Prigogine. The message is essentially millenarian prophecy, older than history, but stated in ways that suggest the coming of the millennium is practically a scientific fact. Fritjof Capra, a promoter of the "new paradigm" idea, says that although "the dynamics of the shift may be different in science and in society . . . a shift of paradigms is occurring in both areas."[14] The essential "new paradigm" belief is that just as scientific theories are sometimes replaced by new theories with greater ability to explain observed phenomena, so will the old culture of Western civilization be replaced by "new paradigm" values: patriarchy will be replaced by feminism, control of nature by cooperation with it, and so forth. It is important to remember that the "new paradigm" ideology is not merely a stand in favor of such values; it is a prediction, offered with as much certainty as a Marxist warning of the coming world revolution, that they *will* prevail, completely and soon. Part of the ideology (and part of its appeal) is its assertion that "changes of paradigms occur in discontinuous, revolutionary breaks."[15] This means that people who are watching for the emergence of the new paradigm take developments that conform to it as evidence that they are right (you can see it's coming) and developments that don't conform to it as evidence that they are right again (you can't tell it's coming until it's here).

Prigogine's work with dissipative models offers another metaphor for such a sudden shift—a metaphor whose fans unfortunately forget that it is a metaphor and not a law of history. Prigogine researched chemical reactions in which there was a sudden and spontaneous reorganization. Certain oils, for example, when heated, began to form complex patterns of hexagons on their surface—a reorganization of the system into a new whole. The temptation to apply the model of such a spontaneous system transformation to the human realm is strong, and New Age writers have given in to it enthusiastically. Marilyn Ferguson tells us in *The Aquarian Conspiracy* that "the theory is immediately relevant to everyday life—to *people*. If offers a scientific model of transformation at every level: molecular, biological, personal, cultural."[16]

It is a long, long leap from describing something that happens in a chemical reaction to forecasting global cultural change. It is also a long leap from describing how a paradigm shift happens within a scientific community (if indeed it happens that way) to applying the same model of change to a global not-quite-yet-civilization made up of many communities, many realities, and many people with their own complex societies of mind. In each case the concept is something less than a scientific theory and something more than a metaphor—more of a new noble lie.

The Green global story is a bit harder to summarize, because the various Green movements are so different and so prone to internal ideological wrangling—Marxists and anarchists versus New Age spiritualists, macho Earth Firsters versus ecofeminists, and so forth. The various factions are in considerable disagreement about where to go or how to get there. But the story in its general outlines is clear enough, and it is basically the opposite of the "progress" story, an attempt to roll back the Industrial Revolution. Greens see the Industrial Revolution not as a producer of goods and freedom, but as a producer of pollution and exploitation; they call for a repudiation of modern-era ideas about progress and a return to a way of life based on simpler technologies and social arrangements.

"Bioregionalism" is one of the more popular elements of the Green ideology, an attractive utopian vision of how to live in the world. Its prescription is to save the earth by restoring the sense of place. The reasoning is that if every person were to be first of all a resident of a specific place, a bioregion, he or she would then of necessity come to know it deeply and would relate to it with reverence and care: Kirkpatrick Sale, a current leading spokesman for bioregionalism, tells us that "to come to know the earth fully and honestly, the crucial and perhaps only all-encompassing task is to understand *place*, the immediate specific place where we live."[17]

Now, this is a reasonable enough proposition, and anyone who has had the good fortune to know and love a particular region would recommend such a way of living to anybody who could afford it. It is when the proposition inflates into an ideology and a prescription for global survival that it begins to turn into pure crackpot politics.

The trouble is that bioregionalism is not such a hot way of arranging things in a world that has over 5 billion people in it, and is adding close to 90 million a year; a world with unprecedented mobility, not only of people but of plant and animal life, so that every bioregion is being constantly transformed; a world massively urbanizing, so that each day a greater portion of the global population is urban rather than rural. Faced with the news that a lot of people live in cities, Sale proposes "relocating" them: "There seems to be no choice," he writes, "but to break down the current multimillion-people cities both by dividing them into smaller cities, each with a surrounding greenbelt, and by resettling them into different-sized communities in the surrounding region," and assures us that "there is plenty of land for such dispersal in any bioregion in North America. . . ."[18] This ignores yet another troubling condition of our time, which is that one of the major reasons why people stream into huge metropolises such as Mexico City is that soil erosion and other forms of ecological deterioration have rendered so much agricultural land incapable of supporting the numbers of people who are already there, busily ruining the bioregions they have had centuries to become deeply acquainted with.

Bioregionalism is an essential part of Green ideology. The West German Green platform declared: "Our policy is a policy of active partnership with nature and human beings. It is most successful in self-governing and self-sufficient economic and administrative units, of a humanly surveyable size."[19] The manifesto of the British Green party proposed scrapping the existing governmental and administrative system and replacing it with an arrangement of local districts.

One of the many questions that the Green/bioregional story fails to confront is personal choice. Although strong in its advocacy of genetic diversity, it is weak in the area of psychological and social diversity. The Greens have little to say about how to deal with people who just don't *want* to live simply in their bioregions, who want to live in another bioregion, or to travel all over and be world citizens, or to identify with communities—of science, art, or religion, for example—that have no geographic base at all. No way of dealing with such people except to sermonize about their wrongness. The trouble with ideological stories that decide how everybody should live is that sooner or later the person who tries to turn the prescription into reality finds it necessary to use force. In Cambodia, the Pol Pot regime, enthusiastically turning back the clock on the corruptions of modernism and relocating people in bioregions, managed to slaughter over a million people in the process. The Sendero Luminoso movement has been equally bloody in its campaign to bring bucolic simplicity to Peru.

I have dwelt extensively on the newer stories here, because they represent ideological positions that have been less extensively examined in public dialogue and because many people are tempted to believe that, being new, they must be free of the defects of older ideologies. They are not. The Greens declare themselves to be neither right nor left, but ahead—but in many ways they are behind, the very model of an obsolete modern-era political movement weighted down with ideology, self-righteousness, simplistic doctrines, and quasi-totalitarian notions about how everybody ought to think and act.

The "new paradigm" model is an attempt to explain certain historical events; turned into political ideology, cited as zealously as redneck preachers quote the Bible, it becomes a rigid prediction of historical inevitability—as rigid as Marxism, and far less intellectually developed. And although the paradigm model as Thomas Kuhn described it is essentially constructivist, it is also linear: it says there is this paradigm, and then there is a revolution, and then there is that paradigm. The paradigm is dead, long live the paradigm. Such a way of looking at things doesn't tell us much about what to do in a world that has lots of paradigms, and lots of paradigms about paradigms, and any number of stories claiming to be the key to the future. New Age scenarios cite Kuhn endlessly, but almost never cite Feyerabend. In many ways, the early-postmodern Green and "new paradigm" ideologies turn out to be more rigidly "modern" than the capitalist and communist ones, which, being more engaged with actual governance, are more flexible and protean, more likely to take on entirely new shapes in response to changing conditions and new information.

Information makes life difficult for anyone who would like to hold on to a story in its pure form. Information acts upon stories as rain acts upon sand castles. It discredits them, deconstructs them, refutes their prophecies, and complicates their lives.

The Western myth of progress has taken a heavy beating from the bad news about the social and psychological tragedies attending industrialization, the environmental deterioration that goes with exploitation of resources, the massive debts built up by "developing" nations. The communist myth is equally shopworn; history in the twentieth century has not turned out according to any of its scenarios—the crystal balls of Marx, Engels, Trotsky, and Lenin now appear equally clouded. Marxists are tired of hearing about how many people Stalin murdered, about how Marxist economies perform. Religious fundamentalists are sick of all the scientists and researchers who keep turning Holy Writ into fairy tales. Greens are hostile toward any scent of scientific progress that might damage their conviction that science and technology only cause problems. New paradigmers leave out of their discussion Thomas Kuhn's declaration that his theory does not apply to social change, and the opinions of those scholars who don't even believe it explains change in science.

Faced with information, the believer becomes either a constructivist or a fundamentalist: the former takes stories lightly, changes them, or abandons them entirely when it becomes necessary; the latter deals with troublesome information through psychological denial and/or political repression.

I see no likelihood whatever that any of the major political or religious belief systems of the contemporary world, or any of the new candidates for that status, will emerge untouched from this century as *the* global story, the structure of reality that will unite all the diverse cultures and societies and movements and worldviews into one global culture. And I see no likelihood that any of the six I have mentioned, or any of their various cousins, is about to go away—information or not.

Each of the stories has something to offer, but the present situation is not exactly a global dialogue. Despite the overlaps and occasional points of agreement among the various stories, *they do not flow together into a single story.* Each has doctrines that are utterly incompatible with others. The feminism of the Green and "new paradigm" stories, for example, does not harmonize with the place assigned to women by fundamentalist religions. And you do not find within the dogma of any organized belief system much in the way of doctrines of reconciliation: not much in contemporary fundamentalist Christian rhetoric about getting along with Marxists, not much in Green talk about mixing Green agendas for the future with those of multinational business. Many of the currently predominant stories are basically conflict stories about a battle between good and evil. A fundamentalist Christian who anticipates Armageddon is not much interested in hearing about the new paradigm. A doctrinaire Marxist who awaits the world revolution as foretold by Marx and Engels does not want to sit down with some conflict-resolution team. Conflict resolution short of victory is incompatible with such reality structures.

These competing ideologies will be part of global civilization, but, at least in their more fundamental aspects, will be more forces for divisiveness than for unification. We have to look beyond them for clues as to what may hold a maturing postmodern civilization together.

CHAPTER 11

The Emergent Fiction

The world, says director Jonathan Miller, is an "emergent fiction," something that, like artists, we fabricate anew in every moment of our lives.[1] That is meant to be a description of individual experience, but it applies equally well to what happens to social groups, anything from small communities to the entire human species, as they create and re-create the realities that are common to all their members.

We all share the good fortune – or the misfortune, depending on how you look at it – of being present at a great historical/evolutionary event: we are seeing now the emergence of a social reality that is different in important ways from anything we have known before, the first global civilization. To say that we are "seeing" it is a bit of a strained metaphor, however: it's not that easy to see.

When we look for evidence that we are indeed moving out of international barbarism, making the transition from global theater to global polis, we are inevitably influenced by our preexisting mental models of what a civilization is: we think of the Greek or Roman civilizations of the past, or of the Western or Islamic civilizations of the present. It is very hard – in fact impossible – to know what to look for when the thing we are trying to observe and define has never existed, when nothing of its class has ever existed. Global civilization will have to accommodate and include all the present civilizations and cultures and nations. It will take its form in a postmodern world in which beliefs about belief – definitely including all the ideologies and religions and cultures that have supported past and present civilizations – have changed, and are changing. And it will be a social construction of reality.

People sometimes get drunk on the idea of social construction of reality and – when they apply it to the subject of global civilization – leap to the grandiose assumption that somehow we can sit down today and make up tomorrow's world. That delusion animates the more militant adherents of various global stories such as those I enumerated in the past chapter, the worst sort of futurism and much New Age foolishness. I have been present at meetings of faction-ridden little groups of a couple of dozen people who fancied they were shaping the future of human thought.

But even the creation of personal experience is a collaborative effort, with evolution and history and all our parents and peers doing their part to help each of us assemble the emergent fiction of the moment. And the manufacture of social reality is an even more crowded operation: no matter how often we repeat the platitude that the future is what we make it, we find much of it being made in mysterious ways, ways that elude our agendas, ways that stretch far back into the past. Huge historical forces march through our time: the future is being shaped by the Reformation, the Enlightenment, the Industrial Revolution; by population growth and global environmental changes; by God knows how many different people and groups with God knows how many different ideas of what they are doing and why. The more skillful we become at creating social realities, the more of us get into the business and the more realities we create. And our deliberate reality-creating, future-making, civilization-building projects always turn out to have unexpected consequences: no plan of social action, and certainly no revolution, has failed to surprise its creators. Much of what happens is the product of actions that people set in motion *without* explicit reality-creating agendas, but that turn out to have them anyway. The German philosopher Jürgen Habermas—one of the great theoreticians on the subject we are discussing here—writes of systems "colonizing the lifeworld": that is, impersonal systems created for the purpose of merely "getting things done"—such as markets and bureaucracies—lead to changes in values and beliefs that are necessary in order to make the systems work more effectively.[2]

And so we hope and blunder our way into the future, worldmakers in spite of ourselves. Things change, and the way things change changes, and we try to build a global polis at the same time that we realize (a) that we don't know how to create social reality, and (b) that we don't know how not to.

GLIMPSES OF A *ZEITGEIST*: FIVE METATRENDS

The belief-about-belief that I (somewhat reluctantly) call the postmodern worldview is not all by itself terribly revolutionary, nor terribly difficult for the average person to begin to understand, nor even, in a certain sense, new. Many cultural traditions have had ideas about the illusory nature of belief, and many people have written and thought about the "culture shock" experiences of encountering other people with different worldviews. I suspect, in fact, that if you penetrate deeply enough into the belief system of any society—even a premodern society with no highly developed consciousness of *having* a belief system—you will find hints of a shadow side, rituals and customs that secretly mock the society's own truths and customs. You will find humor, and humor is our universal way of pushing pinholes in public reality. I suspect that although the ideas I call a postmodern worldview are only now emerging into the sunlight, they have been there always in the background as people have inhabited their symbolic universes, constructed their realities, and occasionally laughed at themselves.

What is new is the pervasiveness of such ideas, and the willingness of so many people to state them clearly. We see postmodern thought emerging from countless different directions—transforming different cultures, belief systems, and intellectual disciplines.

The postmodern worldview is becoming the *zeitgeist*, as modernism was in past centuries. It will be a central element in the global culture, but it is hardly likely to be universally accepted *in any explicit form* or to unite all people; it will be central as a global theme around which people will differ and disagree. Here and there, it will probably appear as something like an ideology. In the past, there were some who understood and embraced modernism—the *philosophes* of the Enlightenment come to mind—and gave it a distinct energy and identity. Others embraced modernism but did not understand it; still others understood it but did not embrace it. And some did not get the news at all, or at least not until much later; there are still societies that have been scarcely touched by the modern age. But nobody will be untouched by the postmodern age. For the first time, things are happening to the entire human species at once. And we know it; the knowing is one of the most important things that is happening.

It would be best if postmodernism were widely understood, *explicitly* understood, debated, and worked through by everybody—but it probably won't be, and many people will be more battered by cultural changes and political innovations and strange shifts of morality and life-style than they might have been. The shift to postmodernism is far more likely to be traumatic if you are convinced that there can be no truth without absolutes, no science without objectivity, no morality without rules, no society without uniform values and beliefs, no religion without a church. Obviously many people hold such convictions—or are trying to. And yet, if you look at all the games that are being played with belief systems such as Christianity and Marxism, it is equally obvious that a sense of the postmodern condition is springing up in the minds of many people who have no name for it—and no idea at all that they are feeling and thinking about life and organizing their experience in profoundly different new ways.

Let me identify some of the new ways. Following are five fundamental characteristics of the postmodern worldview, ways of looking at reality/unreality that are evident in actions people are taking in relation to politics, religion, and culture. I call them metatrends, because we experience them not merely as changes, but as changes in the way things change. I offer them as part diagnosis, part manifesto: diagnosis because they are important but relatively little-noticed aspects of what is going on in our time, and manifesto because I believe we can function more honestly and effectively if we identify and understand these processes so we can use them and not merely be affected by them. The five are (1) changes in thinking-about-thinking (shifts in the public psychology); (2) changes in identity and boundaries; (3) changes in learning; (4) changes in morals, ethics, and values; and (5) changes in relationship to traditions, customs, and institutions.

First, thinking-about-thinking. We can see a growing awareness of the multidimensional, relativistic quality of human experience. This is expressed in many ways: in psychological concepts such as Minsky's society of mind, in theories about multiple personalities and subpersonalities, in Westernizing spiritual traditions such as Buddhism, and in literary images such as Salman Rushdie's idea of mental channel hopping.

The most important part of this is thinking-about-thinking itself, reflexivity: the mind's ability to see itself, and to see itself seeing itself. At a high level of intellectual discourse, the notion of self-reflexivity has become in this century a tool for criticizing (and deconstructing) grand philosophical systems. A leading constructivist, Paul Watzlawick of Stanford, writes:

> *As audacious and powerful as the most sublime philosophical edifice may be, as much as it may appear to be an iron-clad system, it nevertheless has a fatal flaw: It cannot prove its own logic and freedom from contradiction from within itself.* This fundamental condition for the logical construction of every reality we create has been most thoroughly researched by the mathematicians—above all by Kurt Gödel—and their results are valid for all thought systems having a complexity that corresponds at least to that of arithmetic. In order to establish its freedom from contradiction, it is unavoidable that the given system step out of its own conceptual framework to demonstrate its consistency from without by using interpretive principles that it cannot generate from within . . . and so on *ad infinitum*.[3]

This recognition involves two of the main keys to postmodern thought: the admission that all explanations of reality are themselves constructions—human, useful, but not perfect—and the ability to "step out" of reality constructs and see them as such.

The stepping out is the whole theme of Douglas Hofstadter's *Gödel, Escher, Bach*, in which he shows the mind seeing itself in mathematics, music, and art. The Dutch graphic artist M. C. Escher illustrates the idea of reflexivity so beautifully, in so many ways—such as his famous drawing of a hand that is drawing a hand that is drawing the hand—that they are suitable for the symbols of our time, iconoclastic icons of the postmodern era.

Because stepping out is what we all do, all the time; it is the characteristic action of the postmodern era. It is performed with equal regularity by objectivists and constructivists, right-wingers and left-wingers, revisionists and fundamentalists. The Reverend W. A. Criswell, whom we met in chapter 1, steps out when he tells Bill Moyers that the Bible is the final authority for everything. What is his authority for saying the Bible is the final authority? Does it say that in the Bible? If it does, isn't that using a system to prove itself? If it doesn't, isn't he being an errant fundamentalist by relying on another authority?

Anthropologists step out of their cultures to study other cultures, and the people they study step out by describing their culture to anthropologists. We step out of good old American values when we attack them, and we step out when we defend them. We step out of myth when we talk about creating new ones. We step out of language when we deconstruct it, or oppose deconstructing it. To live in a pluralistic world, and to think about how to live in it, is to be continually required to step out.

As we let go of the modern era's idea of progress (everything gets better) we may develop a postmodern idea of it as ever-increasing reflexivity, each era of history seeing previous eras and seeing itself, the individual mind more capable of thinking about its thought. All of postmodernism, in fact, can be summarized as looking at beliefs—including one's own.

As such concepts become more commonly accepted and disseminated, whether through art or cognitive science or popular culture, they become available to us as templates for personal experience. Just as (according to Kuhn's account) a new scientific paradigm sometimes enables researchers to accept and understand observations/data that they might previously have ignored, a new public idea of what human consciousness is *supposed* to be like enables people to organize private experience differently—perhaps to notice, accept, and understand thoughts or feelings that might previously have been overlooked or repressed; perhaps to understand events in new ways. An experience that a premodern person might have understood as possession by an evil spirit might be understood by a modern psychoanalytic patient as more mischief from the Id, and might be understood by a postmodern individual as a subpersonality making itself heard—might even, if you want to get really postmodern about it, be recognized as all three.

Second, and following from the above, people develop a different sense of identity and boundaries. We live in the age of the fading boundary, the twilight of a mind-set that structured reality with sharp lines. The boundaries between nations, races, classes, cultures, species—all become less distinct. Plenty of people of course try to maintain the old boundaries. The United States government is currently digging a moat along the Mexican border and has invested millions in Star Wars research—the latter an attempt to maintain a national boundary in space. Racists continue to oppose the mixing of black and white, aristocrats mourn the breakdown of the old class hierarchies, culture-preservers fret about the dilution into globalism of French *haute couture* or the traditions of primitive peoples. Anti-biotechnology crusaders yearn to legislate the genetic purity of species. Expect many such reactionary efforts—but boundary lines are not what they used to be, either in thought or in practice.

And for most of us, one-dimensional social identities are not what they used to be either. They are simply not adequate to our self-concepts or to the situations in which we function. It is hard for the average contemporary person—especially in the West—to understand what a complete and final definer of the self class once was, and it is becoming equally difficult for many people to maintain their attachment to *any* of the ethnic, national, religious, or other cards of identity that have been so essential to social reality in the past. Some people get a lot out of being Jewish or English or American Indian, and some don't. We all make choices about how seriously we take such identities, and many of us make choices about the identities themselves. A world in which religious conversion is commonplace and millions of people change nationalities is a different world for everybody in it—definitely including those who make no such outward change. It is a world in which the boundaries between religions and nationalities are seen to be artificial and movable.

Most people need some public identifier, some anchor to a historical tradition and a recognized group. Some of us obviously need it more than others, but even enlightened Buddhists seem to want to let you know they are Buddhists. More and more, we find it suitable to identify ourselves with more than one term. Multiple identity becomes a common feature of postmodern life. Whenever we describe ourselves, we should add "etc."

America is probably the leading multiple-identity society, with its growing numbers of Hispanic Americans and Asian Americans and all its older ethnic groups who have still not entirely dehyphenated. But multiple-identity people can now be found everywhere. Life is often difficult for them, as Salman Rushdie's travails dramatized for the world. Their existence is a threat to those who wish to preserve the integrity of the single-identity groups that traditionally gave everybody a sure sense of what they belonged to and who they were expected to hate. But multiple identities must inevitably be accepted, and honored. We are not likely to have any nations that are not pluralistic—especially when so many of the people in them are pluralistic all by themselves. And personal identity-change takes place much more easily when multiple identities are commonplace; you do not have to undergo the stress of complete conversion.

Third, we come to accept the centrality of learning to the life of every individual, to every society, and to the species as a whole. At the individual level learning is best described as growth, at the social level as progress, at the species level as evolution. Perhaps "discovery" is a better word than "learning" for what I am trying to describe here. Most ideas of learning, as found in traditional societies and doctrinal religions, assume that whatever information one may need, whatever understanding, exists somewhere in the society: the task is to get in front of a good teacher, pay attention, and do your homework.

The kind of learning that becomes a necessity for survival in the postmodern age—the discovery kind of learning—is a bit different. It is not so much the constant filling-in of a picture as an ongoing process of reality-construction in which it frequently becomes necessary to step out of the picture, and sometimes to drop the old picture entirely. Science, if properly understood, is a good model for this kind of learning; not scientism, the worship of facts, but science based on the constant attempt to falsify one's hypotheses and find better ones. Pragmatism, the philosophical tradition we associate with American philosophers such as William James and John Dewey and (more recently) Richard Rorty, also has much to contribute to how we go about learning and living in the postmodern world. In the pragmatic view, theories become, as James put it, "instruments, not answers to enigmas, in which we can rest."[4] To be a postmodern pragmatist is to recognize all constructs as theories—and hence as instruments to be used where appropriate and periodically replaced.

Fourth, we come to accept morality, and moral discourse, as a living and central element in human existence. We see our interpersonal relationships as collaborative efforts in constructing values. We see education as, among other things, a training in the skills of moral reasoning—morality not merely handed down but learned and created and re-created out of experience. And when there is conflict about that, as there inevitably will be, we accept the conflict also as an arena for expressing and creating values.

The collapse of belief does not, it turns out, result in a collapse of morality: quite the opposite. Many people turn to old belief systems precisely because they come with ready-to-wear values. Other people find their values in the give-and-take of moral reasoning, in secular humanism, in New Age or mystical religions, in political commitments, in philosophy. Plenty of paths, and plenty of people on all of them. New developments in biotechnology and medical science create a demand for professional ethicists in hospitals. New demands for ethics in politics keep governments everywhere in turmoil; politicians are repeatedly surprised to find that what was kept secret and tolerated a few decades ago is now made public and criticized. The early postmodern years are bringing, instead of a collapse of morality, a renaissance of searching for principles of life that we variously call morals, ethics, values. And this is not merely a single shift of values but a continual dynamic process of moral discourse and discovery. Morals are not being handed down from the mountaintop on graven tablets; they are being created by people out of the challenges of the times. The morals of today are not the morals of yesterday, and they will not be the morals of tomorrow.

Fifth, we inhabit all kinds of SCRs in new ways. A social construction of reality does not have to be discarded the moment one has recognized that that is what it is. The Wizard of Oz, upon being exposed as human, may still be a very good man; and the belief, tradition, value, religion, norm, or Constitution that stands revealed as nothing more than a social construct may still be a very useful item.

When you step out of an SCR, identify it as such and perhaps even perceive its limitations, you may very likely step back again. You can step in, in many different ways. Much of the social behavior and the political position-taking of our time can be identified as different ways of stepping in. You can deny that you have ever stepped out and hunker down as a fundamentalist defender of the eternal rightness of your tradition. You can recognize that it is merely a tradition and deliberately take it on anyway—as, for example, some people choose to observe the customs of Orthodox Judaism—and do so quite seriously. You can do the same thing with a giggle, and call it camp. You can lose the faith, as has probably happened to more priests than we will ever know, and continue to preach it because you think it is good for others. You can come to a point in your life when you see the artificial nature of your society's reality, and continue to live within it anyway simply because it is comfortable to do so.

This is especially important in relation to all the artifacts we call government—norms and laws, and the philosophical principles and cultural traditions they are derived from. These do not merely evaporate, even if all lawyers were to agree on their artificiality. They remain honorable monuments to prior value-creating efforts, they remain literally true for many people in the society, and they remain highly useful guidelines and foundations for new efforts at creativity.

Whenever people step out of a reality construct and step back in again, the stepping in involves both choice and creativity. "In the same river we step and we do not step," wrote Heraclitus. He may have been trying to tell us something about living in social constructions of reality. Every decision to reinhabit a tradition has a bit of the quality of the Scotsmen getting back into their kilts—we have made up something new, even if we don't want to admit it to ourselves or to others. This seems to be a way that people create reality without taking on the stress of consciously doing so.

As we become more sensitive to these various strategies, we discover that we are living in a much more interesting time than we may have suspected—a time in which there are not only many realities, but many ways of living in and with them—and we may become more skilled at making such choices.

Each of these ways of changing can be found all around us, as the life strategies of people who do not think of themselves as postmoderns. Each relates to the other; they are all part of our growing repertoire of ways to construct and reconstruct reality. If this is postmodernism, let us make the most of it.

HINTS OF A CIVILIZATION: SIX NORMS

As we look around for hopeful signs, signs that the world is making the transition from theater to civilization, we can select many kinds of evidence: the fact that we have gotten this far without a nuclear war, the growing number of international organizations, the modest success of groups such as Amnesty International at reducing the sum total of human barbarity. Here I would like to direct attention to the slow but nonetheless impressive emergence of global norms.

A norm is a pattern of behavior that is somewhere along the road to reification, taking on a certain sanctity—becoming accepted as a way that people *ought* to behave. Norms govern commerce, play, politics, love. Any organized society has plenty of norms—sometimes encoded as laws, sometimes supported by tradition and religious belief. Much of the fear of postmodernism is based on the assumption that norms can have no binding force without systems of absolute belief to back them up. The question of whether we can have a civilization in a multicultural, multiple-reality world essentially boils down to whether we can have norms without belief in the traditional sense.

A group of leading scholars made a study of the state of international cooperation and came up with the following list of norms of behavior generally accepted among nations. The list is instructive both for reminding us that we do make some progress, and for reminding us of how far we have yet to go:

> *Territorial integrity.* Since 1945 few countries have had their territory forcibly annexed by another country, as was customary for millennia past. (But the system does not yet inhibit or condemn more subtle forms of take-over.)
>
> *The inviolability of diplomatic missions.* This traditional principle has been codified and strengthened, in an effort to keep pace with the enormous growth in the size and range of diplomatic functions. The violations are dramatic because they are rare.
>
> *The non-use and non-proliferation of nuclear weapons.* The disproportionate destructive power of nuclear weapons has made them unusable even as a last resort in 43 years of turbulent international politics featuring many bloody wars. . . .
>
> *Immunity of civilian aircraft and ships.* Brutal attacks on both have served to strengthen norms against hijacking and firing on innocent craft. Attitudes toward terrorism . . . have been hardening throughout the world in recent years.
>
> *International responsibility for helping refugees.* . . . With some large exceptions (Japan, the Soviet Union) there has been a striking growth in the willingness of governments and peoples to accept and resettle refugees.
>
> *Decolonization.* Non-subjugation of other people, along with the unacceptability of overt, officially sanctioned racial discrimination, are norms now widely and fiercely asserted. As is usual in moral posturing, however, the outrage is selective.[5]

No reader, reviewing the above, is likely to be swept away with the feeling that the world's troubles are over, and the authors of the report are themselves anything but Pollyannaish. Nevertheless, they insist, "significant norms of international behavior have become widely accepted; that is, they pass the test that an obvious violation, however unpunished, brings near-universal opprobrium." Furthermore, these norms are not propped up by any particular religion or ideology; although they are in general terms compatible with most of them, they are actually elements of a global culture, frail harbingers of an emergent global order.

At this point they are quite precarious, and probably still not all that widely held. It might be more accurate to call them norms of the international political subculture—the loose network of diplomats, politicians, journalists, scholars, and activists—than of the world's population. Surveys in the past have revealed that great numbers of Americans don't know anything about the Bill of Rights and a lot of those who do know something about it don't agree with it; norms of international behavior probably have an even narrower base.

Given the mobility of the times, any number of things could happen to this small cluster of global norms. It could, with years and growing observation of the rules, become more solidly reified, and be joined by other norms to fill out a structure of global civilization. Or any or all of them could be—literally—blown away in a few turbulent days.

PROBLEMS FOR EVERYBODY: TWO MEGA-ISSUES

The global not-quite-civilization is being presented with problems of a sort that no civilization—not even relatively stable ones with fully functioning political institutions, clearly defined norms, and common systems of value and belief—has ever had to cope with. Among these are the prospect of massive environmental change, and worldwide demands for human rights.

These problems have a lot to do with the matters we are exploring here. They will be central and visible parts of the world's shared reality, will force themselves into everybody's life, and in that sense will become part of the global superculture. And they are both—although in different ways—social constructions of reality.

People constructed the idea of a spheroid planet a few centuries ago, the idea of evolution less than two centuries ago, and the idea of an environment in the past couple of decades. Before that we had notions roughly *resembling* what people now mean when they talk about the environment—for example, the eighteenth-century concept of "climate"—but only recently has the environment emerged as a general theme of public discussion. Heinz von Foerster writes of how this hit some of his acquaintances:

> I am sure you remember the plain citizen Jourdain in Molière's *Le Bourgeois Gentilhomme* who, nouveau riche, travels in the sophisticated circles of the French aristocracy and who is eager to learn. On one occasion his new friends speak about poetry and prose, and Jourdain discovers to his amazement and great delight that whenever he speaks, he speaks prose. He is overwhelmed by his discovery: "I am speaking Prose! I have always spoken Prose! I have spoken Prose throughout my whole life!"
>
> A similar discovery has been made not so long ago, but was neither of poetry nor of prose—it was the environment that was discovered. I remember when, perhaps ten or fifteen years ago, some of my American friends came running to me with the delight and amazement of having just made a great discovery: "I am living in an Environment! I have lived in an Environment throughout my whole life!"
>
> However, neither M. Jourdain nor my friends have as yet made another discovery, and that is when M. Jourdain speaks, may it be prose or poetry, it is he who invents it, and likewise, when we perceive our environment, it is we who invent it.[6]

The concept of "The Environment"—which is what von Foerster is talking about—is a social construct, like "The Economy." So, in another way, is the actual physical environment we envision when we talk about it. Our ancestors have been moving about the earth for millions of years, modifying it with hunting and gathering, with agriculture, with the systematic and unsystematic transportation of plant and animal life from one place to another, with technology, with industry—so that now even our wilderness areas are human creations.[7]

Environmental politics, like economic politics, depends heavily on information—statistics, trends, "indicators." We evaluate the performance of presidents on the basis of inflation rates and GNP, and in 1929 people jumped out of windows because of the numbers on ticker tapes. Similarly, we rely on measurements—of air and water quality, for example—for our perceptions of the health of the environment. We would not have an environment crisis as a public issue if modern scientists had not developed improved information-gathering capabilities that, in effect, make us better at gathering bad news.

The information basis of environmental politics becomes even more striking as we turn to the alarming prospect of major changes in the biosphere. We confront data of species extinction, soil erosion, deforestation, population growth—information about something happening to the whole world. The information is always incomplete, fallible, capable of being interpreted in different ways—or even of being denied entirely. That is the only kind of information there is. Yet its importance, the urgency of the message it seems to bring, can scarcely be overestimated.

The greenhouse effect and damage to the earth's ozone layer, problems of a kind the human species has never before confronted, arrive as abstract information—not things that we see, or that our neighbors see, but numbers and ideas about them that come from anonymous scientists. The information is incomplete, and different people have entirely different interpretations of it. Some people tell us the buildup in the atmosphere of CO_2 and other gases will lead to global warming. Some say there will be no climate change. Some say the world will get colder. The scientific facts are anything but conclusive, and they do not seem to tell us what to do. Yet we—and "we" in this case means the human species—have to take the information seriously, to do something about it, and to do something fast. The information, with all its inadequacies, calls for actions on a grand scale, global cooperation of a sort never before undertaken. It also calls for turning ideas that many people have scarcely heard about, like energy conservation, into global norms.

The information provides the ground for conflict of all sorts, and it also becomes in its own way a part of the global commons and the global culture. We do become, as the current jargon has it, an information society. And we become a global society, because the information is everybody's property and everybody's business. The picture of the world that we draw with it is part of the emergent fiction.

The idea of human rights was emerging into the public dialogue at roughly the same time that philosophers such as Montesquieu were talking about "climate" as a factor in the progress and prosperity of societies. A few centuries earlier, in the days when the world was flat and there was no environment, there were also no human rights. In Plato you can find some discussion of the rights and duties of citizens of the republic, but no assertion that *all people* naturally possess rights. Not until John Locke's time do we find it stated that God gives every human being rights, which are a kind of personal property. Locke's words were adapted, and turned into a much more vigorous assertion of rights, by Thomas Jefferson in the Declaration of Independence.

Locke had written in his *Second Treatise of Government*: "Man being born, as has been proved, with a title to perfect freedom, and an uncontrolled enjoyment of all the rights and privileges of the law of nature, equally with any other man, or number of men in the world, hath by nature a power . . . to preserve his property, that is, his life, liberty and estate. . . ." Jefferson wrote: "We hold these truths to be self-evident, that all men are created equal; that they are endowed by their Creator with certain inalienable rights: that among these are life, liberty, and the pursuit of happiness." Locke had written that "men unite into societies that they may have the united strength of the whole society to secure and defend their properties. . . ." Jefferson wrote that "to secure these rights, governments are instituted among men, deriving their just powers from the consent of the governed." So rights became the property of all people, and the protection of them the basis of government. A few years after Jefferson's declaration came the French Revolution, with its own declaration of the rights of man.

It took another century or so for governments to take the logical next stop of agreeing that if people did indeed have rights, these rights should be recognized and protected by governments other than their own. Some progress in this area was made after World War I, some more progress after World War II with the United Nations' Universal Declaration of Human Rights, some more in the 1970s when President Jimmy Carter made it a principle of U.S. foreign policy. After two hundred years or so of rhetoric, some human rights are beginning to attain the status of global norms; national governments everywhere are reaching the point of at least professing that they do not violate them.

People create rights—they created the idea of rights, then they created the rights, and finally they created laws to protect rights. At a certain point in history, von Foerster's friends would have come running to him with the announcement that they had rights, had always had rights. Currently some people are trying to create better protections for rights, and others are trying to create new rights. The list has lengthened since Locke and Jefferson. The 1948 U.N. declaration went beyond the then-generally accepted civil and political rights (life, liberty, freedom from arbitrary arrest) to economic, cultural, and social rights such as the right to an education and the right to participate in the cultural life of a community. It is not at all hard to state anything that you want or believe in as a right; I took part in such an exercise some years ago when I helped draft an "environmental bill of rights" that we attempted to get written into the California constitution.

More people are demanding rights, and demanding realization of the rights they are supposed to have already. And we are not at all clear—certainly we do not have international agreement about—what a right is, or where one comes from.

The idea of rights becomes a part of the global superculture, the emergent fiction. But it is extremely difficult to find a basis for agreement about rights—other than might, the one that people generally recognized before Locke's time. When there are so many points of view, so many different interests, so many realities trying to be born, people are easily tempted to ground their position in an absolute: to say rights are God-given; they are "natural." Such claims may slip past when the right in question is life or liberty; when it is the right to day care for children or holidays with pay, it becomes more difficult to make progress without entering into serious dialogue about what is decent and possible—and creating new values in the process.

The temptation to fall back on absolutes, to seek a cosmic anchor for one's own position, is even greater in regard to environmental issues.

As our concern about environmental deterioration grows, we hear more and more political pronouncements based on nature. People preach endlessly about nature, with little thought that it is another reification. But the concept of nature is quite different in different societies, in some hard to locate at all. We tend to think of nature as that which is "untouched by human hands"—so that some areas are still in a "natural" state, some kinds of food are "natural" rather than "artificial"—but the boundary between the natural and the nonnatural is perhaps the fuzziest of all.

We are not going to deal with such problems as the deterioration of the global environment and the worldwide demands for rights without finding that beliefs about belief become part of the dialogue, and that we have to address such meta-issues more explicitly and on a greater scale than people have ever done. To deal with environmental problems and human rights at all requires increasing communication and interaction—in effect, creating a civilization. A tall order in any case, and made more serious by the urgency of the problems and the likelihood that they will not wait forever to be dealt with. The environment and human rights—realities we have created—challenge us to create new realities, to create global culture, and to move continually in and out of our older frameworks of value and belief.

A STORY ABOUT STORIES

The competition between different stories, whether based on religion or ideology, is far less critical to the prospects for peace in the world, and to the emergence of a global civilization, than the competition between different stories about stories—between absolutist/objectivist and relativist/constructivist ideas about the nature of human truth. A pluralistic civilization can only be built with a great amount of tolerance, and the kind of tolerance that comes from people who believe in the cosmic certainty of their truth (and theirs alone) is both limited and patronizing. You can only become truly tolerant of other people's realities by having found some new way to inhabit your own.

To develop tolerance is to develop a story about stories, a perspective on all our values and beliefs. We need such a story desperately now, as much as we need sound environmental management and respect for human rights. And developing such a perspective involves something more than becoming familiar with current trends in cognitive science or critical theory—although both of those are good windows to look though; it involves a view of evolution, and of history. Just as we develop an image of the world and the human species—as we create the world and create humanity—

so do we develop an image of the human species as an indefatigable creator of stories, myths, values, beliefs, theories, morals, laws, and religions. And to know that we create such things need not destroy our respect for the species nor our respect, even reverence, for the things created.

I don't think we ever step entirely out of socially created reality, or ever shut down the story-making parts of our minds, or ever should. When we step out of a reality to examine it, we step in to a reality in which it is possible to examine realities, and that wider terrain is itself a culture, and a custom. The idea of the social construction of reality is itself an SCR, and this book is a story.

Learning about such things, continually reexamining beliefs about beliefs, becomes the most important learning task of all the others needed for survival in our time. And, although achieving some degree of insight into the construction of reality is not beyond anybody, further learning about it isn't easy. We don't really know how to do such learning, or such teaching, and it is likely that wherever people try to do such teaching they will be opposed—as the educators of "moral reasoning" have been—by people who view the effort as inherently evil.

We are seeing in our lifetimes the collapse of the objectivist worldview that dominated the modern era, the worldview that gave people faith in the absolute and permanent rightness of certain beliefs and values. The worldview emerging in its place is constructivist. If we operate from this worldview we see all information and all stories as human creations that fit, more or less well, with our experience and within a universe that remains always beyond us and always mysterious. We honor the search for truth and knowledge and values, but regard what we find as the truth and knowledge and values of people—of people in our time.

Wherever a nation revises its Marxism, wherever a group of Catholics revise their Christianity, wherever a scientist works with two theories at the same time, wherever a person chooses to live within a belief system for the simple comfort it brings and not because he or she considers it the last word, wherever people play in campy irreverence with forms of culture, wherever a person who believes one thing lives with peace and respect near a person who believes something entirely different—a constructivist worldview, by whatever name, is present. And wherever that is happening, the forces of reaction—the urge toward modern, even premodern, certainty—can be found, both in society and within each of us.

The constructivist worldview is a story about stories, and it is also a story. It is a belief, and in some ways an arbitrary one. It presumes, without knowing how to prove it, that there is an objective cosmos that we can seek to understand, even though all our understanding is always in a sense subjective. There are other stories, stories that there is no objective cosmos at all, or that it is what we create. And yet other stories will probably come along.

We all have a lot of work to do to learn our way into the postmodern worldview, and to create the emergent fiction that is the world we live in; but even as that happens, other and better fictions may emerge, hills beyond hills.

Notes

PREFACE

1. Richard J. Bernstein, *Beyond Objectivism and Relativism* (Philadelphia: University of Pennsylvania Press, 1985), 1.

CHAPTER 1. WELCOME TO THE POSTMODERN WORLD

1. Allan Bloom, *The Closing of the American Mind* (New York: Simon and Schuster, 1987), 25.
2. Frances Moore Lappé, *Rediscovering America's Values* (New York: Ballentine, 1989).
3. Robert Bellah et al., *Habits of the Heart* (Berkeley: University of California Press, 1985).
4. James Fallows, *More Like Us* (Boston: Houghton Mifflin, 1989).
5. E. D. Hirsch, Jr., *Cultural Literacy* (Boston: Houghton Mifflin, 1987).
6. *New Options* newsletter, May 29, 1989, 8.
7. Stephen Toulmin, *The Return to Cosmology* (Berkeley: University of California Press, 1982), 254.
8. William Butler Yeats, "The Second Coming" in Richard J. Finneran, ed., *The Poems of W. B. Yeats: A New Edition* (New York: Macmillan Publishing Company, 1924), 187.
9. Riane Eisler, *The Chalice and the Blade* (San Francisco: Harper & Row, 1987).
10. Rachel Sternberg, quoted in Lillian S. Robinson, "Sometimes, Always, Never: Their Women's History and Ours." Unpublished paper, Institute for Research on Women and Gender, Stanford University, 1988.
11. Elizabeth Fox-Genovese, "Androcrats Go Home!" *New York Times Book Review,* Nov. 4, 1987.
12. Sarah B. Pomery, "When No One Wore the Pants," review of Gerda Lerner, *The Creation of Patriarchy, New York Times Book Review,* April 20, 1986.
13. Plato, *The Republic*, trans. Allan Bloom (New York: Basic Books, 1968), 94.
14. W. S. Gilbert, *Iolanthe*, Act. II.
15. Quoted on National Public Radio, April 1987.
16. David Purpel and Kevin Ryan, eds., *Moral Education . . . It Comes With the Territory* (Berkeley: McCutchan, 1976), 84.
17. Richard L. Curwin and Geri Curwin, *Developing Individual Values in the Classroom* (Palo Alto, CA: LEARNING Handbooks, 1974) 9.
18. *Values Clarification: How You Can Effectively Fight It* (Longview, TX: The MEL GABLERs, 1983).

19. *Education Newsletter,* A Publication of the National Association of Christian Educators and Citizens for Excellence in Education, P.O. Box 3200, Costa Mesa, CA 92628.
20. Gary Bower, White House Domestic Affairs Advisor, quoted on National Public Radio, April 1987.
21. *God and Politics: The Battle for the Bible,* Production of Public Affairs Television, Inc. A presentation of WNET/New York.
22. "More Ferment Among Southern Baptists," *Christianity Today,* Nov. 20, 1987, 46.
23. Peter L. Berger and Thomas Luckmann, *The Social Construction of Reality* (New York: Doubleday Anchor, 1967), 121.
24. Fergus M. Bordewich, "Holy Terror," *The Atlantic,* April 1987, 63.
25. William Greider, "Annals of Finance: The Fed," Part II, *The New Yorker,* Nov. 16, 1987, 68.

CHAPTER 2. TO SEE THE WIZARD

1. Karl Mannheim, *Ideology and Utopia* (New York: Harcourt, Brace, 1936), 7.
2. Max Weber, *Wirtschaft und Gesellschaft* and *Religionsoziologie: Stande, Klassen und Religion,* quoted in Mannheim, *Ideology and Utopia,* 7.
3. Philip Lee Ralph, *The Renaissance in Perspective* (London: G. Bell, 1973).
4. Hannah Arendt, *The Human Condition* (Chicago: University of Chicago Press, 1958), 279.
5. Arendt, *The Human Condition,* 281.
6. Roy Wagner, *The Invention of Culture* (Chicago: University of Chicago Press, 1981), 4.
7. Mannheim, *Ideology and Utopia,* 78.
8. Peter L. Berger and Thomas Luckmann, *The Social Construction of Reality* (Garden City, NY: Doubleday, 1967), 89.
9. Alfred Korzybski, *Science and Sanity* (Lancaster, PA: Science Press, 1933), lxiii.
10. Korzybski, *Science and Sanity,* lxiv.
11. Korzybski, *Science and Sanity,* 61.
12. Stuart Chase, *The Tyranny of Words* (New York: Harcourt, Brace, 1938), 10.
13. Quoted in Chase, *The Tyranny of Words,* 99–100.
14. George Orwell, "Politics and the English Language," in Sonia Orwell and Ian Argus, eds. *In Front of Your Nose* (New York: Harcourt, Brace, 1968), 140.
15. Benjamin Whorf, *Language, Thought and Reality* (New York: Wiley, 1956), 214.
16. Theodore Roszak, *The Making of a Counter Culture* (New York: Doubleday, 1969).
17. Alan Watts, *The Joyous Cosmology* (New York: Vintage, 1962).
18. Alan Watts, *Psychotherapy East and West* (New York: Mentor, 1963), 15.
19. R. D. Laing, *The Politics of Experience* (New York: Pantheon, 1967), 101.
20. Laing, *The Politics of Experience,* 43.
21. Todd Gitlin, *The Sixties* (New York: Bantam, 1989), 435.
22. Antonin Artaud, *The Theater and Its Double* (New York: Grove, 1958), 74.
23. Greil Marcus, *Lipstick Traces* (Cambridge: Harvard University Press, 1989), 6.
24. Marcus, *Lipstick Traces,* 83–84.
25. Michael Selzer, *Terrorist Chic* (New York: Hawthorn, 1979), 56.
26. Marcus, *Lipstick Traces,* 77.

CHAPTER 3. SCIENCE AND THE CREATIVE BRAIN

1. Michael S. Gazzaniga, *The Social Brain* (New York: Basic Books, 1985), 72.
2. Such dates are always imprecise, and many would persuasively argue that behaviorism had a longer life span. J. B. Watson popularized it in the mid-1920s, building on earlier experimental work, and research in the behaviorist mode is still being done. The dates I give are the period in which it was clearly predominant.
3. John B. Watson, *Behaviorism* (New York: W. W. Norton, 1925), 19.
4. A. Tversky and D. Kahneman, "Extensional vs. Intuitive Reasoning: The Conjunctive Fallacy in Probability Judgment," *Psychological Review* 90 (1983), 293–315.
5. Howard Gardner, *The Mind's New Science* (New York: Basic Books, 1987), 56–57.
6. On-line computer conference, Western Behavioral Sciences Institute, 1989.
7. Marvin Minsky, *The Society of Mind* (New York: Simon and Schuster, 1986), 51.
8. Jorge Luis Borges, *Other Inquisitions* (New York: Washington Square Press, 1966), 108.
9. B. Berlin and P. Kay, *Basic Color Terms: Their Universality and Evolution* (Berkeley: University of California Press, 1969).
10. B. Berlin, "Ethnobiological Classification," in E. Rosch and B. B. Lloyd, eds., *Cognition and Categorization* (Hillsdale, NJ: Lawrence Erlbaum, 1978).
11. Gardner, *The Mind's New Science*, 348–50; Morton Hunt, *The Universe Within* (New York: Simon and Schuster, 1982), 170–71.
12. M. Sahlins, "Colors and Cultures," *Semiotics* 16 (1976), 1–22.
13. George Lakoff, *Women, Fire, and Dangerous Things* (Chicago: University of Chicago Press, 1987), 93.
14. The essay is included in Stephen Jay Gould, *Hen's Teeth and Horse's Toes* (New York: Norton, 1983).
15. Lakoff, *Women, Fire, and Dangerous Things*, 9.
16. See Clifford Geertz, *Interpretation of Cultures* (New York: Basic Books, 1973), and Kenneth Gergen, "The Social Construction Movement in Modern Psychology," *American Psychologist*, March 1985, 266–75. Gergen uses the term "constructionist" rather than "constructivist" as a general term for the movement as a whole.
17. Hilary Putnam, *Reason, Truth and History* (Cambridge: Cambridge University Press, 1981), 40.
18. Quoted in Ernst von Glasersfeld, "An Introduction to Radical Constructivism," in Paul Watzlawick, ed., *The Invented Reality* (New York: W. W. Norton, 1984), 27.
19. Von Glasersfeld, "An Introduction to Radical Constructivism," 18.
20. Humberto R. Maturana and Francisco J. Varela, *The Tree of Knowledge* (Boston: New Science Library, 1987), 234.
21. Heinz von Foerster, "On Constructing a Reality," in Watzlawick, *The Invented Reality*, 47.
22. Rupert Riedl, "The Consequences of Causal Thinking," in Watzlawick, *The Invented Reality* 70–71.
23. Riedl, "The Consequences of Causal Thinking," 82.
24. Clark Hull, *Principles of Behavior* (New York: Appleton Century Crofts, 1934), 24.

25. Thomas S. Kuhn, *The Structure of Scientific Revolutions*, 2d ed. rev. (Chicago: University of Chicago Press, 1970), vi.
26. Kuhn, *The Structure of Scientific Revolutions*, 111.
27. Paul Feyerabend, *Against Method* (London: Verso, 1975), 30.
28. Kuhn, *The Structure of Scientific Revolutions*, 206.
29. Kuhn, *The Structure of Scientific Revolutions*, 206.
30. Albert Einstein, *Autobiographical Notes*, quoted in Heinz Pagels, *The Dreams of Reason* (New York: Bantam Books, 1989), 153.
31. Von Foerster, "On Constructing a Reality," 46.
32. Nelson Goodman, *Of Mind and Other Matters* (Cambridge: Harvard University Press, 1984), 42.
33. Quoted in Tony Rothman, "A 'What You See Is What You Beget' Theory," *Discovery*, May 1987, 96.
34. H. M. Collins, "The Meaning of Experiment: Replication and Reasonableness," in Hilary Lawson and Lisa Appignanesi, eds., *Dismantling Truth* (London: Weidenfeld and Nicolson, 1989), 88.
35. Jerome Bruner, *Actual Minds, Possible Worlds* (Cambridge: Harvard University Press, 1986), 105.

CHAPTER 4. THE MEANINGS OF LITERATURE

1. The term was coined by John Crowe Ransom. See his *New Criticism* (Westport, CT: Greenwood, 1979).
2. Cleanth Brooks, "The Quick and the Dead: A Comment on Humanistic Studies," in Julien Harris, ed., *The Humanities: An Appraisal* (Madison: University of Wisconsin Press, 1950), 21.
3. For a good historical account of these developments, see William S. Cain, *The Crisis in Criticism* (Baltimore: Johns Hopkins, 1984).
4. William Wimsatt and Monroe Beardsley, *The Verbal Icon* (Lexington: University of Kentucky Press, 1954), 21.
5. Louis Milic, "Unconscious Ordering in the Prose of Swift," in Jacob Leed, ed., *The Computer and Literary Style* (Kent, OH: Kent State, 1966), 276.
6. Richard Ohmann, "Generative Grammars and the Concept of Literary Style," in Glen A. Love and Michael Payne, eds., *Contemporary Essays on Style* (Glenview, IL: Scott, Foresman, 1969), 143.
7. E. D. Hirsch, *Validity in Interpretation* (New Haven, CT: Yale, 1967), 46, 163.
8. E. D. Hirsch, *The Aims of Interpretation* (Chicago: University of Chicago Press, 1976), 13.
9. Stanley Fish, *Is There a Text in this Class?* (Cambridge: Harvard University Press, 1980), 305.
10. Fish, *Is There a Text*, 3.
11. Fish, *Is There a Text*, 10–11.
12. Cain, *The Crises in Criticism*, 130.
13. Henry David Thoreau, *Walden* (New York: Penguin, 1983), 142.
14. Thoreau, *Walden*, 335.
15. Walter Benn Michaels, "*Walden*'s False Bottoms," *Glyph* 1 (1977), 132–49.

16. Terry Eagleton, *Literary Theory* (Minneapolis: University of Minnesota Press, 1983), 131.
17. David Lehman, "The (de) Man Who Put the Con in Deconstruction," *Los Angeles Times*, March 13, 1988.
18. Kenneth E. Melichar, "Deconstruction: Critical Theory or Ideology of Despair," *Humanity and Society*, vol. 12, no. 4 (1988), 366–85.
19. Clare Dalton, "An Essay on the Deconstruction of Contract Doctrine," in Sanford Levinson and Steven Mailloux, eds., *Interpreting Law and Literature* (Evanston, IL: Northwestern University Press, 1988), 285.
20. Calvin Trillin, "A Reporter at Large: Harvard Law," *The New Yorker*, March 26, 1984, 54.
21. Trillin, "A Reporter at Large," 56.
22. Roberto Mangabeira Ungar, *The Critical Legal Studies Movement* (Cambridge: Harvard University Press, 1986).
23. Thomas Pangle, "'Post-Modernist' Thought," *Wall Street Journal*, Jan. 5, 1989, 17.
24. Sanford Levinson, *Constitutional Faith* (Princeton: Princeton University Press, 1989), 86.
25. Pangle, "'Post-Modernist' Thought," 17.
26. Quoted in Calvin Woodard, "Toward a 'Super Liberal' State," *New York Times Book Review*, Nov. 23, 1986, 9.
27. Robert H. Bork, *The Tempting of America* (New York: The Free Press, 1990), 2–3.
28. Robert H. Bork, *The Tempting of America*, 69.
29. Robert H. Bork, *The Tempting of America*, 208.
30. Robert H. Bork, *The Tempting of America*, 144.
31. Paul de Man, *Allegories of Reading* (New Haven: Yale University Press, 1979), p. 216.
32. Susan Sontag, "Notes on 'Camp'," in *Against Interpretation* (New York: Farrar, Straus & Giroux, 1966), 275–92.
33. Brian McHale, *Postmodernist Fiction* (New York: Methuen, 1987), 196.
34. Julio Cortázar, "Continuity of Parks," in *Blow-up and Other Stories* (New York: Pantheon, 1967), 63–64.
35. McHale, *Postmodernist Fiction*, 59.
36. McHale, *Postmodernist Fiction*, 60.

CHAPTER 5. MAKING BELIEFS AND MAKING BELIEVE

1. Nigel Dennis, *Cards of Identity* (New York: The Vanguard Press, 1955), 120.
2. Jean-Paul Sartre, "Childhood of a Leader," in *Intimacy and Other Stories* (New York: New Directions, 1948).
3. Hugh Trevor-Roper, "The Invention of Tradition: The Highland Tradition of Scotland," in Eric Hobsbawm, and Terence Ranger, eds., *The Invention of Tradition* (Cambridge: Cambridge University Press, 1984), 17.
4. Ivan Baillie (1785), quoted in Trevor-Roper, "The Highland Tradition of Scotland," 22.
5. *Letters of Sir W. Scott*, quoted in Trevor-Roper, "The Highland Tradition of Scotland," 29.

6. Bernard Nietschmann, "Third World War: The global conflict over the rights of indigenous nations," *Cultural Survival Quarterly*, reprinted in *Utne Reader*, Nov./Dec. 1988, 84.
7. Thomas S. Martin, "Devolutionism: The new nationalist movements transforming the world," reprinted in *Utne Reader*, Nov./Dec. 1988, 78.
8. Norbert Elias, *The Civilizing Process* (New York: Urizen Books, 1978).
9. Roy F. Baumeister, *Identity* (New York: Oxford, 1986), 125.
10. Robert Jay Lifton, *Thought Reform and the Psychology of Totalism* (New York: Norton, 1961).
11. Eugene Kinkead, *In Every War but One* (New York: Norton, 1959).
12. Nat Hentoff, "Them and Us: Are Peace Protests Self-Therapy?" originally published in *Evergreen Review*, vol. II, no. 48. Reprinted in W. Anderson, ed., *The Age of Protest* (Pacific Palisades, CA: Goodyear, 1969), 254–61.
13. Daniel Boorstin, *The Image* (New York: Atheneum, 1961), 21.
14. Dr. F. Gentry Harris, quoted in *Terrorism, Hearings Before the Committee on Internal Security, House of Representatives*, Part I, Feb.-March 1974, 2954.
15. Andrew Goodwin, "News, Lies, and Videotape," *East Bay Express*, Sept. 1, 1989, 9.
16. F. Scott Fitzgerald, "How to Waste Material: A Note on My Generation," in *Afternoon of an Author* (New York: Scribner's, 1958), 117.

CHAPTER 6. BEING SOMEONE: THE CONSTRUCTION OF PERSONAL REALITY

1. © 1987 SBK April Music Inc./Purple Rabbit Music. Elektra/Asylum Records, A Division of Warner Communications Inc.
2. Abraham Maslow, *Motivation and Personality* (New York: Harper & Row, 1970), 39–46.
3. Ernest Becker, *The Birth and Death of Meaning*, 2d ed. (New York: Free Press, 1971), 139.
4. Erving Goffman, *The Presentation of Self in Everyday Life* (New York: Doubleday Anchor, 1959), 253.
5. Eric Berne, *Games People Play* (New York: Grove, 1964).
6. George Kelly, *Clinical Psychology and Personality* (New York: Wiley, 1969).
7. Jay S. Efran, Robert J. Lukens, and Michael D. Lukens, "Constructivism: What's In It for You?" *Networker*, Sept./Oct. 1988, 27–35.
8. Karl Tomm, and John Lannamann, "Questions as Interventions," *Networker*, Sept./Oct. 1988, 38–41.
9. Donald Polkinghorne, *Narrative Knowing and the Human Sciences* (Albany: SUNY Press, 1988), 160.
10. Polkinghorne, *Narrative Knowing*, 154.
11. Maureen O'Hara, "Constructing Emancipatory Realities," *Association of Humanistic Psychology Perspective*, Aug./Sept. 1989, 5.
12. Andrea Nye, "Woman Clothed With the Sun," *Signs*, Summer 1987, 665.
13. O'Hara, "Constructing Emancipatory Realities," 5.
14. Garry Trudeau, "Doonesbury," March 17, 1989.
15. Joel Selvin, "Del Rubios—Three's a Charm," *San Francisco Chronicle*, Jan. 30, 1989, F1.

16. Trish Donnally, "Look of the '60s returns—it's colorful and Bohemian," *San Francisco Chronicle,* Feb. 3, 1989, B3.
17. Paul Rudnick and Kurt Andersen, "The Irony Epidemic: Suddenly Everything is Amusing," *San Francisco Chronicle,* March 21, 1989, B3. Reprinted from *Spy* magazine.
18. Lewis Yablonsky, *The Hippie Trip* (New York: Pegasus, 1968), 230.
19. Theodore Roszak, *The Making of a Counter Culture* (Garden City, NY: Doubleday, 1969), 169.
20. Lawrence Kohlberg, "Stage and Sequence: The Cognitive-developmental Approach to Socialization," in D. Goslin, ed., *Handbook of Socialization Theory and Research* (Chicago: Rand, McNally, 1969).
21. Carol Gilligan, *In a Different Voice* (Cambridge: Harvard University Press, 1982).
22. Martha T. Mednick, "On the Politics of Psychological Constructs," *American Psychologist,* August 1989, 1122.

CHAPTER 7. DEMOCRACY'S DILEMMA

1. Stanley Kelley, Jr., *Professional Public Relations and Political Power* (Baltimore: Johns Hopkins, 1966), 40.
2. Walt Anderson, *Campaigns: Cases in Political Conflict* (Pacific Palisades, CA: Goodyear, 1970), 125.
3. Carey McWilliams, *California: The Great Exception* (New York: Current Books, 1949), 195.
4. William Kornhauser, *The Politics of Mass Society* (Glencoe, IL: The Free Press, 1960) is the classic study of this subject.
5. Quoted in Kelley, *Professional Public Relations,* 50.
6. Daniel Bell, *The End of Ideology* (Glencoe, IL: The Free Press, 1960), 16.
7. Bill Boyarsky, *The Rise of Ronald Reagan* (New York: Random House, 1968), 22–23, 139–40.
8. Walt Anderson, "Dynamic Duo of California Politics," *Los Angeles Times West Magazine,* Dec. 11, 1966, 22.
9. Mark Hertsgaard, *On Bended Knee* (New York: Schocken Books, 1989), 19–20.
10. Leslie Janka, quoted in Hertsgaard, *On Bended Knee,* 6.
11. Quoted by Chronicle wire services, "Abbie Hoffman, 52, Found Dead," *San Francisco Chronicle,* April 13, 1989, A16.
12. Jerry Rubin, *Growing (Up) at Thirty-seven* (New York: M. Evans, 1976), 49.
13. Christopher Lasch, *The Culture of Narcissism* (New York: Warner Books, 1979), 154.
14. Peter Collier and David Horowitz, *Destructive Generation* (New York: Summit Books, 1989).
15. Joseph Sobran, "Lost Generation," *National Review,* March 24, 1989, 43.
16. David Burner, "We Were Disinformed," *New York Times Book Review,* April 23, 1989, 18.
17. Burke Zimmerman, *Biofuture* (New York: Plenum, 1984), 171.
18. F. C. Butler, *Community Americanization* (Washington, DC: Government Printing Office, 1920), 14.
19. Arthur Schlesinger, Jr., "The Opening of the American Mind," *New York Times Book Review,* July 23, 1989, 1.

CHAPTER 8. THE MAGIC BAZAAR

1. From Anton Szandor LaVey, *The Satanic Bible* (New York: Avon, 1969), quoted in Gordon Melton, *Encyclopedic Handbook of Cults in America* (New York: Garland, 1986), 77–78.
2. Melton, *Encyclopedic Handbook of Cults*, 76.
3. J. Gordon Melton, *The Encyclopedia of American Religions* (Detroit: Gale Research, 1989), 964–66.
4. George D. Abell and Barry Singer, *Science and the Paranormal* (New York: Scribner's, 1986), 165.
5. *Psychic Reader*, June 1989, 4.
6. Melton, *Encyclopedic Handbook of Cults*, 216.
7. Frances Fitzgerald, *Cities on a Hill* (New York: Simon and Schuster, 1986), 378.
8. Don Lattin, "Sect Battling Secularism, Sin and Lawsuits," *San Francisco Chronicle*, May 18, 1989, A2.
9. The classic study of this sort is Leon Festinger, Henry W. Riecken, and Stanley Schachter, *When Prophecy Fails* (New York: Lippincott, 1964).
10. Quoted in Melton, *Encyclopedic Handbook of Cults*, 224.
11. Quoted in Melton, *Encyclopedic Handbook of Cults*, 232.
12. Bob Sipchen, "The Cult Wars," *Los Angeles Times*, Nov. 17, 1988, A11.
13. Anthony and Streiker quotes in Sipchen, "The Cult Wars," A11.
14. Kenneth L. Woodward, "Heaven," *Newsweek*, March 27, 1989, 52–55.
15. Peter de Rosa, *Vicars of Christ* (New York: Crown, 1988), 17.
16. Quoted in de Rosa, *Vicars of Christ*, 283.
17. De Rosa, *Vicars of Christ*, 18.
18. Richard Rodriguez, "Evangelicos," Pacific News Service, August 1989.
19. Quoted in Penny Lernoux, *People of God* (New York: Viking, 1989), 28.
20. Lernoux, *People of God*, 216.
21. De Rosa, *Vicars of Christ*, 18.
22. Bill Kenkelen, "Planned Papal Visit to San Francisco Stirs Growing Gay Protest," Pacific News Service, June 1987.
23. *Catholic Women and Abortion* (Washington, DC: Catholics for a Free Choice, 1981), 18.
24. Eugene Kennedy, *Tomorrow's Catholics, Yesterday's Church* (New York: Harper & Row, 1988), 18–19.
25. Lernoux, *People of God*, 93.
26. "Black priest establishes new Catholic church," Palma (Spain) *Daily Bulletin*, July 6, 1989, 17.
27. Don Lattin, "A Bay Church That Defies the Pope," *San Francisco Chronicle*, Aug. 1, 1988, A2.
28. Michael D'Antonio, "Fortress Catholicism," *San Francisco Chronicle, This World* magazine, Jan. 6, 1985, 18.
29. Wolfhart Pannenberg, *The Kingdom of God and Theology* (Philadelphia: The Westminster Press, 1969).
30. Jürgen Moltmann, *Theology of Hope* (New York: Harper & Row, 1967).
31. Alfred North Whitehead, "God and the World," in Ewert Cousins, ed., *Process Theology* (New York: Newman Press, 1971), 86.

32. Whitehead, "God and the World," 91.
33. Alfred North Whitehead, *Science and the Modern World* (New York: Mentor, 1948), 19.

CHAPTER 9. THE TWO FACES OF GOD

1. Zen Koans quoted from various sources including Isshu Miura and Ruth Fuller Sasaki, *The Zen Koan* (New York: Harcourt, Brace & World, 1965), and Alan Watts, *The Spirit of Zen* (New York: Grove Press, 1958).
2. Alexandra David-Neel, *Buddhism* (London: John Lane the Bodley Head, 1939; and New York: St. Martin's Press, 1939), 122.
3. "When the Waters Were Changed," quoted in Idries Shah, *Tales of the Dervishes* (New York: Dutton, 1970), 21.
4. Daisetz T. Suzuki, *Zen and Japanese Culture* (Princeton, NJ: Princeton University Press, Bollingen Series, 1970), 222.
5. Fyodor Dostoevsky, *The Brothers Karamazov*, trans. Constance Garnett (New York: Heritage Press, 1933), 193.
6. Frances Fitzgerald, *Cities on a Hill* (New York: Simon and Schuster, 1986), 314–15.
7. Quoted in Mary Luytens, *Krishnamurti: The Years of Awakening* (New York: Farrar, Straus and Giroux, 1975), 272.
8. From the Kalama Sutra, which can be found in any collection of basic Buddhist teachings.
9. Ernest Becker, *The Denial of Death* (New York: The Free Press, 1973), 274.

CHAPTER 10. ALL THE WORLD'S A STAGE

1. Neil Postman, *Amusing Ourselves to Death* (New York: Penguin, 1986), 86.
2. Edward Jay Epstein, *Deception* (New York: Simon and Schuster, 1989), 25.
3. Epstein, *Deception*, 27.
4. James J. Angleton, quoted in Epstein, *Deception*, 29.
5. Epstein, *Deception*, 117.
6. Nathan Miller, *Spying for America* (New York: Paragon, 1988).
7. Epstein, *Deception*, 103.
8. David Wise, *The Politics of Lying* (New York: Vintage, 1973), 270–71.
9. Steven Kull, *Minds at War* (New York: Basic Books, 1988), 116.
10. Kull, *Minds at War*, 137.
11. Salman Rushdie, *Satanic Verses* (New York: Viking, 1989), 463.
12. William Pfaff, "Cultural Collision in Rushdie Affair," *San Francisco Chronicle*, March 3, 1989, A32.
13. Donald N. Michael and Walter Truett Anderson, "Norms in Conflict and Confusion: Six Stories in Search of an Author." The article was printed, in slightly different versions, in Howard F. Didsbury, Jr., ed., *Challenges and Opportunities* (Bethesda, MD: World Future Society, 1986); *Technological Forecasting and Social Change*, vol. 31 (1987); and *Journal of Humanistic Psychology*, vol. 29, no. 2, Spring 1989.

14. Fritjof Capra, "The Concept of Paradigm and Paradigm Shift," *ReVISION*, Summer/Fall 1986, 11.
15. Capra, "The Concept of Paradigm," 14.
16. Marilyn Ferguson, *The Aquarian Conspiracy* (Los Angeles: Tarcher, 1980), 123.
17. Kirkpatrick Sale, *Dwellers in the Land* (San Francisco: Sierra Club, 1985), 42.
18. Sale, *Dwellers in the Land*, 116.
19. Quoted in Sale, *Dwellers in the Land*, 174.

CHAPTER 11. THE EMERGENT FICTION

1. Quoted in Penelope Gilliatt, "Doctor in Spite of Himself," *The New Yorker*, April 17, 1989, 87.
2. Jürgen Habermas, *Reason and the Rationalization of Society* (London: Heinemann, 1984).
3. Paul Watzlawick, "Components of Ideological 'Realities,'" in *The Invented Reality*, (New York: W. W. Norton, 1984), 214–15.
4. William James, *Pragmatism* (New York: New American Library, 1974), 46.
5. Harlan Cleveland and Lincoln P. Bloomfield, *Rethinking International Cooperation* (Minneapolis: Hubert H. Humphrey Institute of Public Affairs, University of Minnesota, 1988), 26–27.
6. Heinz von Foerster, "On Constructing a Reality," in Paul Watzlawick, ed., *The Invented Reality*, 41–42.
7. I have discussed this theme in more detail in other works, most recently *To Govern Evolution* (Boston: Harcourt Brace Jovanovich, 1987).

Index